T0329460

THE BRILLIANT REIGN OF

THE KANGXI EMPEROR

THE BRILLIANT REIGN OF THE KANGXI EMPEROR

CHINA'S QING DYNASTY

HING MING HUNG

Algora Publishing
New York

Library of Congress Cataloging-in-Publication Data —

Names: Hung, Hing Ming, author.
Title: The brilliant reign of the Kangxi emperor: China's Qing dynasty /
    Hung Hing Ming.
Description: New York: Algora Publishing, 2017. | Includes bibliographical
    references and index.
Identifiers: LCCN 2017044795 (print) | LCCN 2017044879 (ebook) | ISBN
    9781628943115 (pdf) | ISBN 9781628943092 (soft cover: alk. paper) | ISBN
    9781628943108 (hard cover: alk. paper)
Subjects: LCSH: Kangxi, Emperor of China, 1654-1722. |
    China—History—Kangxi, 1662-1722. | China—History—Qing dynasty,
    1644-1912.
Classification: LCC DS754.6 (ebook) | LCC DS754.6 .H86 2017 (print) | DDC
    951/.032—dc23
LC record available at https://lccn.loc.gov/2017044795

Printed in the United States

Table of Contents

Introduction

This book is about Aisin Gioro Xuanye (1654–1722), the Kangxi Emperor, the greatest emperor of the Qing Dynasty (1644–1721).

The Aisin Gioro Clan rose in Northeast China. Legend has it that they were descendents of Fokulun, a fairy from Heaven.

Aisin Gioro Bukuliyongshun unified the Manchu people in Northeast China and became their king. Bukuliyongshun's descendants became commanders of the Jianzhou Army Station (in Xinbin, Liaoning Province) established by the government of the Ming Dynasty (1368–1644).

Many generations later Aisin Gioro Nurhaci conquered the State of Hada (in Xifeng, Liaoning Province) in 1599, the State of Huifa (in Huinan, Jilin Province) in 1607, the State of Wula (in Wulajie, Jilin Province), and the State of Yehe (in Lishu, Jilin Province) in 1619. In 1616 Nurhaci established the (Later) Jin Dynasty and he ascended the throne as emperor of this dynasty. He was on the throne for 10 years.

Aisin Gioro Huangtaiji succeeded his father Nurhaci as the Emperor of the (Later) Jin Dynasty in 1626. He carried out expeditions against the Ming Dynasty. In 1629 Huangtaiji commanded his army to attack Beijing, the capital of the Ming Dynasty. But later he gave up the attack and withdrew back to Shenyang (in Liaoning Province), the capital of the (Later) Jin Dynasty, in 1630. In 1636 he changed the name of the dynasty from Jin Dynasty to Qing Dynasty. He was on the throne for 17 years.

Aisin Gioro Fulin succeeded his father Huangtaiji as the Emperor of the Qing Dynasty in 1643. The title of his reign was Shunzhi. Historians refer to him as the Shunzhi Emperor — or Emperor Shunzhi. In March 1645 Li Zi Cheng, the leader of the great peasant uprising, took Beijing, the capital of the Ming Dynasty. Emperor Zhu You Jian of the Ming Dynasty committed suicide by hanging himself to a tree on the Coal Hill. The Ming Dynasty fell. Li Zi Cheng commanded a great army to march to Shanhaiguan Pass. Wu San Gui, the general of the Ming Dynasty defending Shanhaiguan Pass, asked help from the Qing Dynasty. In April 1645 Duoergun, the Prince Regent of the Qing Dynasty, commanded a great army to Shanhaiguan Pass. Wu San Gui welcomed the Qing army commanded by Duoergun into Shanhaiguan Pass. The Qing troops and the troops under Wu San Gui defeated Li Zi Cheng's army by Shanhaiguan Pass. Li Zi Cheng escaped back to Beijing. The Qing army and Wu San Gui's troops pursued Li Zi Cheng to Beijing. Then they attacked Beijing and took it. Li Zi Cheng ran away to the west. In September 1645 Emperor Shunzhi entered Beijing. From then on Beijing became the capital of the Qing Dynasty. Shunzhi sent troops to attack the different provinces. Wu San Gui was made King of Pingxi. He fought all the way from Beijing to Yunnan Province which was situated in the southwest of China. Shunzhi ordered him to garrison Yunnan Province. During his reign, Emperor Shunzhi pacified the most part of China. He was on the throne for 18 years.

Aisin Gioro Xuanye succeeded his father Shunzhi as Emperor of the Qing Dynasty on 9 January 1661 at the age of eight. His reign title was Kangxi, so historians refer to him as the Kangxi Emperor, or Emperor Kangxi. During his reign, he advanced the interests of the Chinese people in a reamarkable way.

Zhu You Lang, the Emperor of the South Ming Dynasty, escaped to Burma from Yunnan Province. In 1661 Kangxi ordered Wu San Gui to command his troops to march into Burma to arrest Zhu You Lang. In December 1661 the King of the Kingdom of Burma had to deliver Zhu You Lang and his family members to Wu San Gui. The South Ming Dynasty was totally destroyed.

When Emperor Kangxi ascended the throne, he was 8 years old. His father Emperor Shunzhi appointed four regent ministers to assist him in a posthumous edict. Aobai was one of them. He arrogated all powers in himself. In 1667 Kangxi reached the age of 16 and he took up the reins of government. But Aobai still held the power in his own hands and would not return the power to Kangxi. Aobai was a strongly built warrior. It would be very difficult to arrest him. Kangxi secretly trained some young body guards as wrestlers. On 16 May 1669 the young wrestlers successfully arrested Aobai at court. From then on Kangxi really held the power in his own hands.

In 1673 Kangxi decided to deprive the power of the military governors. In December 1673 Wu San Gui, the Military Governor of Yunnan Province, held a rebellion. He declared himself to be King of Zhou. His troops marched from Yunnan Province to Guizhou Province, then into Hunan Province. His troops took most of Hunan Province, and they took Changsha, the capital city. Kangxi sent generals to defend the critical places such as Wuchang (in Hubei Province) and Jingzhou (in Hubei Province). In March 1674 Geng Jing Zhong, the Military Governor of Fujian Province, held a rebellion in response to Wu San Gui's rebellion. He took Fujian Province and most part of Zhejiang Province.

When Wu San Gui held the rebellion, Kangxi was only a young man of 20 years old. Wu San Gui thought that Kangxi was young and inexperienced in military commanding. But to Wu San Gui's great surprise, he found that Kangxi dispatched his army in a right way. He knew that his rebellion would fail. Many battles were fought in Hunan Province, Jiangxi Province and Hubei Province. Wu San Gui's troops were seriously defeated. Seeing that there was no hope for him, Wu San Gui ascended the throne of the Emperor of the Zhou Dynasty in 1678 when he was 67 years old. In September 1678 Wu San Gui died. He passed the throne to his grandson Wu Shi Fan. After Wu San Gui died, the army of the Qing Dynasty started a great offensive. In February 1681 the troops of the Qing Dynasty attacked Kunming, the capital city of Yunnan Province. In September 1681 the troops of the Qing Dynasty took Kunming. Wu Shi Fan committed suicide. Wu San Gui's rebellion was at last totally destroyed.

Kangxi performed great deeds in reuniting Taiwan. Taiwan had been occupied by the Dutch in 1624. Zheng Cheng Gong, a general of the Ming Dynasty, drove the Hollanders away and recovered Taiwan in 1661. But he refused to submit to the Qing Dynasty. After Zheng Cheng Gong died, his son Zheng Jin succeeded his father as the ruler of Taiwan. When Geng Jing Zhong held a rebellion in Fujian Province, Zheng Jin sent troops to help him. In 1681 Zheng Jin died. His son Zheng Ke Shuang took over. In June 1683 Kangxi sent Shi Lang to command the naval troops to attack Taiwan. They started from Tongshan Island of Fujian Province. They attacked and took Penghu Island. Then they sailed to Tainan, the capital city of Taiwan at that time. Zheng Ke Shuang surrendered. Taiwan was reunified.

By the end the Ming Dynasty, while China was in great chaos, the Russians took the chance and sent troops to occupy Yakesa (now Albanzino, Russia) and Nibuchu (now Nerchinsk, Russia) which were situated within the territory of China. In order to recover Yakesa, in 1683, Emperor Kangxi sent troops to station along Heilong River in Heilongjing Province to get ready to attack and recover Yakesa. In May 1685 the Qing troops started an attack on Yakesa. The Russian soldiers surrendered and were sent back home. But in 1689 the Russian soldiers secretly turned back to Yakesa. Kangxi sent troops to lay siege to them. In 1689 the representatives of Russia and the representatives of China held negotiations in Nibuchu and concluded the Treaty of Nibuchu. According to the treaty, Yakesa belonged to China and the Russians in Yakesa should go back to Russia; the Ergun River should be the boundary; the area to the south of the river belonged to China; the area to the north of the river belong to Russia; and since Nibuchu was situated to the north of the river, it belonged to Russia.

One of the great deeds of Emperor Kangxi was that he defeated Galdan, the Khan of the Dzungar Khanate. Dzungar Tribe was a subtribe of Elute Tribe of Mongolians. In 1671 Galdan became the Khan of the Dzungar Khanate. In the vast area of the south part of Mongolia, there lived the Khalkha Mongolians. In 1688 war broke out between Galdan's Dzungar Khanate and the Khalkha Mongolians. The Khalkha Mongolians were defeated and rushed into the border areas of the Qing Dynasty for protection. Kangxi allowed them to stay in the border areas. Galdan commanded his troops into the Chinese border areas to chase the Khalkha Mongolians. In order to defeat Galdan, Kangxi carried out three expeditions against Galdan. The first expedition took place in 1690. A battle was fought in Ulan Butung (situated in the southwest of Hexigten Qi, Inner Mongolian Autonomous Region, China). Galdan was defeated and ran away to the north part of Mongolia. In 1695 Galdan commanded his army to Bayan Ulaan (situated by the upper reach of Kerulen River, Mongolia). Kangxi decided to carry out the second expedition against Galdan. A battle was fought in Dzuunmod (a place south to Ulan Bator, Mongolia). Galdan was defeated. He ran away to the area of Tamir River (in the central part of Mongolia). In September 1696 Galdan and his troops moved to Altay (in the west part of Mongolia). In January 1697 Kangxi carried out the third expedition against Galdan. When Kangxi and his great army reached Ningxia Province, he got the information that Galdan had committed suicide by taking poison.

After Galdan died, his nephew Tsewang Rabtan became the Khan of the Dzungar Khanate. In 1717 Tsewang Rabtan sent Tzeren Dondub to command 6,000 men to invade Tibet. When they reached Lhasa, they killed Lha-bzang Khan, the ruler of Tibet. In 1720 Kangxi sent troops to march into Tibet from Qinghai Province and Sichuan Province. In August 1720 the Qing army from Sichuan Province took Lhasa. In the same month the Qing army from Qinghai Province defeated Tzeren Dondub in the north part of Tibet. Tzeren Dondub ran away back to the Dzungar Khanate. The Qing army from Qinghai Province also marched to Lhasa. Tibet was pacified.

In November 1722 Kangxi passed away at the age of 70. Before he died, he appointed Yinzhen, his fourth son, to succeed him to the throne. Kangxi stayed on the throne for 61 years. He was the emperor who stayed on the throne the longest in Chinese history. During his reign China was strong and prosperous.

Aisin Gioro Yinzhen succeeded his father as the Emperor of the Qing Dynasty in September 1722. His reign title was Yongzheng. Historians call him Emperor Yongzheng, or the Yongzheng Emperor.

In 1723 Lobsang Tendzin, the head of the Mongolian Khoshut Tribe, held a rebellion in Qinghai Province against the Qing Dynasty. Emperor Yongzheng ordered General Nian Geng Yao and General Yue Zhong Qi to suppress the rebellion. Lobsang Tendzin commanded his army to attack Xining, the most important city in Qinghai Province. The Qing army defeated him. He had to run away to the Dzungar

Khanate for protection. From then on Qinghai was pacified and was put under the direct control of the government of the Qing Dynasty.

Yongzheng carried out several reforms in China. He ordered to replace the cruel native chieftains of the minority nationalities by officials appointed by the Qing government; he reformed the tax system to lessen the burden of the poor people.

Yongzheng passed away in August 1735. He was on the throne for 13 years. Before he died, he appointed his fourth son Hongli to succeed him to the throne.

Aisin Gioro Hongli ascended the throne of the Qing Dynasty in September 1735. His reign title was Qianlong. Qianlong was a highly accomplished emperor.

In November 1751 there was a rebellion in Tibet. Emperor Qianlong sent troops to suppress the rebellion. From then on the rule of the Qing Dynasty in Tibet was strengthened.

In January 1756 Emperor Qianlong sent troops to attack the Dzungar Khanate. The Qing army took Ili (now Yining, in the west part of Xinjiang Uygur Autonomous Region) and captured Dawachi, the Khan of the Dzungar Khanate. From then on the Dzungar Khanate was pacified and the area of the Dzungar Khanate (now the area of Xinjiang Uygur Autonomous Region) became part of the territory of China.

In 1774 Qianlong ordered to compile Siku Quanshu (Complete Library in Four Sections). In 1783 the compilation of Siku Quanshu was completed. This great book included 3,500 volumes, 78,000 chapters and 36,000 titles with 800 million Chinese characters. It was the greatest work in the world at that time.

In 1796 Qianlong had been on the throne for 60 years and he was already 86 years old. In December 1796 he passed the throne to his 15th son Yongyan. But he still attended to the state affairs. He worked till he passed away in January 1800 at the age of 89.

All the materials used in writing this book are taken from the following books:

"Draft History of the Qing Dynasty" (Chinese: 清史稿or qingshigao) compiled by Zhao Er Xun (趙爾巽: 1844-1927) et al.

"Veritable Records of Kangxi Emperor Period" (Chinese: 康熙朝實錄 or kangxichaoshilu) by Ma Qi (馬齊 1652-1739), Zhang Ting Yu (張廷玉 1672-1755), Jiang Ting Xi (蔣廷錫 1669-1732), Zhu Shi (朱軾 1665-1732) of the Qing Dynasty (1636-1912).

"Veritable Records of the Yongzheng Emperor Era" (Chinese: 雍正朝實錄 or yongzhengchaoshilu) by Ortai (鄂爾泰 1677-1745), Zhang Ting Yu (張廷玉 1672-1755), Fumin (福敏 1675-1756), Xu Ben (徐本 ?-1732), Santai (三泰 ?-1758) of the Qing Dynasty (1636-1912).

"Veritable Records of Qianlong Era" (Chinese: 乾隆朝實錄 or qianlongchaoshilu) by Qinggui (慶桂 1737–1816), Dong Gao (董誥 1740–1818), Cao Zhen Yong (曹振鏞 1755–1835).

"Veritable Records of Taizu of the Qing Dynasty" (Chinese: 清太祖武皇帝實錄 or qingtaizuwuhuangdishilu) by Jueluoledehong (覺羅勒德洪), Ming Zhu (明珠 1635–1708), Wang Xi (王熙 1628–1703), Song De Yi (宋德宜 1626–1687) of the Qing Dynasty (1636–1912).

"History of the Ming Dynasty" (Chinese: 明史 or mingshi) by Zhang Ting Yu (張廷玉 1672–1755) of the Qing Dynasty (1636–1912).

1. Portrait of Aisin Gioro Xuanye, The Kangxi Emperor of the Qing Dynasty

Map of China

Chapter One: The Roots of the Qing Dynasty

Section One: Establishing the (Later) Jin Dynasty

1. The Legendary Origins of the Aisin Gioro Clan and the Manchu Nationality

In Northeast China there lies a great mountain range called Changbai ("perpetually white," as it is covered with snow all year round). At the foot of one of the eastern mountains is Bu'erhuli Lake. Legends say that long, long ago, three fairy sisters descended to Bu'erhuli Lake from Heaven. The eldest was Engulun; the second was Zhenggulun; the youngest was Fokulun. They took off their clothes and went into the water to take a bath. When they finished bathing in the lake, a magpie holding a red fruit in its mouth flew to the bank of the lake and put the red fruit on Fokulun's clothes. Fokulun liked the red fruit very much. She put it in her mouth and got dressed. But while she was putting on her clothes, the fruit slipped down her throat and into her belly. And then she found that she was pregnant. She said to her two sisters, "Now I am very heavy and cannot fly. What shall I do?" Engulun said, "You are a fairy. Don't worry. After you have given birth, you will surely be able to fly back to Heaven." So her two sisters Engulun and Zhenggulun flew back to Heaven and left Fokulun behind.

Soon she gave birth to a baby boy. She named him Aisin Gioro Bukuliyongshun. ("Aisin Gioro" was the clan name. Bukuliyongshun was the given name.) Of course, he was no ordinary boy. When he grew up, he ended the strife and fighting among the three tribes in the southeast part of the Changbai Mountains, and the people of the three tribes supported him as their king. Bukuliyongshun named the people of these tribes the Manchu people, and he is regarded as the first ancestor of what many years later became the royal clan of the Qing Dynasty.

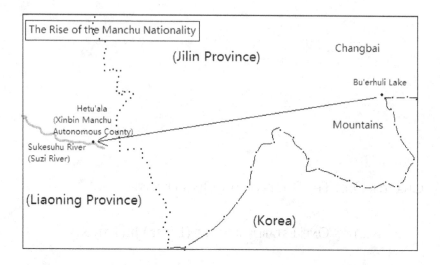

2. Aisin Gioro Nurhaci Conquers the Tribes in Northeast China

The government of the ruling Yuan Dynasty (1271–1368, just around the time Marco Polo was traveling in Asia) established an office to govern the people in these areas. Next, the government of the Ming Dynasty (1368–1644) established Jianzhou Army Station in the Changbai Mountains. Aisin Gioro Bukuliyongshun's descendants were appointed commanders of this army station.

Many generations later, Aisin Gioro Mengtemu was the commander of Jianzhou Army Station. He took all his soldiers and people and moved to Hetu'ala (now Xinbin Manchu Autonomous County, in the east part of Liaoning Province) by the Sukesuhu River (now Suzi River) and stayed there. Jianzhou Army Station was also moved to Hetu'ala.

Mengtemu had two sons, Chongshan and Chuyan. Chongshan then had three sons. The third of them had only one son — but he went on to have six sons. That's the way dynasties are built.

The third son, Juechang'an, succeeded his father as the commander of Jianzhou Army Station and he dispatched his brothers to build new cities throughout the area. He had five sons of his own.

At that time the Shuosena Tribe and the Jiahu Tribe were living along the lower reaches of the Sukesuhu River. These two tribes attacked the Manchu tribes near Jianzhou Army Station. Juechang'an and his eldest son Lidun commanded their troops and defeated these two tribes; they took control of the area and conquered all the tribes around.

Nurhaci Brings Peace to Jianzhou

In February 1559, Takeshi's wife Xitala gave birth to a baby boy. Takeshi named him Nurhaci. When Nurhaci grew up, he was a strong, handsome young man with strong character. He was magnanimous and was a man of talent and bold vision. He had a younger brother named Shurhaci.

In 1583 Li Cheng Liang, the Commander-in-chief of the Ming Dynasty army stationed in Liaodong (now Liaoning Province), commanded a great army from Guangning (now Beizhen, Liaoning Province) to attack Gule City (now Shangjiahe, Liaoning Province). Atai, the master of Gule City, had married Juechang'an's grand-daughter. Juechang'an and Takeshi went to Gule City with Nurhaci and Shurhaci to visit Atai.

Nikanwailan, the master of Tulun City (now Tangtu Village, situated to the southeast of Fushun, Liaoning Province), took his army to join forces with the Ming army under Li Cheng Liang to attack Gule City. Nikanwailan deceived the defenders of Gule City by saying that they would be spared if they opened the city gate to let the Ming army into the city. Atai and the defenders of Gule City believed him and opened the city gate to let the Ming army in. But the Ming army started a massive slaughter. Atai was immediately killed. Juechang'an and Takeshi were also killed in the great confusion. Nurhaci and Shurhaci were captured by the Ming troops. Li Cheng Liang's wife saw them and had pity on them. She secretly set them free and let them go.

Nurhaci went back to Hetu'ala. His grandfather Juechang'an had left thirteen sets of armor. Nurhaci put on one set and gave the rest to Shurhaci and other men. He established an army, with Eyidu and Anfeiyanggu as officers. He sent an envoy to Gule City to ask the officials of the Ming Dynasty, "What crimes have my grandfather and father committed that they have been killed by your soldiers?" The Ming officials had to return the dead bodies to Nurhaci. Nurhaci again sent an envoy to say to the officials of the Ming Dynasty, "Nikanwailan is my enemy. You should arrest him and turn him over to me." But the officials of the Ming Dynasty would not do so.

Nomina, the master of Sa'erhu City (situated to the east of Fushun, Liaoning Province), together with Gehashanhasihu, the master of Jiamuhu City (now a place in Fushun County, Liaoning Province), and Changshu, the master of Zhanhe City (in Jilin Province), took their troops to join Nurhaci. Now Nurhaci, Nomina, Gehashanhasihu and Changshu formed an alliance.

In May 1583 Nurhaci took a large army to attack Tulun City, where his enemy Nikanwailan was. But his ally Nomina did not come to join forces with Nurhaci as he had promised. When Nikanwailan heard that Nurhaci was coming, he fled to Jiaban City (now Dajiabang, in the east outskirt of Fushun). Nurhaci took Tulun City without much effort, so Nikaiwailan ran further to Hekoutai, a stronghold of the Ming army. Nurhaci led his army to chase down Nikanwailan to Hekoutai. The Ming army came out to resist Nurhaci's army. Nikanwailan fled to E'erhun. In this action Nurhaci could not achieve his purpose because Nomina failed to honor his promise; and he secretly revealed to Nikanwailan the time when Nurhaci's army was planning to attack. Nurhaci was enraged by Nomina's treachery, and he took the opportunity to launch an attack on him. Nurhaci killed him and his younger brother, and took Sa'erhu City.

2. Aisin Gioro Nurhaci, Emperor Taizu of the Qing Dynasty

In December 1583 Lidai, the Master of Zhaojia City (now in Xinbin Manchu Autonomous County, Liaoning Province), who was one of Nurhaci's clansmen, colluded with the people of Hada Tribe to loot the Huji Stronghold. Nurhaci sent Anfeiyanggu and Baxun to lead 12 soldiers to go after Lidai's soldiers and the Hada soldiers. They got back everything that had been looted.

In January 1584 Nurhaci decided to attack Zhaojia City so as to revenge Lidai's looting of Huji Stronghold. When Nurhaci's troops were on their way to Zhaojia City, a heavy snow suddenly started to fall. The officers suggested that they should turn back. Nurhaci said, "Lidai is my clansman. But he colluded with the people of Hada Tribe to attack me. I will never forgive him." Nurhaci commanded his troops to march on to Zhaojia City resolutely. When they reached Zhaojia City, they started a fierce attack and took the city. Lidai was captured.

Five months later, Nurhaci commanded 400 soldiers to attack Ma'erdun City (in Xinbin Manchu Autonomous County) defended by four officers. The attack lasted for four days. When Nurhaci at last took Ma'erdun City, Nashen escaped but the other three leaders were killed.

In September that year, Nurhaci led 500 soldiers to attack Qijida City (in what is now Huanren Manchu Autonomous County, Liaoning Province) where the people of Dong'e Tribe lived. Ahai, the head of Dong'e Tribe, commanded 400 soldiers to defend the city. Again a sudden, heavy snow fell. Nurhaci had to withdraw. Ahai sent troops from the city to pursue Nurhaci's troops. Nurhaci sent 12 cavalrymen to fight the pursuing troops and beat them back.

On his way back to Hetu'ala, Nurhaci attacked Wengkeluo City, but he was seriously wounded by an arrow. He had to ride back to Hetu'ala. When he had recovered from the wound, he commanded his troops to attack Wengkeluo City again and this time they took it.

In the area where the Suzi River and Hun River joined, lived the Zhechen people, a Manchu tribe. In February 1585, Nurhaci ordered his troops to attack Jiefan City (now in Xinbin Manchu Autonomous County, Liaoning Province). The Jiefan City defense force was well prepared for the attack. Nurhaci saw that it was not going to be easy to conquer the city, so he commanded his troops to retreat. When they retreated southward to Tailangang, Nashen, the master of Jiefan City, who had been defeated in the battle of Ma'erdun in June 1584, ordered his troops to go after Nurhaci. At the same time Sa'erhu City, Dongjia City, and Ba'erda City also sent their troops to attack Nurhaci. Nurhaci turned back to fight them single handedly. Nashen broke Nurhaci's horse whip with his sword. Nurhaci moved to Nashen's back, slashed with his sword and cut Nashen in half from behind. Then Nurhaci drew his bow and shot at Bamuni, one of Nashen's subordinates, and killed him. The enemy troops did not dare to press on. Nurhaci and his troops retreated slowly and calmly.

Much of this action took place in the region around Fushun, in the east of Liaoning Province. For clarification, let's note here that in modern China, Qingyuan remains one of 11 Manchu autonomous counties in China, and Qingyuan and two other counties still fall under the administration of Fushun City.

In May 1586, Nurhaci commanded his troops to attack the Hunhe Tribe's Boyihun Stronghold (south of Fushun, Liaoning Province) and took it. In July he conquered the Zhechen Tribe's Tuomohe City (east of Fushun). Nurhaci got news that Nikanwailan was in E'erhun (northeast of Fushun). He immediately commanded his troops on a swift march to E'erhun, and very soon his troops conquered the city. They searched the whole city for Nikanwailan but could not find him.

Nurhaci went up to the top of the city wall to observe. He saw a man wearing a felt hat and green armor, riding a horse. A common man could not afford a horse and armor. He thought that man must be Nikanwailan. He jumped up on his horse and rode out of the city to track that man down. But he was surrounded by the local people, and he had to fight them off. Nikanwailan escaped to an area controlled by the Ming army.

Nurhaci sent envoys to see the officials there, demanding they hand over Nikanwailan. In the end, the officials had to agree to let Nurhaci send his officers to execute Nikanwailan. Nurhaci sent Zhaisa there, and he executed Nikanwailan. Nurhaci at last had avenged his grandfather and father. Since the Ming officials had permitted Nurhaci to send his representatives to kill Nikanwailan, Nurhaci also showed signs of friendship to the Ming Dynasty by paying tribute to their royal court.

Battles in the Area Near Fushun

In January 1587, Nurhaci ordered that a new city be built in a place south of Hetu'ala. He named this city Fo'ala (now in Xinbin Manchu Autonomous County, Liaoning Province). Palaces were built and the new city was ringed by three protective walls: the outer wall, the inner wall and the wall around the palaces. In Fo'ala City, Nurhaci declared himself Beile (meaning "king" in the Manchu language) of a Manchu state, and he established policies and laws for the state.

In June of that year, Nurhaci attacked Keshan Stronghold, which was held by the troops of Zhechen Tribe. Nurhaci took Keshan Stronghold and killed A'ertai, the master of Keshan Stronghold. He sent E'erdu, one of the generals under him, to attack Ba'erda City (in Qingyuan). E'erdu commanded his troops to cross the Hun River secretly and make a surprise attack on the city at night. E'erdu urged his troops to fight fiercely and they took the city. Nurhaci granted E'erdu the title of "Batulu" (meaning "great warrior" in Manchu). Nurhaci personally led some soldiers to attack Dong City (in Qingyuan). Zahai, the master of Dong City, surrendered. From then on Nurhaci successfully conquered the whole Zhechen Tribe.

In April 1588 Hu'ergan, the son of the king of the State of Hada (Liaoning Province), with his daughter, came to submit to Nurhaci. Nurhaci treated Hu'ergan very politely and married his daughter. This was followed by a series of submissions,

Suo'erguo, the head of Suwan Tribe (in Shuangyang, Jilin Province), with his son Feiyingdong, led all his armed forces and people to submit to Nurhaci. Nurhaci made Feiyingdong a First Class Official. Likewise, Heheli, the grandson of the head of Dong'e Tribe, led all his troops and people to submit to Nurhaci, and Nurhaci appointed him too to be a First Class Official. Hu'erhan, the head of the Dong'e Tribe's Ya'ergu Stronghold, brought his troops and people, too, to submit to Nurhaci. Nurhaci appointed Hu'erhan as a First Class Official. In September 1588 Nurhaci commanded his troops to attack Wangjia City (situated thirty kilometers to the northeast of Xinbin Manchu Autonomous County, Liaoning Province) of Wanyan Tribe and took it. From 1583 to 1588 Nurhaci spent five years to unify all the Manchu tribes in Jianzhou area. In January 1589 the court of the Ming Dynasty appointed Nurhaci as the Commander-in-chief of Jianzhou Army Station.

In June 1593, Buzhai and Nalinbulu, the two kings of the State of Yehe (in Jilin Province), colluded with Menggebulu, the king of the State of Hada (in Liaoning Province), Mantai, the king of the State of Wula (in Jilin Province), and Baiyindali, the king of the State of Huifa (in what is now Huinan, Jilin Province), to command the soldiers of the four states to attack the Hubucha Stronghold of Jianzhou which was under Nurhaci's jurisdiction.

Nurhaci commanded his troops in beating back the troops of the four states. He pursued the defeated troops to the Hada stronghold, Fu'erjiaqi. The king of Hada fought back resolutely, and Nurhaci called a retreat. He personally brought up the rear. Menggebulu commanded his cavalrymen to go after Nurhaci. One of them got ahead of Nurhaci, who pulled his bow and prepared to shoot him. Suddenly three more enemy cavalrymen closed in and Nurhaci's horse was spooked; Nurhaci was nearly thrown to the ground. The cavalrymen lifted their swords, intending to kill Nurhaci. At this critical moment, Anfeiyanggu, a general under Nurhaci, intervened and killed all the three enemy cavalrymen and saved Nurhaci. Nurhaci then used his bow and arrows to shoot at Menggebulu, and killed his horse. Menggubulu changed horses and rode away. After the battle, Nurhaci honored Anfeiyanggu with the title of "Batulu" ("great warrior").

The Battle by Gule Mountain

A grand alliance was formed in September 1593, when Buzhai, the king of the State of Yehe, joined with several local kings and Mongolian tribes, mainly from Heilongjiang Province and Jilin Province, to invade Jianzhou. This army united 30,000 men from nine states. They closed in on the city by three different routes.

When Nurhaci heard of this plan, he sent Wulikan to the north to gather information about the oncoming enemy. When Wulikan reached the bank of the Hun River (in Liaoning Province), it was already evening. He could see the enemy troops on the northern bank of the river cooking their supper. After eating, they began to cross the river and marched southward. Wulikan sped back to Fo'ala, reaching the place by midnight. He reported what he had seen to Nurhaci.

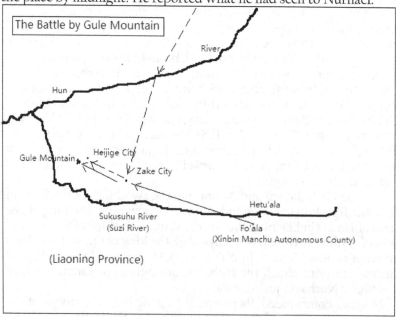

The Battle by Gule Mountain

Hun — River

Gule Mountain

Heijige City

Zake City

Sukusuhu River
(Suzi River)

Hetu'ala

Fo'ala
(Xinbin Manchu Autonomous County)

(Liaoning Province)

Nurhaci said, "So the Yehe troops have really come. If our troops go out of the city this late at night, the people of the city will be alarmed. Tell the generals that we shall march out of the city at dawn." Then he went to bed and fell soundly asleep. Lady Fucha, his concubine, woke him up. She said, "Are you out of your mind? Aren't you scared? The troops of the nine tribes are coming. How sleep at such a time?" Nurhaci said, "If a person is scared, he cannot fall asleep even if he lies in bed. If I were really scared, how could I fall into a sound sleep? A few days ago I got word that the troops of Yehe Tribe and the others were coming by three different routes, but I did not know the exact date they would come. That is why I have been worried. Now they are here. All my worries have been removed and I feel at ease. If I had done something wrong to the people of Yehe Tribe, Heaven would punish me. Then I would be afraid. But I have been obedient to the will of Heaven and have done my best to bring peace and tranquility to the people of my state. Now the head of Yehe Tribe hates me and has colluded with the other eight tribes to harm the innocent people. So I know very well that Heaven will surely not help them." Then Nurhaci went to bed again and enjoyed a sound sleep.

At dawn Nurhaci commanded his army of 10,000 men to march out of Fo'ala. Before marching, Nurhaci told his generals and soldiers, "Take off your hand protectors and neck protectors so that you can move flexibly. Otherwise you will be bound by these things and it will not be convenient for you to fight with your enemy." Then he said, "The troops of the nine tribes are just a disorderly mob. They are not determined. If we defeat their vanguards, the main force will retreat. Then we may overtake them and we will surely win."

When Nurhaci and his troops reached the outskirts of Zaka City, thirty kilometers to the northwest, two men came out to let him know, "The enemy troops arrived at our city at eight in the morning. They surrounded our city and attacked fiercely. But they could not take it. Now they have gone north to attack Heijige City." Nurhaci decided to stay in Zaka City for the night.

And during that night a soldier from Yehe came to surrender. He told Nurhaci, "There are 10,000 soldiers from the State of Yehe, 10,000 from the State of Hada, the State of Wula and the State of Huifa, and 10,000 from the three Mongol tribes. There are 30,000 men in all in the united army." This news was a bit intimidating to the generals and men, but Nurhaci just told them, "Don't worry. You won't need to fight a hard battle. We shall establish our camps in strategic locations by the mountain. I will lure our enemies to come to attack us there, and when they come, I will arrange the troops in battle formation. The troops of the nine tribes are just a disorderly mob. They have no great will to fight and will not go forward to attack us. Only the heads of the tribes will urge their troops to go forward. We shall wait at our ease for the exhausted enemy. If we kill one or two of the leaders of the tribes, the enemy forces will collapse. Although we have fewer soldiers, if we spare no effort in the battle, we shall surely win."

The next morning Nurhaci and his army marched to Gule Mountain (Xinbin Manchu Autonomous County, Liaoning Province). They pitched camp by the mountain across from Heijige City. The day before, the united army had attacked Heijige but could not take it. Now, the united army attacked Heijige again. Nurhaci arranged his troops in battle formation and then he ordered Eyidu to lead 100 soldiers to ride to the enemy to challenge them in battle. When the united troops saw the enemy coming, they dropped their attack on Heijige City.

Buzhai, the king of Yehe, with the three heads of the Mongol tribes, commanded their troops to attack Nurhaci's army at the foot of Gule Mountain. Buzhai rode at the head of his army. Suddenly Buzhai's horse stumbled on a log on the ground and Buzhai was thrown. A soldier named Wutan dashed forward, sat on Buzhai, drove his sword into Buzhai's chest and killed him. When Buzhai's generals and soldiers saw that their master had been killed, they all shrieked in horror. The heads of the other states were terrified and their armies collapsed. Ming'an, the head of Mongolian Horqin Tribe, and his horse got stuck in the mud and could not get out. Ming'an had to jump onto a spare horse without saddle and ride away.

Nurhaci ordered his troops to charge at the enemy. Many enemy soldiers were killed. Nurhaci's troops pursued them to the southern part of the State of Hada (still in Liaoning Province). The next day one of Nurhaci's soldiers caught Buzhantai, the younger brother of Mantai, the king of Wula. Buzhantai was bound tightly and brought before Nurhaci. Nurhaci untied Buzhantai and set him free.

Thus in the battle by Gule Mountain, Buzhai, the king of the State of Yehe was killed. His son Buyanggu succeeded him as the king of the State of Yehe.

In January 1597, the kings of Yehe, Hada, Huifa and Wula sent envoys to Nurhaci to beg him to pardon them for their crime of invading Jianzhou. They promised to make peace. In order to show his sincerity, King Buyanggu of the State of Yehe promised to marry his younger sister to Nurhaci. Nurhaci granted his permission. A ceremony was held to make their vows to form an alliance with Nurhaci. After the ceremony, Nurhaci said, "If any of you goes against your vows and breaks the agreement of alliance, I will wait for three years for you to reform. If you do not reform in three years, I will carry out an expedition against you."

Nurhaci Conquers the State of Hada

In autumn 1599, Nalinbulu, Buyanggu's uncle, who was also a king of the State of Yehe (in Lishu, Jili Province), commanded his troops to attack the State of Hada. Menggebulu, the king, could not withstand the attack, so he sent his three sons to Nurhaci as hostages in a plea for help.

Nurhaci sent Feiyingdong and Gegai with 2,000 soldiers to station themselves in the territory of the State of Hada. When Nalinbulu heard this, he had a clever plan. He colluded with an official of the army of the Ming Dynasty stationed in Kaiyuan and asked him to write a letter to Menggebulu for him. The letter suggested, "If you arrest the two generals sent by Nurhaci, you can use them to redeem your three sons. You may kill all the 2,000 soldiers under the two generals. I will marry my daughter to you as your wife, and you and I shall form an alliance."

Menggebulu believed what Nalinbulu had said in the letter, and he made an appointment to meet Nalinbulu in Kaiyuan. But this secret was somehow revealed. Nurhaci was very angry with Menggebulu and decided to mount an expedition against the State of Hada (in Xifeng, Liaoning Province). Shurhaci, Nurhaci's younger brother, offered to lead the vanguards, and Nurhaci agreed.

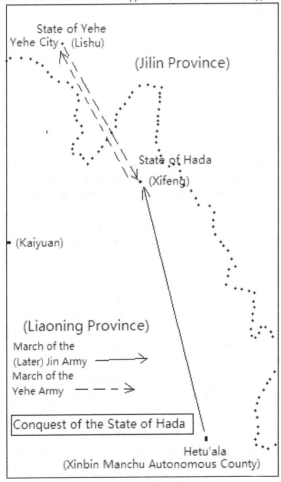

State of Yehe
Yehe City • (Lishu)

(Jilin Province)

State of Hada
(Xifeng)

(Kaiyuan)

(Liaoning Province)

March of the
(Later) Jin Army ⟶

March of the
Yehe Army — — ⇢

Conquest of the State of Hada

Hetu'ala
(Xinbin Manchu Autonomous County)

When the troops reached Hada, the city defense troops came out to fight. Shurhaci held his men where they were and would not go forward to fight. He just said to Nurhaci, "The enemy troops have come out!" Nurhaci responded very angrily, "Have we come to attack an empty city?" Then he commanded his troops to go forward — but Shurhaci's troops blocked the way. So Nurhaci had to command his troops to go along the city wall. The enemy soldiers on the top of the city wall shot arrows down and many of Nurhaci's soldiers were killed or wounded.

Finally, Nurhaci ordered his troops to attack the city. After six days fighting, Nurhaci at last won. General Yangguli caught Menggebulu alive, and brought him before Nurhaci. Menggebulu crawled on all fours to the feet of Nurhaci. Nurhaci spared Menggebulu and set him free.

Nurhaci sent envoys to all the other cities of the State of Hada to call upon the defenders to surrender. Then all the people of the other cities submitted to Nurhaci. Nurhaci's troops did not do the slightest harm to the people of these cities. All of Menggebulu's subordinates were moved to the area of Jianzhou, and Menggebulu was brought back to Jianzhou. Nurhaci treated him politely. Nurhaci intended to let Menggebulu go back to the State of Hada later, but it was found out that Menggebulu was colluding with Gegai, the general under Nurhaci, to plan a rebellion. So Menggebulu and Gegai were executed.

In 1601, the Ming emperor Zhu Yi Jun heard about this. He sent an envoy to ask Nurhaci, "Why have you attacked the State of Hada and taken the whole of it? Now you must send the king's son Wu'ergudai back to be the king of the State of Hada." Nurhaci had to obey Emperor Zhu Yi Jun's order and send troops to escort Wu'ergudai back to the State of Hada to be the king.

Not long later, Nalinbulu plotted with the Mongol tribes to loot the people of the State of Hada several times. Nurhaci sent envoys to say to Emperor Zhu Yi Jun of the Ming Dynasty, "I obeyed Your Majesty's order and have sent troops to escort Wu'ergudai back to his state. Now the troops of Yehe have invaded the State of Hada many times. Why should the state I conquered be taken by the Yehe?" But Emperor Zhu Yi Jun of the Ming Dynasty ignored Nurhaci.

At that time there was a great famine in the State of Hada. There was no food for the people. Wu'ergudai sent envoys to Kaiyuan, which was under the control of the Ming army, to beg the officials for food. But the officials of the Ming Dynasty refused to give any. Wu'ergudai had to ask Nurhaci for help. Nurhaci took the opportunity to annex the State of Hada.

Nurhaci Conquers the State of Huifa

The people of the Huifa Tribe lived along the Huifa River (in the southwest part of Jilin Province). King Wangjichu had built a very strong city on Hu'erqi Mountain (to the Southeast of Huinan, Jilin

Province) and surrounded with three rings of walls. When he died, his grandson Baiyindali killed seven of his uncles and took the seat of the king of the State of Huifa for himself. In June and September 1593, Buzhai (of the State of Yehe) joined with the other states to invade the territory of Jianzhou twice. Baiyindali had commanded his troops to join with the army of Yehe to invade Jianzhou.

But in 1603, many of Baiyindali's clansmen betrayed him and fled to the State of Yehe, where they submitted to Nalinbulu. Many of Baiyindali's subordinates were planning a rebellion. Baiyindali sent the sons of his seven high-ranking officials to Nurhaci as hostages, begging Nurhaci to send troops to help him. Nurhaci agreed and sent 1,000 men. Nalinbulu of the State of Yehe sent an envoy to trick Baiyindali by saying, "If you recall the seven hostages, I will turn over to you those who have betrayed you."

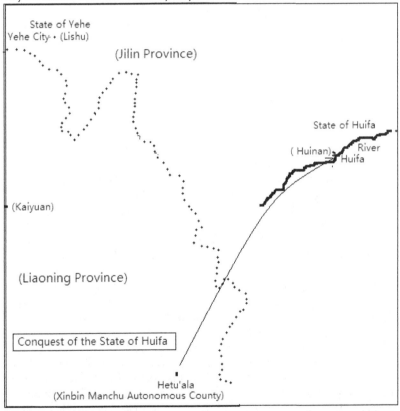

Baiyindali believed what Nalinbulu said and recalled the sons of his seven officials from Jianzhou. Then he sent his own son to Nalibulu as a hostage; but Nalinbulu did not hand over those who had betrayed Baiyindali. Therefore, Baiyindali sent an envoy to tell Nurhaci, "I have been deceived by Nalinbulu. Now I really hope that you will grant me favors. I beg that you will marry your daughter to me." Nurhaci gave his permission and promised to marry his daughter to Baiyindali. But later Baiyindali broke the agreement and refused to marry Nurhaci's daughter. Nurhaci sent an envoy to ask Baiyindali, "In the past you assisted the State of Yehe in invading my territory twice. I pardoned you for your crimes. I gave permission for you to marry my daughter. But now you have broken the agreement and refused to marry my daughter. Why have you done so?" Baiyindali lied again, "When my son comes back from the State of Yehe, I will marry your daughter and form an alliance with you." Then Baiyindali ordered his soldiers to fortify the defenses of the city on Hu'erqi Mountain.

After Baiyindali's son returned from the State of Yehe, Nurhaci sent an envoy to ask Baiyindali sternly, "Your son has come back. Now what are your plans?" Baiyindali thought that his city on Hu'erqi Mountain was strong enough to protect him from Nurhaci's army, so he broke his agreement. In September 1607, Nurhaci led his great army along the Huifa River to attack the city on Hu'erqi Mountain. When Nurhaci's army reached the city, they surrounded it and pounded the city fiercely, day and night. Several days later, they conquered the city and slew Baiyindali and his sons. Nurhaci took the people of the State of Huifa and moved them to Jianzhou. The State of Huifa no longer existed.

Nurhaci Conquers the State of Wula

Buzhantai, the younger brother of Mantai, the king of the State of Wula, was captured in the battle by Gule Mountain back in September 1593. Nurhaci had treated him with dignity. Three years later, in July 1596, Nurhaci decided to send him back to the State of Wula. He sent Generals Tu'erkunhuangzhan and Bo'erkunfeiyangzhan to escort him. Before Buzhantai arrived in Wula, Mantai and his son raped two women in a village and were killed by women's husbands at night. Now Xingniya, Buzhantai's uncle, wanted to be king so he intended to kill Buzhantai. But when Buzhantai arrived, he was protected by Nurhaci's two generals. Xingniya had no chance to kill him, so he high-tailed it to the State of Yehe. Buzhantai duly became the king of the State of Wula. After that, the two generals went back to Jianzhou.

Buzhantai was grateful to Nurhaci for sparing his life and helping him regain the seat of the king; he respected Nurhaci like his father. In December 1596, Buzhantai married his younger sister to Shurhaci, Nurhaci's younger brother. But the very next month, Buzhantai changed sides and allied with the Yehe. He captured Luotun, Geshitun and Wangjinu, the three heads of the Wa'erke Tribe who had submitted themselves to Nurhaci, and turned them over to the State of Yehe. Then he sent an envoy to present the valuable copper hammer kept by Dudugu, Mantai's wife, to Nalinbulu of the State of Yehe so as to please him. Then in December 1598, in order to show his gratitude to Nurhaci for sparing his life, Buzhantai came to visit

Nurhaci with three hundred followers. Nurhaci married his younger brother Shurhaci's daughter to Buzhantai. Nurhaci granted him fifty sets of armor and saw him back with due courtesy.

Buzhantai asked Ming'an, the head of the Mongolian Horqin Tribe, to marry his daughter to him. Buzhantai gave Ming'an many sets of armor, valuable furs, quantities of gold and silver and many horses and camels as betrothal gifts. Ming'an took the gifts but refused to give his daughter to Buzhantai. In January 1603 Buzhantai sent an envoy to tell Nurhaci, "When I was captured, you spared my life. Then you sent me back to be the king of the State of Wula. You married a princess to me. I am very grateful to you. But I failed to live up to your expectations. I did something wrong and I did not dare to tell you. I asked Ming'an to marry his daughter to me. Ming'an took all my betrothal gifts but refused to give his daughter to me. I feel very shameful for this. I hope you will marry a princess to me again. I will come to visit you every year with the two princesses." Nurhaci gave his permission and married another of Shurhaci's daughters to him.

In January 1607, Cemutehei, the head of Feiyou City (Jilin Province) of the Wa'erka Tribe, came to have an audience with Nurhaci. He told Nurhaci that he had submitted to Buzhantai but had been treated badly by him. He begged Nurhaci to allow his whole family and the people in Feiyou City to move to Jianzhou to submit to Nurhaci. Nurhaci sent his younger brother Shurhaci, his eldest son Chuying, and his second son Daishan to lead Generals Feiyingdong, Hu'erhan and Yangguli with 3,000 soldiers to Feiyou City to escort the family members of Cemutehei and the 500 households in Feiyou and the surrounding villages to Jianzhou. When they got to Feiyou City, they collected the people of the 500 households. General Hu'erhan and General Yangguli had orders to take 300 soldiers in the lead to escort the people of the 500 households first.

When Buzhantai got this information, he had his uncle Bokeduo lead more than 10,000 men to attack Nurhsci's army and the people of Feiyou City as they made their way to Jianzhou. The two armies met by the side of a mountain. General Hu'erhan arranged the civilians on the top of the mountain and sent 100 soldiers to protect them. Then he and General Yangguli commanded 200 soldiers to fight with the 10,000 soldiers commanded by Bokeduo. At that time Chuying, Daishan and Feiyingdong brought up the main force of 2,700 men to the battlefield. They fought very bravely. The Wula troops were disastrously defeated. Daishan caught up with Bokeduo and killed him. Bokeduo's son was also killed. In this battle, 3,000 soldiers of the State of Wula were killed, and Nurhaci's troops captured 500 horses.

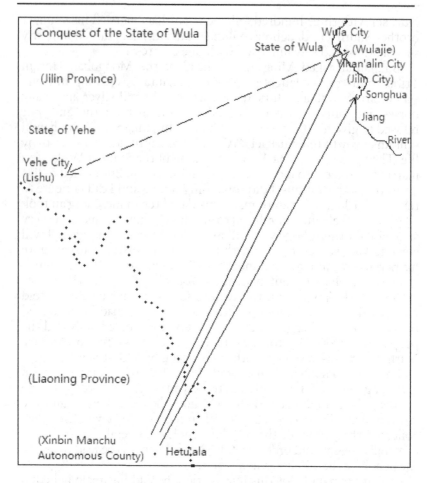

Conquest of the State of Wula

(Jilin Province)

State of Yehe

Yehe City
(Lishu)

(Liaoning Province)

(Xinbin Manchu
Autonomous County)   · Hetu'ala

Wula City
State of Wula   (Wulajie)
Yihan'alin City
(Jilin City)
Songhua
Jiang
River

In January 1608 Nurhaci ordered Chuying, his eldest son, and Taiji'amin, his nephew, to take 5,000 men to carry out an expedition against the State of Wula. Chuying's troops marched to Yihan'alin City (now Jilin City, Jilin Province) of the State of Wula. They attacked the city and took it, killing more than 1,000 soldiers. At that time Buzhantai and Weng'adai, the head of Mongol Horqin Tribe, commanded their troops to march out of Wula City, the capital the State of Wula. They marched for about 10 kilometers and watched the battle from afar. Buzhantai knew that his army was no match for Nurhaci's army. So he sent his army and the Mongolian army back to Wula City.

Since Yihan'alin City had been taken by Nurhaci, Buzhantai was very much afraid. In September 1608 Buzhantai sent an envoy to Nurhaci to make peace. In order to show his sincerity, he arrested 50 Yehe officials that had been sent by Nalinbulu of the State of Yehe. He asked Nurhaci to send envoys to the State of Wula to kill these

50 Yehe officials. Then he sent an envoy to speak to Nurhaci, saying, "I have violated our agreement of alliance several times and have offended Your Highness. I am ashamed of myself. If Your Highness marries your daughter to me and treats me as your own son, I will be devoted to you all my life." Nurhaci decided to marry his own daughter Mukushi to Buzhantai. He sent envoys to escort Mukushi to the State of Wula to marry Buzhantai.

In September 1612, Buzhantai violated the alliance with Nurhaci again. He commanded his army to attack the Hu'erha Branch of the Woji Tribe (in an area between the Songhua Jiang River and Wusuli Jiang River, Heilongjiang Province), who had been submitted to Nurhaci. He wanted to marry Buzhai's daughter, who was betrothed to Nurhaci. He used whistling arrows to shoot at Mukushi, Nurhaci's daughter.

When Nuhaci heard about this, he was really outraged. He commanded a great army to carry out an expedition against the State of Wula. Manggu'ertai, Nurhaci's fifth son, and Huangtaiji, Nurhaci's eighth son, went with him. When his great army reached the State of Wula, Nurhaci ordered his men to set up a big yellow umbrella. His army marched along the Wula River (now the upper branch of the Songhua Jiang River, Jilin Province) with loud drums beating. Buzhantai commanded his troops to meet Nurhaci's army. When they reached the riverside, they saw that Nurhaci's army was very strong. All of them were very afraid. They did not dare to fight with Nurhaci's army. Nurhaci's troops took control of five cities along the river. Then they took Jinzhou City, across the river just one kilometer west of Wula City, the capital of the State of Wula.

On 1 October 1612 Nurhaci sent some troops to the north of Wula City and destroyed the food stores of Buzhantai's army. Nurhaci's troops stayed there for three days. Buzhantai came out of the city with his army to face Nurhaci's army across the river in the daytime and went back into the city for the night. Nurhaci's sons Manggu'ertai and Huangtaiji asked Nurhaci's permission to cross the river to attack Wula City. Nurhaci said to them, "That is not the right way to conquer the State of Wula. Wula is a big, strong state, about equal in strength with our state. We cannot conquer them in one action. Conquering this state will be like felling a massive tree with a big, strong trunk. We cannot fell this big tree with one blow. We should chop at the trunk of this tree with an axe. When the trunk has been chopped many times and becomes small enough, the tree will fall. Our best strategy is to take all the cities around Wula City. Then Wula City will be isolated. It will not be able to stand alone for long."

So Nurhaci ordered his troops to destroy the six cities around Wula and burn all the houses and food stores. Buzhantai with six of his officials took a boat and sailed up the river to the place where Nurhaci was staying. Nurhaci put on his armor and rode a horse into the river and stood there. Buzhantai knelt down on his knees and touched his head to the floor boards of his boat and said in a very sad voice, "The State of Wula also belongs to Your Highness. I beg that Your Highness not burn all my food supplies." Nurhaci scolded him sternly for violating their agreements and for shooting at his daughter with whistling arrows. Nurhaci and his army stayed in the State of Wula for five more days. Then he commanded his main force to go back to Jianzhou.

In December 1612 Buzhantai violated his alliance with Nurhaci again. He decided to send his daughter Sahalian, his son Chuoqinai, and the sons of seventeen high officials to the State of Yehe as hostages. He put Nurhaci's daughter and Shurhaci's daughter in jail. He married Buzhai's daughter who had been betrothed by Nurhaci.

In January 1613 Nurhaci commanded his son Daishan, his nephew Amin and several generals to carry out an expedition with 30,000 men against the State of Wula. Nurhaci's army marched very quickly and soon took three cities of the State of Wula. Buzhantai had stationed 30,000 soldiers in Fu'erha City, south of Wula City. He ordered his second son Dalamu to defend Wula City. When Nurhaci's army marched near Fu'erha City, Buzhantai commanded his troops to come out of the city and array themselves in battle formation just 100 feet away from the battle formation of Nurhaci's army. The two armies met and fought heatedly.

Buzhantai's army was disastrously defeated. More than half of his soldiers were killed. The rest of Buzhantai's soldiers ran away in all directions. Swept up in the momentum of victory, Nurhaci commanded his soldiers to storm Wula City and they took it. Buzhantai had only 100 men following him. He rode back to Wula City. To his great surprise, he saw that Nurhaci was sitting on the top of the city wall at the west gate. He turned back but met with Nurhaci's son Daishan and his elite troops. Half of Buzhantai's remaining soldiers were killed. Buzhantai had a very narrow escape and rode to the State of Yehe. Nurhaci sent troops to take over the whole territory of the State of Wula. He took all the people to Jianzhou. The State of Wula became extinct.

Nurhaci Attacks the State of Yehe

After Buzhantai escaped to the State of Yehe, Nurhaci sent envoys to demand the kings of the State of Yehe to hand him over. But King Jintaishi and King Buyanggu of Yehe refused to do so. In September 1613, Nurhaci commanded 40,000 men to attack the State of Yehe. They captured 19 cities and strongholds. Then Nurhaci ordered his soldiers to burn the cities and the strongholds, and he brought the people to Jianzhou.

At that time, Yehe City (Lishu, Jilin Province), the capital of the State of Yehe, was divided into two: the West City and the East City. King Jintaishi stationed his army in the East City and King Buyanggu stationed his in the West City. They sent envoys to the authorities of the Ming Dynasty in what is now Liaoning Province, saying, "Nurhaci has taken the State of Hada, the State of Huifa and the State of Wula. Now he is invading our state. His intention is to invade the Ming Dynasty after he has taken all the four states. He will take the city of Liaodong and establish his capital there. Then the areas of Kaiyuan and Tieling will fall into his hands and become pasturelands for his horses."

The authorities of the Ming Dynasty believed that and sent envoys to order Nurhaci to stop invading the State of Yehe. They sent Commanders Ma Shi Nan and Zhou Da Qi with 1,000 soldiers carrying guns to the East City and the West City of Yehe. When Nurhaci heard all this, he personally went to Fushunsuo (now Fushun, Liaoning Province) to see Li Yong Fang, the Commander-in-chief of the Ming army in Northeast China. He delivered a letter to Li Yong Fang which read, "In the past, the State of Yehe, the State of Hada, the State of Huifa, the State of Wula, the Mongolian Horqin Tribe, Mongolian Xibo Tribe, Mongolian Gua'ercha Tribe, Zhusheli Tribe, and Nayin Tribe all united together to invade my state. I led my army to resist their attacks. With the help of Heaven, I won. My troops killed Buzhai, the king of the State of Yehe, and captured Buzhantai. In 1597, the kings of the four states vowed to form an alliance with me. King Buyanggu of the State of Yehe promised to marry his younger sister to me. But very soon King Buyanggu broke the agreement and refused to send his sister. I treated Buzhantai with dignity after he was captured and helped him to go back to be the king of the State of Wula. But he was devoid of gratitude. He acted as my enemy. So I carried out an expedition against him and conquered the State of Wula. Buzhantai went away to the State of Yehe, and the king of Yehe granted him asylum there. I demanded the king of Yehe to hand Buzhantai over to me several times. But he refused to do so. This is why I have attacked the State of Yehe. There is no hatred between you and me. I will not attack your territory." Having delivered the letter, Nurhaci went back to Jianzhou.

3. Nurhaci Establishes the (Later) Jin Dynasty and Ascends the Throne

Nurhaci Establishes the Eight Banners Army System

Nurhaci organized his army in the following way: 300 men formed a basic unit called a "Niulu," and each Niulu had a commander; five Niulu (1,500 men) formed a bigger unit called "Jiala," and each Jiala had a commander; five Jiala (7,500 men) formed a "Gushan," and each Gushan had a commander and two deputy commanders. At first all the troops were put under four pure color banners: the pure yellow banner, the pure red banner, the pure blue banner and the pure white banner. Each pure color banner was quadrilateral with a dragon design on it, with the head of the dragon facing back. Later, as his army grew greater, Nurhaci established four more banners: the red banner with a white border, the yellow banner with red border, the blue banner with red border and the white banner with red border. Each banner with borders was pentagon-shaped with a dragon design on it, with the head of the dragon facing forward.

When the army marched in a wide area, all the troops under the eight banners marched side by side. When the army marched in a narrow place, all the troops under the eight banners marched in a line one after another. The troops marched with great discipline and no noise was allowed to be made. On the battlefield, those who had strong armor, long spears, and broad swords, were put in the front as a vanguard. Those who had lighter armor and were good at shooting arrows stood behind the vanguard. The elite equestrian troops were ready to reinforce the vanguard and the archers. In every battle, all the officers and soldiers were eager to establish their reputation by making military contributions. Nurhaci and his generals planned each battle carefully. So Nurhaci's troops were sure to win in each battle, and when they attacked a city, they were sure to take it. After each battle, Nurhaci granted rewards to those who had made the most significant contributions and punished those who showed themselves to be cowards. So Nurhaci's army was invincible.

Nurhaci Establishes His Dynasty and Ascends the Throne

As early as in March 1602, Nurhaci ordered workmen to build a big city outside the city of Hetu'ala with grand palaces in it. This new city became the capital of the new dynasty.

On 1 January 1616, Nurhaci ascended the throne as emperor at the age of 58. He declared the establishment of the Jin Dynasty. He gave his reign the title of "Tianming," meaning "the Will of Heaven." So 1616 was the first year of Tianming. In order to distinguish the Jin Dynasty founded by Nurhaci in 1616 from the Jin Dynasty founded by Wanyuan Hao in 1114, historians call the dynasty established by Nurhaci the "Later Jin Dynasty." Nurhaci made Daishan, his second son, the Grand King; Amin, his younger brother's son, the Second King; Manggu'ertai, his fifth son, the Third King; and Huangtaiji, his eighth son, the Fourth King. (By that time Chuying, his eldest son, had died — he was imprisoned for committing an offense against his father.) Nurhaci appointed Eyidu, Feiyingdong, Heheli, Hu'erhan and Anfeiyanggu as the Five Grand Officials. He let the Four Kings and the Five Grand Officials attend to the state affairs together with him. Nurhaci instructed the Four Kings and the Five Grand Officials that they should be fair in handling state affairs and they should exert themselves to make the country prosperous.

4. Nurhaci Wages War against the Ming Dynasty

Nurhaci Declares the Seven Reasons for His Hatred for the Ming Dynasty

In April 1618 Nurhaci decided to mount an expedition against the Ming Dynasty. Before his army started out, a ceremony was held to pledge its determination. In the ceremony, Nurhaci read out his declaration of the seven reasons for his hatred for the Ming Dynasty. Nurhaci declared, "My grandfather and my father did not do the slightest harm to the Ming Dynasty. But the court of the Ming Dynasty sent troops to invade our territory and killed my grandfather and my father without any basis. That is the first reason for my hatred for the Ming Dynasty. Although the Ming Dynasty has started the quarrel, I still tried to be friendly with the Ming Dynasty. We set up boundary tablets marking the boundary of the two sides, and the two sides agreed that neither would cross the boundary. But the army of the Ming Dynasty went against the agreement and crossed our boundary to support the State of Yehe. This is the second reason for my hatred for the Ming Dynasty. Every year Ming troops have crossed the boundary into the territory of my state to loot the people. I sent troops to kill some of the Ming intruders. But the authorities of the Ming Dynasty accused me of violating the agreement and executed my two envoys and another ten people on the boundary. This is the third reason for my hatred for the Ming Dynasty. The troops of the Ming Dynasty went across the boundary to assist the State of Yehe, and the king of Yehe married Buzhai's daughter whom I had been betrothed to. This is the fourth reason for my hatred for the Ming Dynasty. The people of the tribes in Chaihe, Sancha and Fu'an are my people. They have grown crops in these places for generations. But the Ming Dynasty does not allow them to harvest the crops and send troops to drive the people away. This is the fifth reason for my hatred for the Ming Dynasty. The king of the State of Yehe acted against the Will of Heaven and was punished by Heaven. The authorities of the Ming Dynasty believed the king of Yehe's one-sided story and sent envoys to insult me. This is the sixth reason for my hatred for the Ming Dynasty. The State of Hada supported the State of Yehe in invading my territory twice. With the help of Heaven, I defeated the State of Hada and captured the king. The Ming emperor forced me to send his son back to be king of Hada. Later, the State of Yehe invaded the State of Hada several times and the king of the State of Hada asked the Ming Dynasty for help. But the authorities of the Ming Dynasty allowed the State of Yehe to invade Hada. The authorities of the Ming Dynasty are partial to and sided with the State of Yehe against me; they confused right and wrong. This is the seventh reason for my hatred for the Ming Dynasty. For these reasons, I will begin military operations against the Ming Dynasty." In conclusion, Nurhaci prohibited his troops from insulting captives, raping women, and killing those who surrendered.

Nurhaci Takes Fushun and Qinghe City

The second day after the ceremony, Nurhaci commanded his army of 20,000 men to march towards Fushun. That night, it was raining, and Nurhaci asked the Kings and the Grand Officials if they felt they should turn back? Daishan, the Grand King, said, "All our soldiers have waterproof coats. There is no problem for them to march in the rain. Heaven has sent this rain to make the troops of the Ming Dynasty slack off in their preparation against our attack. Then we can take our enemy by surprise. So the rain is favorable for us but unfavorable for our enemy."Nurhaci agreed with him and ordered his troops to continue their march forward.

Not long after, the rain stopped and the sky became clear. The bright moon came out. So Nurhaci's troops made quick progress. On 15 April 1618, Nurhaci's troops reached Fushun and laid siege to the city. Nurhaci wrote a letter to Li Yong Fang, the commander-in-chief of the Ming army defending Fushun City and asked a local person to take the letter to him. The letter read, "You will surely be defeated if you resist my army. But if you surrender without a fight, I will let you remain the commander-in-chief of your army. If you come out of the city to surrender, my troops will not enter the city so that the people of the city will not be frightened, and family members will not be separated from one another. Think about it and make up your mind quickly."

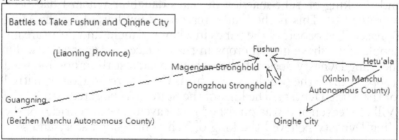

Battles to Take Fushun and Qinghe City

After Li Yong Fang had read the letter, he stood at the top of the city wall and looked out of the city. He saw Nurhaci's troops were strong indeed, and were ready to attack the city with long ladders. So he decided to surrender. Nurhaci accepted his surrender with due courtesy. He appointed Li Yong Fang as commander-in-chief to lead the Ming troops who had surrendered. He ordered his troops to escort the people from Fushun City to Jianzhou. Then he sent 4,000 soldiers to destroy the city of Fushun.

On the same day, Nurhaci's army taking the eastern route took Dongzhou Stronghold (in the southeast of Fushun) and Magendan Stronghold (just to the south). Then all the troops under Nurhaci retreated to the border between the area under the rule of the Ming Dynasty and Jianzhou.

When Zhang Cheng Yin, the Commander-in-chief of the Ming army in Guangning (now Beizhen Manchu Autonomous County, Liaoning Province), his Deputy Commander-in-chief, and the local general got information that Nurhaci's troops had taken Fushun, Dongzhou Stronghold and Magendan Stronghold, they commanded 10,000 troops to counterattack. Nurhaci ordered Daishan, the Grand King, and Huangtaiji, the Fourth King, to take some troops to fend off the Ming troops. When the Ming troops came, they pitched three camps by the hillside. They dug ditches around the camps and shot guns at Nurhaci's troops. Nurhaci's two sons commanded their troops to attack.

Suddenly a strong wind rose and blew sand directly at the Ming troops. The troops under the two kings took the chance to charge at the enemy. They destroyed the three camps and killed many Ming soldiers. The Commander-in-chief of the Ming army, the Deputy Commander-in-chief and General Pu Shi Fang were all killed in the battle.

In June 1618, Nurhaci attacked Qinghe City (Liaoning Province). All the Kings and Grand Officials went with him. Zhou Chu Xian, the Deputy Commander-in-chief of the Ming army defending Qinghe City, led 10,000 men in a stout defense of the city. They had 1,000 guns and cannons. Nurhaci's soldiers clambered up the city wall with their long ladders, in spite of the rain of gun-fire, arrows and stones. They succeeded in reaching the top of the city wall, and the Ming soldiers ran away. Nurhaci took Qinghe City.

The Great Battle of Sa'erhu

In February 1619, Emperor Zhu Yi Jun of the Ming Dynasty saw that the (Later) Jin Dynasty had become stronger and stronger and he was afraid that they would bring great trouble to the Ming Dynasty. So he decided to send a great army to carry out an expedition against them. The court of the Ming Dynasty sent Du Song, the Commander-in-chief of the Ming army in Shanhaiguan (in the northeast part of Hebei Province), Wang Xuan, the Commander-in-chief of the Ming army in Baoding (in the middle of Hebei), Liu Ting, the Commander-in-chief of the Ming army in Liaoyang, Li Ru Bai, the Commander-in-chief of the army in Liaodong (in eastern Liaoning Province), Ma Lin, the Commander-in-chief of the army in Kaiyuan and Tieling (all in Liaoning Province), to command their forces to carry out this expedition.

There were 200,000 men in this great army. They were divided into four routes. Du Song commanded the army of the West Route with 60,000 men, intending to attack Hetu'ala, the capital of the (Later) Jin Dynasty, from the west. They would march along Hun River through Fushun Pass. Li Ru Bai commanded the army of the

South Route, with 60,000 men. They were to attack Hetu'ala from the south, marching from Qinghe through Yagu Pass. Ma Lin commanded the army of the North Route, with 40,000 men. They were to attack Hetu'ala from the north. The army of the State of Yehe would join them, marching from Kaiyuan. Liu Ting commanded the 40,000-man army of the East Route. More than 10,000 Korean soldiers joined them. This route of the army would march from Kuandian to Dong'e (now Huanren Manchu Autonomous County, Liaoning Province).

On 29 February 1619, Du Song commanded 60,000 men to march out of Fushun Pass at night. Du Song's troops held torches in their hands. Nurhaci's scouts saw the Ming troops marching out of Fushun Pass from afar, and raced back to report what they had seen to the Kings as they sat in court early the next morning. Before this information was reported to Nurhaci, the scouts from the south came to report that the Ming army had reached Dong'e. The Kings and the officials reported all the information to Nurhaci.

Nurhaci said, "It is certain that the Ming armies have come. We have 500 troops stationed in the south. They can hold off the Ming troops coming from that direction. The Ming approach from the south is simply to lure my army off track. The Ming army marching from Fushun, however, must be a great army. We should fight this army first. If we defeat this branch of the Ming army, the other branches will be easily dealt with."

So in the morning of 1 March 1619 Nurhaci, with Daishan, the Grand King, other Kings and the Grand Officials, commanded the troops in Hetu'ala to march out of the city. Nurhaci ordered Daishan to take the vanguard to march ahead of the main force. When Daishan and his troops had passed Zaka Pass, Daishan ordered the men to stop. He intended to stay there and wait for his father and the main force. Then Huangtaiji, the Fourth King, arrived. He said to Daishan, "In the mountains in Jiefan, there are 15,000 workmen who are building a new city. They have no weapons and there are only a few troops to protect them. If the Ming troops come, all the workmen will be killed. Our troops should speed over there to save them." Daishan agreed with him and off they went towards Jiefan Mountain (near the confluence of the Suzi River and Hun River).

When the troops reached Tailangang (south of Jiefan Mountain), Daishan wanted to station the troops in a concealed place and wait for his father and the main force. But Huangtaiji said, "Now it is the time for our troops to set up their battle formations so as to show the enemy how strong our troops are. The workmen on the mountain will see us and will be inspired and will fight with all their might. Why should you hide the troops?" All the generals and officials agreed with him. So the troops under Daishan and Huangtaiji marched towards Jiefan in battle formation. When they reached Jiefan, the workmen joined forces with them. They pitched camps by Jilinya Cliff. On 1 March 1619, Du Song and the Ming troops arrived at Sa'erhu Mountain.

He ordered 40,000 soldiers to pitch camp. He himself commanded 20,000 men to cross the Suzi River and attack Jilinya Cliff.

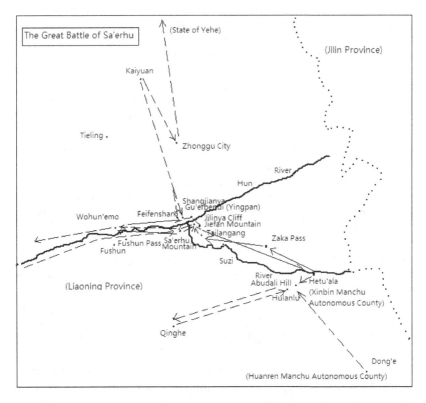

The Great Battle of Sa'erhu

(State of Yehe)

(Jilin Province)

Kaiyuan

Tieling

Zhonggu City

River

Hun

Wohun'emo   Feifenshan   Shangjianya Gu'erbengai (Yingpan)
Jilinya Cliff
Jiefan Mountain

Zaka Pass

Fushun Pass Sa'erhu   Tailangang
Fushun   Mountain

Suzi

River
Abudali Hill   Hetu'ala

(Liaoning Province)   Hulanlu   (Xinbin Manchu
Autonomous County)

Qinghe

Dong'e

(Huanren Manchu Autonomous County)

By sunset, Nurhaci arrived at Jilinya Cliff commanding the troops under the eight banners. After discussion with the Kings and the officials, he decided to send troops under six banners to attack the Ming troops on Sa'erhu Mountain and send troops under two banners to attack the Ming troops attacking Jilinya Cliff. The next morning Nurhaci personally commanded the troops under six banners in crossing the Suzi River and attacking the Ming troops on Sa'erhu Mountain. The Ming troops were arranged in battle formation and they had guns. The (Later) Jin troops shot arrows at the Ming soldiers on the mountain. After a fierce fight, the Ming encampment was destroyed by the (Later) Jin troops. Many Ming soldiers were killed in the battle.

At the same time the (Later) Jin troops on Jilinya Cliff dashed down the hill to attack the Ming troops. The troops under the two banners started their attack from the back the of the Ming troops. The Ming troops were attacked from the front and from behind. The Ming troops were routed. Du Song and several of his generals were killed. The West Route of the Ming army was totally destroyed.

At night of the same day Ma Lin, the Commander-in-chief of the North Route of the Ming army, led 40,000 men to Shangjianya. The main force pitched camp there. Pan Zong Yan, the Supervisor of the North Route, led some troops to pitch camp in Feifenshan, two kilometers to the west. General Gong Nian Sui and General Li Xi Mi, two commanders in the West Route, led about 10,000 men to Wohun'emo. The (Later) Jin scouts reported the situation to Nurhaci. Nurhaci took some men to attack the Ming forces in Wohun'emo. The Ming troops were defeated and ran away. The (Later) Jin troops went after them. General Gong Nian Sui and General Li Xi Mi were killed in battle.

Then Nurhaci commanded his troops to attack the Ming troops in Shangjianya. Again, the Ming troops were wiped out. Ma Lin, the Commander-in-chief of the North Route of the Ming army, narrowly escape. Then Nurhaci commanded all his troops to launch a fierce attack on the troops in Feifenshan. The Ming soldiers there were thoroughly routed and the Supervisor of the North Route was killed. The two kings of the State of Yehe, commanding their troops, were marching southward intending to join forces with the North Route but when they reached Zhonggu City, they heard the news and turned back immediately to the State of Yehe.

Having defeated two branches of the Ming army, Nurhaci took all his troops on 3 March 1619 to Gu'erbendi (now Yingpan, east of Fushun). There, they learned that Liu Ting, the Commander-in-chief of the East Route of the Ming army, had reached Dong'e, and Li Ru Bo, the Commander-in-chief of the South Route of the Ming army, had reached Hulanlu. They were planning to attack Hetu'ala, Nurhaci's capital.

Nurhaci sent Hu'erhan with about 1,000 men to go first to resist the Ming troops coming from the south, and on 4 March 1619 Nurhaci held a grand ceremony in Jiefan to offer sacrifices to Heaven. The next day, Nurhaci and his great army went back to Hetu'ala. He sent Daishan, the Grand King, and Huangtaiji, the Fourth King, to command 10,000 elite cavalrymen to resist Liu Ting and the East Route of the Ming army. Liu Ting commanded a vanguard of 20,000 men to march towards Abudali Hill (south of Hetu'ala). Huangtaiji led his troops in occupying Abudali Hill. Daishan ordered the soldiers to put on the hats and clothes of the Ming soldiers who were captured in the battle against Du Song and the West Route of the Ming army. Daishan disguised himself as a general of the Ming army. At that time Liu Ting did not know that the West Route of the Ming army had been destroyed. When he and his troops reached the foot of Abudali Hill, he saw some troops in Ming army uniforms holding Ming banners. Liu Ting did not have the slightest idea that they were the (Later) Jin troops. Suddenly these troops attacked Liu Ting's forces. At the same time Huangtaiji and thirty cavalrymen rode swiftly down the hill to attack the Ming troops. They fought valiantly. Liu Ting's troops were in a total confusion and many of the Ming soldiers were killed. Liu Ting was killed, too.

Then Daishan and Huangtaiji commanded their troops to march further south and they defeated the remainder of Liu Ting's army. From then on, the East Route of the Ming army was thoroughly routed. Nurhaci successfully destroyed three routes of the Ming army in four days.

Yang Gao, the Supreme Commander of the Ming army in Liaodong Area, urgently sent envoys to Hulanlu to order Li Bo Ru, the Commander-in-chief of the South Route of the Ming army, to withdraw immediately. So Li Bo Ru commanded the South Route of the Ming army to withdraw back to Qinghe.

The Battles to Take Kaiyuan and Tieling

On 10 June 1619 Nurhaci commanded 40,000 troops to march north to attack Kaiyuan (now Kaiyuan, in the north part of Liaoning Province). His troops marched for three days. There was a heavy rain and the roads were muddy. It was difficult for his troops to march north and cross the Hun River (now Hun River, Liaoning Province). Nurhaci was afraid that the information of his plan of attacking Kaiyuan would be reported to the Ming army in Kaiyuan. So he sent 100 soldiers to march to Shenyang (now Shenyang, Liaoning Province) so as to show to the Ming army that his purpose was to attack Shenyang. These 100 soldiers marched to Shenyang and killed 30 Ming soldiers and captured 20 Ming soldiers. At the same time Nurhaci sent scouts to find out if there was heavy rain in Kaiyuan and whether the roads to Kaiyuan were muddy. The scouts came back and reported to Nurhaci that there had been no rain in Kaiyuan and the roads were not muddy. Nurhaci commanded his troops to march to Kaiyuan quickly. In early morning of 16 June 1619 Nurhaci's troops reached Kaiyuan and started a fierce attack. Very soon the city of Kaiyuan was taken by the (Later) Jin army. Ma Lin, the Commander-in-chief of the Ming army defending Kaiyuan, Yu Hua Long, the Deputy Commander-in-chief of the Ming army, and Gao Zhen, the Chief of the General Staff, were all killed in battle.

Having taken Kaiyuan Nurhaci did not go back to Hetu'ala, the capital, but commanded his army to Jiefan and stayed there. He said to the Kings and the officials that his army could have a rest there and the horses of the army could feed on the grasslands there. And the more important reason was that it would be convenient for them to start their next military action from Jiefan.

On 25 July 1619 Nurhaci commanded his troops to attack Tieling (now Tieling, Liaoning Province) which was situated to the south of Kaiyuan. The troops of the (Later) Jin laid siege to the city. They climbed up the city wall by long ladders against a rain of arrows and stones and they successfully took the city. Yu Cheng Ming, Shi Feng Ming and Li Ke Tai, the generals of Ming army defending Tieling, were all killed in battle.

Nurhaci Conquers the State of Yehe

On 19 August 1619 Nurhaci commanded his army to carry out an expedition against the State of Yehe. Nurhaci's army marched to Yehe City (situated in Lishu, Jilin Province), the capital of the State of Yehe. There were two cities in Yehe City: the East City and the West City. King Jintaishi of the State of Yehe lived in the East City. King Buyanggu of the State of Yehe lived in the West City. On 22 August the (Later) Jin army reached Yehe City, Nurhaci ordered the four kings to take their troops and attack the West City where Buyanggu was. Nurhaci himself attacked the East City where Jintaishi was.

The four kings and their troops laid siege to the West City. Nurhaci commanded his troops to lay siege to the East City and started a fierce attack on the city.

Very soon Nurhaci's troops destroyed the four walls of the city. The troops of the (Later) Jin army surrounded Jintaishi's house and urged him to surrender. Jintaishi shouted to Nurhaci, "Your son, the Fourth King, is my younger sister's son. If he can come to meet me and tell me his pledge not to kill me, I will go down." Nurhaci immediately sent an envoy to the West City to call Huangtaiji, the Fourth King, to the East City to persuade Jintaishi, his uncle, to surrender. But when Huangtaiji came and tried to persuade his uncle to surrender, Jintaishi said that he had never seen his nephew and was not sure that this man was really him. So he refused to surrender.

The (Later) Jin troops started a fierce attack. Jintaishi set fire to himself and tried to kill himself. But the (Later) Jin soldiers broke into his house. They extinguished the fire and hanged Jintaishi to death with a rope. When Buyanggu knew that the West City had been taken by the (Later) Jin troops, he decided to surrender. He ordered his soldiers to open the city gates and let the (Later) Jin troops to go into the city. Daishan, the Grand King, brought Buyanggu to see Nurhaci. When Buyanggu was brought before Nurhaci, he refused to kneel down on both knees and touch his head to the ground. He just knelt on one knee. He was ordered to pay respects to the emperor with courtesy several times. But he refused to do so. Nurhaci was very angry and ordered soldiers to execute Buyanggu that night. Nurhaci at last conquered the State of Yehe. Then he commanded his army back to Jiefan and stayed there.

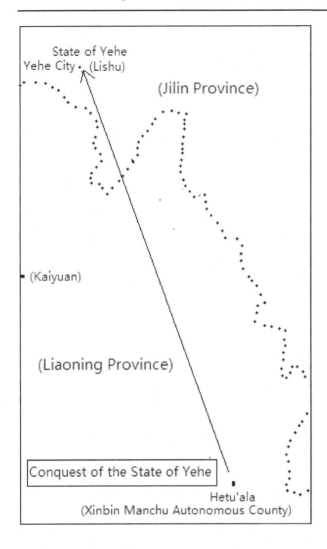

State of Yehe
Yehe City • (Lishu)

(Jilin Province)

(Kaiyuan)

(Liaoning Province)

Conquest of the State of Yehe

Hetu'ala
(Xinbin Manchu Autonomous County)

Nurhaci Takes Shenyang and Liaoyang

In 1620 there were great changes in the Ming Dynasty. In July 1620 Emperor Zhu Yi Jun died at the age of fifty-eight. In August 1620 his son Zhu Chang Luo ascended the throne of the Ming Dynasty. But in September 1620 he died a sudden death at the age of thirty-eight. In the same month his son Zhu You Jiao ascended the throne of the Ming Dynasty. The political situation of the Ming Dynasty was unstable. Nurhaci took this chance to attack Shenyang (now Shenyang, in the central part of Liaoning Province). On 10 March 1621 Nurhaci commanded his great army to march to Shenyang. The soldiers of the (Later) Jin army put all the city attacking equipments on boats and sailed down the Hun River (now Hun River, in Liaoning Province). The foot troops and cavalrymen marched along the Hun River. At night of 11 March when the (Later) Jin troops were marching towards Shenyang, they were found out by the scouts of the Ming army. The scouts rode very quickly to Shenyang to report to He Shi Xian, the Commander-in-chief of the Ming army defending Shenyang, and You Shi Gong, the Deputy Commander-in-chief. They immediately ordered their soldiers to go up to the top of the city wall to resist the attack. In the early morning of 12 March, the (Later) Jin army reached Shenyang. They pitched camps in a place three kilometers east to the city of Shenyang. On 13 March Nurhaci ordered his troops to start a fierce attack on the city of Shenyang. The (Later) Jin soldiers pushed shielded carts to the foot of the city wall and put long ladders on the city wall and climbed very quickly to the top of the city wall. Very soon the city of Shenyang was taken by the (Later) Jin army. He Shi Xian and You Shi Gong were killed in battle.

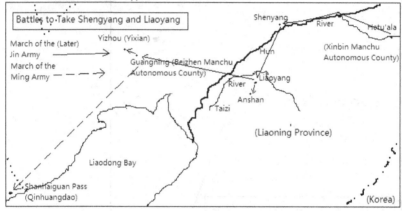

On 18 March 1620 Nurhaci commanded his victorious army to march from Shenyang south towards Liaoyang. Liaoyang was the capital city of Liaodong Province (now Liaoning Province) of the Ming Dynasty. It was a big and strong city. Yuan Ying Tai, the Commander-in-chief of the Ming army in Liaodong Province, commanded the Ming army to defend Liaoyang. When he got the information that the (Later) Jin troops were marching towards Liaoyang, he ordered his soldiers to lead water in Taizi River (now Taizi River, Liaoning Province, which flows past the north of Liaoyang City) to the moat around the city of Liaoyang. At noon of 19 March 1620 Nurhaci and his great army reached Liaoyang and were crossing Taizi River. The scouts of the Ming army found out this information and ran back to Liaoyang to report this information to Yuan Ying Tai. Yuan Ying Tai sent Li Huai Xin, Hou Shi Lu, Cai Guo Zhu, Jiang Bi and Tong Zhong Qui, the generals of the Ming army defending Liaoyang, to command 50,000 men to go out of the city. They arranged their troops in battle

formations in a place two kilometers from the city. Huangtaiji, the Fourth King, having crossed the river, commanded his troops to march to Liaoyang City. He commanded his troops to attack the left wing of the battle formation of the Ming army. At this moment the (Later) Jin troops under two banners arrived. These troops and the troops under Huangtaiji attacked the Ming army from two sides. The Ming troops were seriously defeated and ran away to the south. Huangtaiji commanded his troops to pursue the Ming troops to Anshan (now Anshan, Liaoning Province) which was thirty kilometers south to the city of Liaoyang. Then he commanded his troops back to Liaoyang. On 20 March Nurhaci ordered some troops to dig ditches to drain the water in the moat and some troops to build a dike to block the ditch that led water from Taizi River to the moat. Then the (Later) Jin troops started a fierce attack on the city. Huangtaiji commanded his troops to climb up the city wall. The Ming troops outside the city were totally destroyed. On 21 March the (Later) Jin army started a general offensive. Yuan Ying Tai went up to the tower on top of the city wall to supervise the defense of the city. When the city fell, Yuan Ying Tai set fire to the tower and burned himself to death. At noon that day, Nurhaci went into the city of Liaoyang. On that day Nurhaci decided to move his capital to Liaoyang.

In January 1622 Nurhaci commanded his army to march to the west part of Liaodong. On 23 January Nurhaci's army took Guangning (now Beizhen Manchu Autonomous County, Liaoning Province). Then Nurhaci commanded his great army to march towards Shanhaiguan Pass (now Shanhaiguan Pass, situated in Qinhuangdao, Hebei Province). Xiong Ting Bi, the Governor of Liaodong Province of the Ming Dynasty, commanded his troops to retreat towards Shanhaiguan Pass (in Qinhuangdao, Hebei Province), burning all the towns and villages on his way. Then Nurhaci commanded his army to march westward and took Yizhou (now Yixian, Liaoning Province) and all the cities in the west part of Liaodong.

In March 1625 Nurhaci moved his capital from Liaoyang to Shenyang.

5. Last Days of Nurhaci, and Defeat in Ningyuan

In January 1626 Nurhaci took 130,000 men and marched westward towards Ningyuan (now Xingcheng, in the southwest part of Liaoning Province). Nurhaci and his great army crossed Liao River (now Liao River, Liaoning Province), Daling River (now Daling River, Liaoning Province), and Xiaoling River (now Xiaoling River, Liaoning Province) and went over Tashan Mountain. On 23 January they reached Xingcheng which was a strategically important place because it was situated close to Shanhaiguan Pass (situated in Qinghuangdao, Hebei Province) which was the first pass of the Great Wall. Nurhaci sent envoys into the city to persuade Yuan Chong Huan, the Commander-in-chief of the Ming army defending Ningyuan, to surrender. But Yuan Chong Huan refused. On 24 January Nurhaci ordered his troops to attack the city. Carrying shields in their hands the soldiers pressed to the foot of the city wall. They tried to dig big holes on the city wall so that the city wall would fall. They dug many big holes on the wall but the wall did not collapse because it was winter and the city wall was frozen. The Ming troops defending Ningyuan fired cannons and shot arrows on the top of the city wall and killed many soldiers of the (Later) Jin army. The next day Nurhaci's army continued to attack the city of Ningyuan. The defenders of the city of Ningyuan fought resolutely and caused great casualties on the (Later) Jin army. The (Later) Jin army had to retreat. In these two days, four high ranking officers and more than 500 soldiers of the (Later) Jin army were killed. On 26 January Nurhaci got to know that Huajue Island was situated on the sea eight kilometers south to the city of Ningyuan. Nurhaci sent Wunage, a Mongolian general, to command the Mogolian soldiers under him to attack Huajue Island. Wunage and his troops crossed the sea while the sea water was frozen. They started an attack and killed all the soldiers defending the island, 7,000 in all. They killed all the people on the island. They burned 2,000 ships and all the food supplies stored on the island. Then the Mongolian troops withdrew back to Ningyuan. On 27 Nurhaci commanded all his troops to retreat back to Shenyang. Nurhaci was very angry because, since he had taken up arms, he had been invincible — and Ningyuan was the only city he had not been able to conquer.

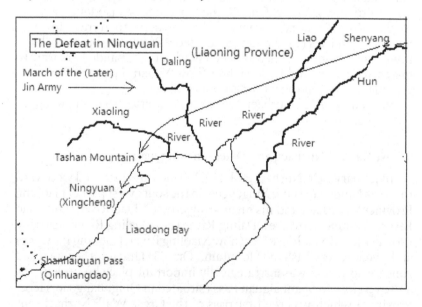

Nurhaci's Last Days

On 23 July 1626 Nurhaci fell ill. He went to the hot springs at Qinghe (now Qinghecheng, Liaoning Province) for treatment. On 7 August his illness became serious. He decided to go back to Shenyang, the capital, by boat along the Taizi River (now in Liaoning Province). On 30 September when the boat reached Aijibao (twenty kilometers from Shenyang City), Nurhaci passed away at the age of sixty-eight. Nurhaci had ruled for eleven years. He was buried in Fu Mausoleum, in the eastern outskirts of Shenyang City. He was given the posthumous title of Emperor Wu and the temple title of Taizu (meaning Supreme Ancestor).

SECTION TWO: AISIN GIORO HUANGTAIJI ESTABLISHES THE QING DYNASTY

1. Aisin Gioro Huangtaiji Ascends the Throne of the (Later) Jin Dynasty

3. Aisin Gioro Huangtaiji, Taizong of the Qing Dynasty

When Nurhaci died he did not appoint any of his sons to succeed to the throne. Daishan, the Grand King, his sons Yuetuo and Sahalian, strongly recommended Huangtaiji, the Fourth King, because Hungtaiji was virtuous and had great ability. All the kings and officials invited Huangtaiji to ascend the throne. They invited him three times and he declined three times. But at last he agreed. On 1 September 1626 Huangtaiji ascended the throne of the (Later) Jin Dynasty in Shenyang. He decided that the title of his reign was "Tiancong" (in Chinese characters天聰) meaning "Born Clever." The year of 1627 would be the first year of Tiancong. The name Huangtaiji (in Chinese characters皇太極) was given by his father Nurhaci in Manchu language. This name coincided with the Chinese words "Huangtaizi" (in Chinese characters 皇太子) meaning "the Crown Prince." So all the people said that it had been the will of Heaven that Huangtaiji should ascend the throne.

2. Expedition against the Ming Dynasty

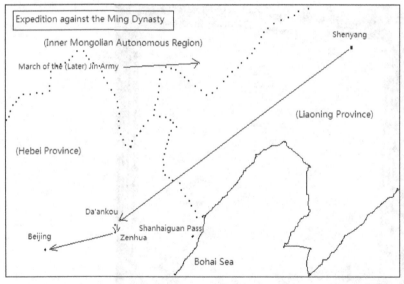

On 2 October 1629 Huangtaiji commanded his great army to carry out an expedition against the Ming Dynasty. On 30 October Huangtaiji and his army reached Zunhua (now Zunhua, Hebei Province). The (Later) Jin army attacked and took Da'ankou, a pass of the Great Wall situated in the north part of Zunhua. Huangtaiji and his great army passed the Great Wall through this pass. On 3 November the (Later) Jin army attacked Zunhua and took the city. On 11 November, the great army of the (Later) Jin Dynasty pressed forward to Beijing (now Beijing), the capital of the Ming Dynasty. On 20 November the (Later) Jin army reached Beijing. Huangtaiji and his main force camped in

Tuchengguan (a place outside Desheng Gate, the north gate of the city wall of Beijing). The rest of his army camped on the northeast outside Beijing. The Ming troops under General Man Gui and General Hou Shi Lu stationed on Desheng Gate. General Yuan Chong Huan who had defeated Nurhaci in Ningyuan, and General Zu Da Shou commanded their troops to station on Shawo Gate (now Guangqu Gate, the east gate of the city wall of Beijing). Huangtaiji commanded Daishan, the Grand King, King Jierhalang, King Yuetuo, King Dudu and King Sahalian to attack General Man Gui and General Hou Shi Lu in Desheng Gate. Mangguertai, the Grand King, King Abatai, King Ajige, King Duoergun, King Duoduo and King Haoge attacked General Yuan Chong Huan and General Zu Da Shou in Shawo Gate.

On 27 November, General Yuan Chong Huan and General Zu Da Shou stationed their troops on the southeast corner of the city wall. The Kings of the (Later) Jin Dynasty commanded their troops to press forward and camped face to face against the Ming troops. Huangtaiji rode to that part of the city wall to watch the situation. The Kings suggested to Huangtaiji that they should attack the city. But Huangtaiji said, "The road is narrow and dangerous. Many of my officers and soldiers will be killed in attacking the city. It is not worthwhile to take the city with great loss of my soldiers." So he ordered to stop the attack. At that time two eunuchs of the Ming Dynasty were captured. Huangtaiji ordered Generals Gao Hung Zhong and Bao Cheng Xian to carry out a secret plan. Then Generals Gao Hung Zhong and Bao Chen Xian sat close to the two eunuchs and said to them in a very low voice, "Today we withdrew. This is our emperor's secret plan. Just now our emperor rode forward singlehandedly to meet two men sent by Yuan Chong Huan. They talked for some time. There is an agreement between our emperor and Yuan Chong Huan. We will surely win." The next day the two eunuchs were set free. They went back to the palace of the Ming Dynasty and told what they had heard to Emperor Zhu You Jian. Emperor Zhu You Jian immediately ordered to arrest Yuan Chong Yuan and put him in jail. Zu Da Shou was very afraid and commanded his troops to run away to Jinzhou (now Jinzhou, Liaoning Province) through Shanhaiguan Pass (now Shanhaiguan Pass, in the northeast part of Hebei Province). Then the Kings and officials suggested to Huangtaiji that they should attack the city. But Huangtaiji said, "If we attack the city, many of my generals and soldiers will be killed. I am not hardhearted enough to do that."

In March 1630 Huangtaiji went back to Shenyang, the capital of the (Later) Jin Dynasty. The Kings and their troops also withdrew back batch by batch.

In March 1634 Kong You De and Geng Zhong Ming, two generals of the Ming army stationed in Northeast China, surrendered to the (Later) Jin Dynasty. In March 1635 Shang Ke Xi, a general of Ming army stationed in Guanglu Island (now Guanglu Island, Liaoning Province), surrendered to the (Later) Jin Dynasty. Huangtaiji appointed Kong You De, Geng Zhong Ming and Shang Ke Xi as high ranking generals and let them command their troops. He ordered them to use black banners with white color rims so as to distinguish their troops from the Manchu troops.

3. Huangtaiji Establishes the Qing Dynasty and Ascends the Throne

In April 1636 Huangtaiji changed the name of the dynasty from Jin Dynasty into the Qing Dynasty. In the same month after a ceremony of offering sacrifices to Heaven and Earth, he ascended the throne of the Qing Dynasty. He changed his title of reign from Tiancong into Chongde (in Chinese characters: 崇德) meaning "Respect for Virtue." He made his sons, brothers and his brothers' sons "Heshuo Princes" (in Chinese characters和碩親王) meaning the "Prince of the First Order" (simplified as "Prince"). He made his elder brother Daishan "Prince Li," Jierhalang "Prince Zheng," Duoergun (Huangtaiji's younger brother) "Prince Rui," Duoduo (Daishan's son) "Prince Yu," Haoge (Huangtaiji's eldest son) "Prince Su," Yuetuo (Daishan's eldest son) "Prince Cheng". Huangtaiji made some former generals of the Ming Dynasty who had submitted to him Kings. He made Kong You De "King of Gongshun" (meaning "respectful and submissive), Geng Zhong Ming "King of Huaishun" (meaning "thankful and submissive), and Shang Ke Xi "King of Zhishun" (meaning "resourceful and submissive").

4. The Great Battle in Jinzhou and Songshan

Jinzhou (now Jinzhou, Liaoning Province) was an important city in Northeast China because it was situated between Shenyang, the capital of the Qing Dynasty, and Shanhaiguan Pass which led to Central China. In December 1640 Huangtaiji ordered Duoergun, Haoge, Duoduo and Abatai to command the army of the Qing Dynasty to lay siege to Jinzhou. The general of the Ming army defending Jinzhou was Zu Da Shou. Huangtaiji sent several envoys to Jinzhou to persuade Zu Da Shou to surrender, but Zu Da Shou refused. In March 1641 the Qing army took the outer city of Jinzhou. In May 1641 General Hong Cheng Chou of the Ming Dynasty commanded 60,000 troops to reinforce Jinzhou. He stationed his troops in a place outside the city of Jinzhou. The Qing army started an attack and defeated Hong Cheng Chou's troops. 2,000 men of the Ming army were killed. On 1 August 1641 Huangtaiji gave promotion to General Aobai, General Laosa and General Yierdeng, who had performed great deeds in the battles outside Jinzhou. On 2 August Zu Da Shou divided his troops into three parts and tried to make a breakthrough in three directions, but they were all beaten back. On 14 August General Qiu Min Yang of the Ming Dynasty commanded more Ming troops to reinforce Jinzhou. These troops joined forces with the Ming troops under Hong Cheng Zhou. There were 130,000 Ming troops in all. They were stationed in Songshan (now Songshan, situated to the south of Jinzhou, Liaoning Province). Huangtaiji personally commanded a great army to attack the Ming army stationed in Songshan.

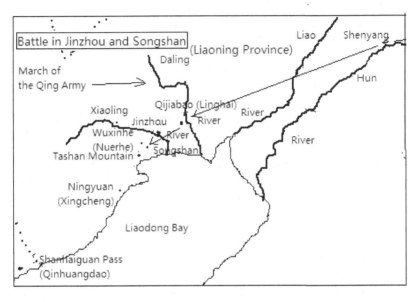

On 15 August Huangtaiji and his great army crossed Liao River (now Liao River, Liaoning Province). Hong Cheng Chou sent troops to attack the right ring of Hungtaiji's army but these troops were defeated by the Qing army under Haoge. On 19 August Huangtaiji reached Qijiabao (now a place situated to the southwest of Linghai City, Liaoning Province). He summoned Duoergun to join forces with him. Duoergun suggested that Huangtaiji should stay near Songshan. Huangtaiji accepted his suggestion and stayed near Songshan. At that time, some troops of the Ming army stationed in Rufengshan (a place in the southwest of Linghai City, Liaoning Province). They established seven camps from Rufengshan to Songshan. The cavalrymen of the Ming army were stationed in the north, east and west around the city of Jinzhou. Huangtaiji stationed his troops from Wuxinhe (now Nüerhe, Liaoning Province) to the sea to cut all the roads leading to Jinzhou. Huangtaiji said to his generals, "There are many enemy troops. There will not be sufficient food for so many soldiers. Now that we have cut all the roads for their food supplies, they will have no will to fight. If we lay ambushes to wait for them, we will be able to extinguish all the enemy troops." On 20 August some Ming troops

came to attack the Qing army and they were beaten back. On the same day Huangtaiji sent some troops to attack the Ming troops in Tashan (now Tashan, Liaoning Province) and defeated them. The Qing troops captured a lot of food supplies of the Ming army. On 21 August the Ming army under Hong Cheng Chou had run out of food. So he decided to run away to Ningyuan (now Xingcheng, Liaoning Province) for food. Huangtaiji knew that Hong Cheng Chou and his troops would run away. He ordered his troops to lay ambushes on the ways to Tashan, to Ningyuan and to Jinzhou. That night Wu San Gui, Wang Pu, Cao Bian Jiao and Wang Ting Chen commanded the Ming troops under them to go out of Songshan. In the dark, they fell into the ambushes. The Ming troops were disastrously defeated. Cao Bian Jiao and Wang Ting Chen escaped back to Songshan. On 22 August Wu San Gui and Wang Pu escaped to Xingshan (now Xingshan Town, Linghai City, Liaoning Province). On 26 August Wu San Gui and Wang Pu went out of Xingshan trying to escape to Ningyuan but fell into an ambush on the way. Nearly all the Ming troops under them were killed. Wu San Gui and Wang Pu had a narrow escape. In this great battle of Jinzhou and Songshan, more than 50,000 Ming soldiers were killed. The Qing army captured 7,000 horses and a lot of military supplies. Hong Cheng Chou collected about 10,000 remaining soldiers and withdrew into the city of Songshan. The Qing army laid siege to Songshan. In September Huangtaiji went back to Shenyang, the capital of the Qing Dynasty. The Qing troops continued their siege to Jinzhou and Songshan.

In February 1462 the Qing troops under Haoge and Duoduo took Songshan and captured Hong Cheng Chou, the Commanding General of Ming army defending Songshan. In March 1462 the Qing troops took Jinzhou. Zu Da Shou led 7,000 men to surrender to the Qing army. In April 1462 the Qing troops under Duoergun and Haoge took Tashan. In May 1462 Hong Cheng Chou and Zu Da Shou were brought before Huangtaiji. They knelt down and said that they deserve death penalty. But Huangtaiji comforted them and set them free.

5. Huangtaiji, Emperor of the Qing Dynasty, Passes Away

Huangtaiji passed away suddenly without any sign of illness in the night of 9 August 1643 at the age of fifty-two. He had ruled for seventeen years. In September 1643 he was buried in Zhaoling Mausoleum in Shenyang. He was given the posthumous title as Emperor Wen. His temple title was Taizong (meaning Supreme Ancestor).

SECTION THREE: AISIN GIORO FULIN ASCENDS THE QING THRONE AND UNIFIES THE WHOLE OF CHINA

4. Aisin Gioro Fulin, Shunzhi Emperor of the Qing Dynasty

1. Aisin Gioro Fulin Ascends the Throne of the Qing Dynasty

When Huangtaiji died, he did not appoint any of his sons to be the successor to the throne of the Qing Dynasty. Daishan (Prince Li) and other Princes and all the officials recommended Aisin Gioro Fulin, Huangtaiji's ninth son, to succeed to the throne of the Qing Dynasty. On 26 August 1643 Aisin Gioro Fulin ascended the throne of the Qing Dynasty at the age of six. It was decided that the title of his reign was "Shunzhi" and 1644 would be the first year of Shunzhi. So Emperor Aisin Gioro Fulin is often referred to as "the Shunzhi Emperor" or Emperor Shunzhi. When Shunzhi ascended the throne, he was too young to attend to state affairs. So Duoergun (Prince Rui) and Jierhalang (Prince Zheng) were appointed Regents to attend to the state affairs.

2. Li Zi Cheng's Great Uprising and the Fall of the Ming Dynasty

In 1628 (the first year of Emperor Zhu You Jian's reign during the Ming Dynasty) there was a great famine in Shaanxi (now Shaanxi Province). Gao Ying Xiang, a man of Ansai (now Ansai, in the north part of Shaanxi Province), led the hungry people there to hold an uprising. He named himself "Daring King." In 1631 Zhang Xian Zhong, a man of Yan'an (now Yan'an, Shaanxi Province), led the people in Yan'an to hold an uprising. In 1632 Li Zi Cheng, a man of Mizhi (now Mizhi, in the north part of Shaanxi Province), who was Gao Ying Xiang's nephew, went to join Gao Ying Xiang. In that year Gao Ying Xiang united with Zhang Xian Zhong.

The Great Uprisings

In 1633 the rebel army crossed the Yellow River and took many prefectures and counties of Shanxi (now Shanxi Province). In 1634 the uprising army entered Henan (now Henan Province). In the spring of 1635 Li Zi Cheng became the head of an uprising army. In 1636 Gao Ying Xiang, Zhang Xian Zhong and Li Zi Cheng commanded their troops to the east. Later Gao Ying Xiang and Li Zi

Cheng commanded the troops under them to turn back to Shaanxi. In spring of 1637 Gao Ying Xiang and Li Zi Cheng commanded their troops to attack Luzhou (now Lujiang, Anhui Province) but could not take it. Then they marched northeast and took Hanshan (now Hanshan, Anhui Province) and Hezhou (now Hexian, Anhui Province). Then they marched northward to attack Chuzhou (now Chuzhou, Anhui Province) but could not take it. Many Ming troops came to reinforce Chuzhou. So Gao Ying Xiang and Li Zi Cheng had to lead their troops to turn back to Shaanxi. In July 1367 Gao Ying Xiang was defeated in Zhouzhi (now Zhouzhi, Shaanxi Province) and was captured. He was brought to Beijing (now Beijing) and was executed. All the generals of the uprising army elected Li Zi Cheng as the Daring King to lead all the troops of the uprising army. In 1638 Li Zi Cheng commanded the uprising army to march into the area of Shu (now Sichuan Province) and took several cities. Then his army attacked Chengdu (now Chengdu, Sichuan Province) but they could not take it. On 1 January 1645 Li Zi Cheng declared himself King of the "Great Shun Dynasty" in Xi'an (now Xi'an, Shaanxi Province). He had 400,000 foot soldiers and 600,000 cavalrymen. In February 1645 Li Zi Cheng commanded his great army to cross the Yellow River and took Taiyuan (now Taiyuan, Shanxi Province). Then he commanded his army to march north and took Datong (now Datong, Shanxi Province). On 13 March 1645 Li Zi Cheng commanded his army to attack Changping (now Changping, Beijing). On 17 March 1645 Li Zi Cheng commanded his troops to attack the nine gates of the city wall of Beijing, the capital of the Ming Dynasty. On 18 March the troops under Li Zi Cheng attacked the city more fiercely. In the late afternoon of that day, Li Zi Cheng's army broke into the city of Beijing. Emperor Zhu You Jian of the Ming Dynasty walked out of the palace and went up the Coal Hill in the royal park (now Jingshan Park within the Forbidden City) which was the highest point in Beijing. He saw that the flames of war rose very high everywhere in the city. He exclaimed, "My people will suffer a lot!" He paced back and forth for a long time. Then he went back to Qianqing Palace (Palace of Heavenly Purity, the residence palace for the emperor). He used his sword to hack his eldest daughter trying to kill her. Then he forced his wife Empress Zhou to commit suicide by hanging. At dawn of 19 March the troops under Li Zi Cheng broke into the Forbidden City. Emperor Zhu You Jian personally sounded the bell to summon the court officials. But none of them came. Then Emperor Zhu You Jian walked up the Coal Hill again. There he committed suicide by hanging himself to a tree by the side of a pavilion on the Coal Hill. The Ming Dynasty fell.

On 19 March 1645 Li Zi Cheng entered the palace of the Ming Dynasty. He ascended the throne for the emperors of the Ming Dynasty in Huangji Hall.

3. The Qing Troops Enter Shanhaiguan Pass and Bring Order to Most of China

When Li Zi Cheng's army was marching towards Beijing, Emperor Zhu You Jian of the Ming Dynasty sent an envoy to Ningyuan (now Xingcheng, Liaoning Province) to order Wu San Gui to command his troops to protect the capital. At that time, Wu San Gui had 500,000 men under him. He commanded his troops to relieve Beijing. On 16 March 1645 Wu San Gui entered Shanhaiguan Pass (now Shanhaiguan Pass, Hebei Province). On 20 March Wu San Gui reached Fengrun (now Fengrun, Hebei Province). But on 19 March Li Zi Cheng had already taken Beijing. He sent some troops to march east to attack Luanzhou (now Luanxian, Hebei Province). Wu San Gui's troops defeated the troops sent by Li Zi Cheng in Luanzhou. Then Wu San Gui commanded his troops to withdraw to Shanhaiguan Pass. Li Zi Cheng forced Wu Xiang, Wu San Gui's father, to write a letter to urge Wu San Gui to surrender. Li Zi Cheng sent a general to take 40,000 ounces of silver to Wu San Gui. Then Wu San Gui decided to surrender. Li Zi Chen sent a general to command 20,000 men to defend Shanhaiguan Pass for Wu San Gui. Then Wu San Gui commanded his troops to go westward to surrender. But when he reached Luanzhou (now Luanxian, Hebei Province), he got to know that Chen Yuan Yuan, his most loved concubine, was taken by Liu Zong Min, a high ranking general under Li Zi Cheng, as his wife. Wu San Gui was very angry and commanded his troops to go back to Shanhaiguan Pass. His troops defeated the troops sent by Li Zi Cheng and occupied Shanhaiguan Pass. He sent two generals as his envoys to take a letter to Duoergun, the Prince Regent of the Qing Dynasty, asking him for help. On 14 April 1645 Duoergun was in Wenghou (a place in Fuxin, Liaoning Province), carrying out a western expedition. When he got the letter, he immediately sent a reply letter to Wu San Gui. Then he commanded the Qing army to march to Shanhaiguan Pass. On 20 April Duoergun and his army reached a place five kilometers north to Shanhaiguan Pass. Wu San Gui sent an envoy to tell Duoergun that Tang Tong, a general under Li Zi Cheng, had stationed his troops outside the pass. Duoergun ordered two generals to command the Qing troops to attack the enemy troops and defeated them. Then Wu San Gui went out of the pass to welcome Duoergun and his troops into the pass.

5. The Great Wall

On 22 April Li Zi Cheng personally led 200,000 men to attack Shanhaiguan Pass. He arranged his troops in battle formations from the mountain to the sea. Duoergun arranged his troops in battle formations face to face with Li Zi Cheng's battle formations. He arranged Wu San Gui's troops on the right wing of the battle formations. When the battle began, Wu San Gui commanded his troops to fight with Li Zi Cheng's army first. After some time Ajige and Duoduo commanded the Qing troops under them to dash into Li Zi Cheng's battle formation from the side of Wu San Gui's battle formation. Li Zi Cheng rode up a hill to survey the situation. When he saw the Qing troops, he exclaimed, "Manchu soldiers!" Then he rode down the hill and ran away to the west. When his soldiers saw this, they collapsed and also ran away to the west. The Qing troops pursued them for 20 kilometers.

On the same day, Duoergun made Wu San Gui King of Pingxi (meaning "Pacification of the West"). Duoergun ordered Wu San Gui to command his troops to pursue Li Zi Cheng. When Li Zi Cheng fled to Yongping (now Lulong, Hebei Province), he killed Wu Xiang. When he sped back to Beijing, he killed all Wu San Gui's family members.

Li Zi Cheng ascended the throne of the Great Shun Dynasty in Wuying Hall (the Hall of Martial Valor) of the palace on 29 April 1645. That night he ordered his soldiers to burn the palace and the nine gates of the city wall, and at dawn he commanded his troops to flee to the west.

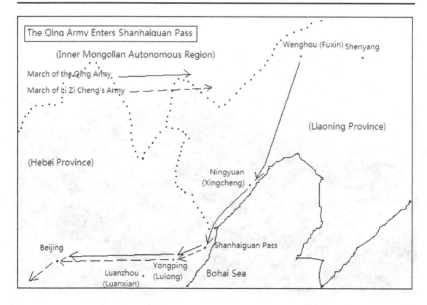

The Qing army entered Beijing on 2 May. Duoergun entered Wuying Hall (Hall of Martial Valor) to attend to the military affairs. The generals and officials of the fallen Ming Dynasty came to see him. Duoergun ordered Wu San Gui and Ajige to command the troops under them to pursue Li Zi Cheng. They caught up with Li Zi Cheng in Qingdu (now Tangxian, Hebei Province) and defeated his troops. Li Zi Cheng escaped to the west. The Qing army pursued him to Zhending (now Zhengding, Hebei Province); Li Zi Cheng was defeated and fled further west.

On 11 June 1645 Duoergun and the officials suggested to Emperor Shunzhi that Beijing should be the Qing capital. On 20 September 1645 Emperor Shunzhi entered Beijing through Zhengyang Gate (the south gate of the city wall of Beijing) to the palace. Ten days later he went to the southern outskirts of Beijing to hold a ceremony to warship and offer sacrifices to Heaven and Earth. Then he ascended the throne in Beijing, in the palace. Since Duoergun had played an important role in bringing these successes, Emperor Shunzhi made him King Regent.

Back in May 1644 Zhu You Song, King of Fu of the Ming Dynasty, had declared himself Emperor of the Ming Dynasty in Jiangning (now Nanjing, Jiangsu Province). He arranged his army along the Yangtze River. He appointed Shi Ke Fa, the Grand Scholar, to command a great army to defend Yangzhou (now in Jiangsu Province). Now, Duoergun wrote a letter to urge Shi Ke Fa to surrender. But Shi Ke Fa resolutely refused.

On 19 October 1645 Ajige was appointed as Grand General of Jingyuan (meaning pacification of faraway places) to head an

expedition to the west against Li Zi Cheng. On 25 October Duoduo
was appointed as Grand General of Dingguo (meaning pacification
of the state) to command a great army to carry out an expedition
to the south of the Yangtze River. On 8 November Shi Ting Zhu, a
general under Duoduo, defeated Li Zi Cheng's army in Pingyang (now
Fenyang, Shanxi Province). The whole Shanxi Province was pacified.
On 14 December Duoduo's army reached Shaanzhou (now Shaanxian,
in the west part of Henan Province) and defeated Zhang You Zeng, a
general under Li Zi Cheng, in Lingbao (now Lingbao, in the west part
of Henan Province).

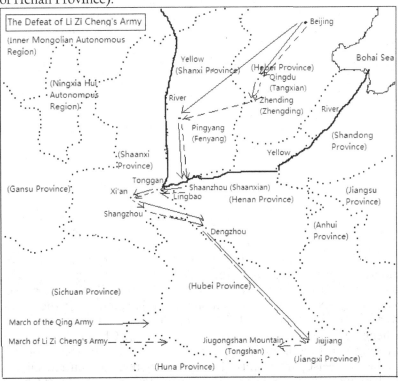

On 3 January 1646 Tulai, a general under Duoduo, defeated Li
Zi Cheng in Tongguan (now Tongguan, in the east part of Shaanxi
Province). Li Zi Cheng ran away to Xi'an (now Xi'an, Shaanxi
Province). On 17 January 1646 Duoduo commanded his army to march
to Xi'an. Li Zi Cheng ran away to Shangzhou (now Shangzhou, in the
south part of Shaanxi Province).

On 6 February 1646 Duoduo commanded his army to pacify the
areas to the south of the Yangtze River. On 7 March Duoduo's army
marched out of Hulaoguan Pass (in Xingyang, Henan Province).
In April 1646 Duoduo's army reached Sizhou (now Sixian, Anhui
Province). The Qing army under Duoduo reached Huai River and

crossed it at night. Duoduo commanded his troops to march to Yangzhou (now Yangzhou, Jiangsu Province). On 26 April, the Qing army attacked and took the city of Yangzhou. Shi Ke Fa, the Grand Scholar of the Ming Dynasty, was captured. He refused to surrender and died heroically. On 5 May 1646 Duoduo's army reached the north bank of the Yangtze River. The Qing troops crossed the Yangtze River by the section of Guazhou (now Guazhou, Jiangsu Province) at night. The Ming troops on the south bank of the Yangtze River were defeated and ran away. On 15 May Duoduo's troops reached Nanjing. Zhu You Song, Emperor of the Ming Dynasty, ran away to Taiping (now Dangtu, Anhui Province). On 10 June 1646 Duoduo sent troops to run after Zhu You Song to Wuhu (now in Anhui Province). After a battle, Zhu You Song was captured. This pretty much brought peace to the area south of the Yangtze River

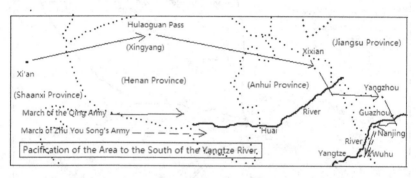

On 3 the second June (1646 was an intercalary year, with two months of June) Ajige defeated Li Zi Cheng in Dengzhou (in the southwest part of Henan Province). Li Zi Cheng fled to the south. The Qing troops gave a hot pursuit to Jiujiang (now in the north part of Jiangxi Province). Thirteen battles were fought there. Li Zi Cheng's troops were seriously defeated. Li Zi Cheng ran away to Jiugongshan Mountain (situated to the south of Tongshan County, in the southeast part of Hubei Province). There he committed suicide by hanging himself to death. The uprising troops led by Li Zi Cheng were basically wiped out.

On 22 the second June Duoduo sent Boluo, Baiyitu and Ashan to command the troops under them to take Hangzhou (now Hangzhou, Zhejiang Province). Zhu Chang Fang, King of Lu of the Ming Dynasty, came out of the city of Hangzhou to surrender. And Zhu Chang Qing, King of Huai of the Ming Dynasty, came to surrender from Shaoxing (now Shaoxing, Zhejiang Province). Then the Qing army took Jiaxing (now Jiaxing, Zhejiang Province), Huzhou (now Huzhou, Zhejiang Province), Yanzhou (now the area around Tonglu, Zhejiang Province) and Ningbo (now Ningbo, Zhejiang Province).

On 1 November 1647 Boluo sent Tulai to command his troops to march southward to take the area of Fujian (now Fujian Province).

Tulai's troops defeated Huang Ming Jun, a minister of the Ming Dynasty, in Xianxiaguan Pass (situated to the south of Jiangshan, Zhejiang Province). Then Tulai's troops took Pucheng (now Pucheng, Fujian Province) and Yanping (now Nanping, Fujian Province). Zhu Yu Zhao, King of Tang of the Ming Dynasty, ran away to Tingzhou (now Changting, Fujian Province). Ajige and Nikan commanded their troops to run after him and killed him. Then Tingzhou, Zhangzhou (now Zhangzhou, Fujian Province), Quanzhou (now Quanzhou, Fujian Province) and Xinghua (now Putian, Fujian Province) were taken. Then the Qing army marched to Fuzhou (now Fuzhou, Fujian Province). Then peace reigned throughout the whole area of Fujian Province.

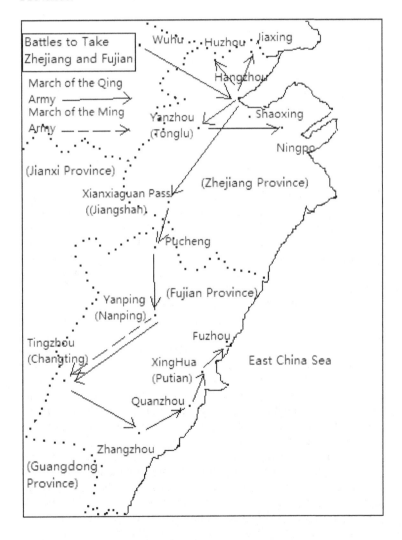

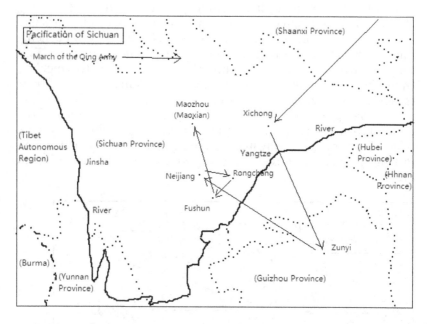

In November 1647 Haoge commanded his troops to the southern part of Sichuan Province. At that time Zhang Xian Zhong, the leader of the peasant uprising, stationed his troops in Xichong (now Xichong, Sichuan Province). Aobai commanded his troops to march very quickly to Xichong and defeated the uprising troops there. Zhang Xian Zhong was killed in this battle. Then the Qing troops defeated the remaining uprising troops in other places. The area around Xichong was pacified. In August the Qing army under Haoge took Zunyi (now Zunyi, Guizhou Province), Neijiang (now Neijiang, Sichuan Province), Rongchang (now Rongchang, Sichuan Province), Fushun (now Fushun, Sichuan Province) and Maozhou (now Maoxian, Sichuan Province). Now, most of Sichuan Province was quiet.

In December 1647 the great army of the Qing Dynasty marched from Yuezhou (now Yueyang, Hunan Province) southward to take Changsha (now Changsha, Hunan Province). He Teng Jiao, the Governor of Hunan Province of the Ming Dynasty, ran away. The Qing army took Changsha. Then they marched southward and took Xiangtan (now Xiangtan, Hunan Province). Huang Chao Xuan, a general of the Ming Dynasty, had 130,000 men in Yanziwo (now a place in Youxian, Hunan Province). The Qing army defeated Huang Chao Xuan and his army there. Then the Qing army defeated them in Hengzhou (now Hengyang, Hunan Province). The Qing army took Baoqing (now Shaoyang, Hunan Province), then went southwest to take Wugang (now Wugang, Hunan Province). Zhu You Lang, King of Gui of the Ming Dynasty, was in Jingzhou (now Jingzhou

Miao Nationality and Dong Nationality Autonomous County, in the Southwest part of Hunan Province). The Qing army marched west and took Jingzhou. Then the Qing army marched northward and took Yuanzhou (now Zhijiang Dong Nationality Autonomous County, Hunan Province). Zhu Yan Jun, the King of Min of the Ming Dynasty, surrendered in Liping (now Liping, in the east part of Guizhou Province). Then the whole area of Hunan Province was at peace.

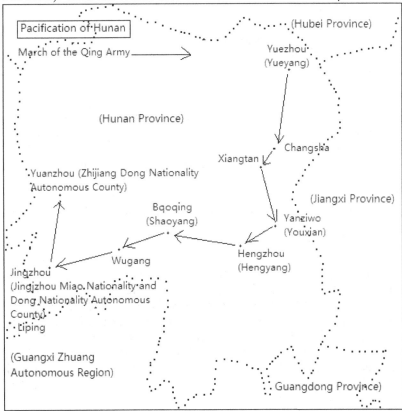

On 10 March 1649 Wang Yong Qiang, a general of the army stationed in Yan'an (now Yan'an, Shaanxi Province), held a rebellion and took the city of Yan'an. Then his rebellion army took nineteen prefectures and counties in Shaanxi Province including Yulin (now Yulin, Shaanxi Province). On 14 March Wang Yong Qiang took Tongguan (now Tongchuan, Shaanxi Province). On 29 March Wu San Gui commanded the Qing army to Tongguan and defeated Wang Yong Qiang. The Qing troops under Wu San Gui recovered Tongguan and Yijun (now Yijun, Shaanxi Province). On 9 April 1649 Wu San Gui took Puxian (now Pucheng, Shaanxi Province).

On 20 May 1649 Shunzhi made Kong You De King of Dingnan (Dingnan means "Stabilizing the South"), Geng Zhong Ming King of

Jingnan (Jingnan means "Tranquillizing the South"), and Shang Ke Xi King of Pingnan (Pingnan means "Pacifying the South"). The Emperor ordered Kong You De to carry out an expedition to Guangxi (now Guangxi Zhuang Autonomous Region), and ordered Geng Zhong Ming and Shang Ke Xi to carry out an expedition to Guandong (now Guangdong Province).

4. Under the Reign of Emperor Shunzhi

In September 1650 Duoergun fell ill. He made a hunting trip in the border area. On 8 December 1650 he died in Kala City (now Luanping, Hebei Province) at the age of thirty-nine. Shunzhi was very sad at the news of his death. On 16 December Duoergun's dead body was carried back to Beijing, the capital. On 19 December a grand memorial ceremony for an emperor was held to memorize Duoergun. Shunzhi granted him the posthumous title of "Emperor Yi," and the temple title of "Chengzong."

On 3 January 1651 Shunzhi appointed Budan as government minister. On 7 January he appointed Suhasaha and Zhandai as government ministers. On 12 January Shunzhi assumed reins of government. He sat on the throne to accept the congratulations chanted by the court officials. On 29 January Emperor Shunzhi appointed Gongadai and Aobai as government ministers. On 30 January he appointed Batuluzhan and Duerma as government ministers.

On 15 February 1651 Suhasaha, Zhandai and Mujilun accused the late Duoergun of betrayal. They listed his following crimes: at first Duoergun and Jierhalang were both appointed as regents to assist the young emperor, but Duoergun took all the power in his own hands and did not allow Jierhalang to attend to the government affairs; he was very proud of himself and named himself "Father King Regent"; the insignia carried before him, the music for him, his retinue and his residence were as grand as those of an emperor; and he said that Huangtaiji should not have been made the emperor according to the order of succession so as to challenge the legitimacy of Emperor Shunzhi. After investigation, all the facts of Duoergun's crimes were found true. Emperor Shunzhi sent officials to search Duoergun's house and confiscate his property. On 21 February Duoergun's crimes were publicly announced, and he was stripped of his posthumous title of Emperor Yi and temple title of Chengzong.

In September 1651 Shunzhi ordered Wu San Gui to carry out an expedition to Sichuan (now Sichuan Province). In July 1652 Wu San Gui took Zhangla (now a village in Songpan, Sichuan Province), Songpan (now Songpan, in the north part of Sichuan Province), and Chongqing (now Chongqing, in the southeast part of Sichuan Province). Then he commanded his troops to march to Chengdu (now Chengdu, in the central area of Sichuan Province) and laid siege to it. In October 1651 Sun Ke Wang, a general of the former Ming Dynasty, commanded his troops to attack Baoning (now Langzhong, Sichuan Province). Wu San Gui commanded his troops to Baoning and defeated Sun Ke Wang. On 19 August 1653 Shunzhi married his younger sister Princess Heshuo to Wu San Gui's son Wu Ying Xiong.

Zheng Cheng Gong was a general of the South Ming Dynasty in Fujian (now Fujian Province). In December 1653 Zheng Cheng Gong commanded his naval troops to attack Wusong (now Wusong, Shanghai). The Qing army defending Wusong beat them back. In January 1654 Zheng Cheng Gong and his troops attacked Chongming (now Chongming, Shanghai), Jingjiang (now Jingjiang, Jiangsu Province) and Taixing (now Taixing, Jiangsu Province). The Qing troops defending these cities beat them back. In December 1654 Zheng Cheng Gong took Zhangzhou (now Zhangzhou, Fujian Province) and laid siege to Quanzhou (now Quanzhou, Fujian Province). In 1655 Zhu You Lang, the Emperor of the South Ming Dynasty, made Zheng Cheng Gong Duke of Yanping. Shunzhi appointed Jidu as Grand General of Dingyuan (meaning "Pacification of the Far Away Place") to carry out an expedition against Zheng Cheng Gong.

In January 1659 Zhu You Lang, the Emperor of the South Ming Dynasty, ran away to Yongchang (now Baoshan, in the west part of Yunnan Province). In February 1659 Wu San Gui, Shangshan and Zhaobutai commanded their troops to march to Kunming (now Kunming, Yunnan Province, the captital city of Yunnan Province) and took it. Then they marched their troops westward to take Yongchang. Zhu You Lang ran away to Tengyue (now Tengchong, in the west part of Yunnan Province). From Tengyue Zhu You Lang ran to Muse which was within the territory of Burma. The King of the Kingdom of Burma sent some officials to welcome Zhu You Lang and his followers to Mandalay, the capital of the Kingdom of Burma.

In March 1659 Shunzhi ordered Wu San Gui to garrison Yunnan Province, Shang Ke Xi to garrison Guangdong Province, and Geng Ji Mao to garrison Sichuan Province.

In July 1659, Zheng Cheng Gong commanded his naval troops to sail up the Yangtze River and to Zhenjiang (now Zhenjiang, Jiangsu Province) and Guazhou (now Guazhou, Jiangsu Province). On 18 July Zheng Cheng Gong commanded his troops to attack Jiangning (now Nanjing, Jiangsu Province). On 1 August the Qing troops defending Jiangning defeated Zheng Cheng Gong. The Qing troops burned more than 500 warships of the troops of Zheng Cheng Gong. Zheng Cheng Gong ran away. The Qing troops chased him to Guazhou (now Guazhou, Jiangsu Province). Zheng Cheng Gong had to give up Guazhou and Zhenjiang and sailed out to sea and back to Fujian.

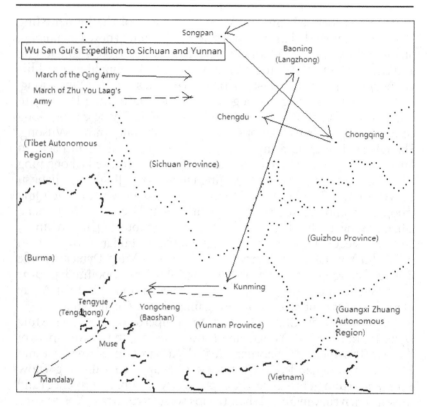

After Zheng Cheng Gong was defeated and ran back to Fujian, he planned to recover Taiwan (now Taiwan Province). Taiwan was an island situated in the sea. Taiwan and Fujian faced each other across the Taiwan Strait. It was China's territory since ancient times. In 1624 the Hollanders invaded Taiwan and occupied it. The Hollanders built two cities. One was Chikan City, situated in the west part of what is now Tainan. The other was Taiwan City, situated in what is now Anping. The port leading to these two cities was Lu'ermen. The water there was shallow. Ships could not sail into this port, so the Hollanders did not station troops to guard this port.

In March 1661 Zheng Cheng Gong took a fleet of more than 25,000 naval soldiers on several hundred warships to start from Jinmen, a small island near Xiamen, Fujian Province, to sail across the Taiwan Strait. When Zheng Cheng Gong's fleet reached Lu'ermen, the sea water there suddenly grew three meters deeper than usual. The warships sailed into Lu'ermen one by one. The Hollanders gave up Chikan City and concentrated all the troops to defend Taiwan City. Zheng Cheng Gong sent an envoy to the commander-in-chief of the Hollanders and told him, "The land of Taiwan is our territory. You should return it to us. You may take all the treasure with you and go away." The commander-in-chief of the Hollanders refused. Zheng

Cheng Gong ordered his troops to lay siege to Taiwan City, and they maintained this blockade for seven months. Many Hollanders died.

At last the Hollanders had to surrender. Zheng Cheng Gong sent them back to where they came from. He made Tainan (now in Taiwan Province) the Eastern Capital of the South Ming Dynasty. He made laws, appointed officials and established schools, and promoted the development of the area.

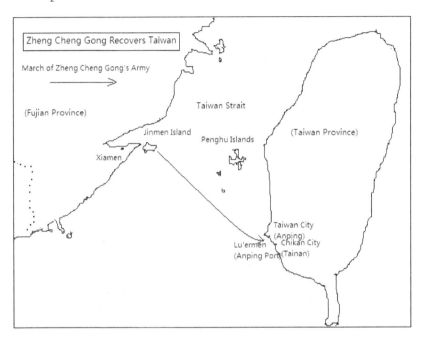

5. Emperor Shunzhi Departs

On 2 January 1661 Emperor Shunzhi fell ill. On 6 January he became seriously ill. On 7 January Shunzhi passed away in Yangxin Hall at the age of twenty-four. He left his testamentary edict which read, "My son Xuanye was given birth by Concubine Tong. He is a man with exceptional wisdom. He has the ability to succeed to the throne. I hereby make him Crown Prince. After I die, he should follow the regulation to wear the mourning apparel for twenty-seven days. After that he should take off the mourning apparel and take the throne. I hereby appoint Suony, Suhasaha, Ebilong and Aobai as the regent ministers. You are my trusted officials. I have entrusted the most important duty on you. You should be utterly loyal to my son and assist him. You should help him to take care of the government affairs. This should be publicly announced so that everyone knows my will."

In March 1661 Shunzhi was buried in Xiao Mausoleum in Eastern Qing Tombs (in Zunhua, Hebei Province). He was given the posthumous title of Emperor Zhang and the temple title of Shizu.

1. The Birth of Aisin Gioro Xuanye

Lady Tong, Emperor Shunzhi's concubine, was General Tong Tu Lai's daughter. In spring 1654 she went to the Empress Dowager's palace to wish her good health. When she was leaving, the Empress Dowager saw that there was a dragon coiling around her gown. She was greatly surprised and asked her what had happened. Concubine Tong told the Empress Dowager that she was pregnant. The Empress Dowager said to the maids waiting on her, "When I was carrying the present Emperor, there was a dragon coiling around me. Now Concubine Tong also has this sign. The son to whom she is going to give birth will enjoy good fortune." On 18 March 1654 Concubine Tong gave birth to a baby boy. When he was born, the whole palace was filled with fragrance. And there was a five-colored bright light in the palace. He was the third son of Emperor Shunzhi. He was given the name Xuanye. When he was five years old, he liked to study very much. He read books for emperors and kings, Confucian classics, philosophy and history. One day when he was six years old, he went to see his father with Fuquan, Shunzhi's second son, and Changning, the fifth son. Shunzhi asked them what they wanted to be when they grew up. Changning was only three years old and could not answer the question. Fuquan said, "I want to be a virtuous and able king." Xuanye said, "When I grow up, I will follow Father Emperor's good example and do my best to make the country prosperous." Shunzhi marveled at his answer and had the idea to make him successor to the throne.

On 7 January 1661 Shunzhi passed away. He left a testamentary edict to make Xuanye Crown Prince to succeed to the throne and appointed Suony, Sukesaha, Ebilong and Aobai as the regent ministers.

2. Aisin Gioro Xuanye Ascends the Throne of the Qing Dynasty

On 9 January 1661 Aisin Gioro Xuanye ascended the throne of the Qing Dynasty at the age of eight. In the early morning that day, he sent Muchen, Commander-in-chief of the army of one of the Eight Banners, to offer sacrifices to Heaven and read out the following prayers, "Today is the ninth of January. I, Xuanye, the Crown Prince, declare before the mighty Heaven that my father, the Great Emperor, has passed away. I scrupulously follow the testamentary edict and the public sentiment to ascend the throne on this day, the ninth of January. I intend to make this clear to all. I respectfully present this memorial to you."

At the same time, he sent Jishiha, Commander-in-chief of the army of one of the Eight Banners, to offer sacrifices to the God of the Earth; he sent Mulima, Commander-in-chief of another one of the armies, to offer sacrifices to the ancestors in the Imperial Ancestral Temple; he sent Ming'andali, a minister, to offer sacrifices to the God of Land and the God of grain. They all read out the same prayers as the prayers to Heaven. Xuanye went to the hall where the memorial tablet of the late Emperor was kept on a big table. He went before the memorial tablet and knelt down on his knees three times and touched his head to the ground nine times. Then he put on a ceremonial robe and went to the Empress Dowager's palace to pay his respects to her.

After that he went into the Hall of Supreme Harmony and ascended the throne. At that time the bells and drums sounded simultaneously. All the kings, military officials and civil officials, wearing court dress, lined up before the Emperor according to their ranks. The official in charge of ceremony presented his memorial of congratulations to the new Emperor. All the kings and officials saluted to the Emperor. Then the Emperor issued his imperial edict which read, "Heaven has shown great concern for our country. My ancestors committed great deeds and laid down a solid foundation. My father, the late Emperor, was a virtuous and benevolent person. He carried on the great course of the ancestors and unified the whole country. His benevolence reached every corner of the country. He carried out policies which conformed to the will of Heaven. While he was doing his best to make our country strong and prosperous, he passed away. He has appointed me, an inexperienced boy, to succeed to the throne. I hesitated. All the kings, peers, ministers, and officials say that the late Emperor has passed the throne to me, and it is improper to delay the ascension to the throne. They urged me to ascend the throne repeatedly. So I contain my sadness over the demise of the late Emperor and have ascended the throne on this ninth of January. Heaven has shown great favor on me. My ancestors have entrusted the important task to me. Although I am still young, I am determined to accept this important task and carry forward the great course my ancestors have started to a successful end and bring peace and prosperity to my country. I have decided that the title of my reign is 'Kangxi' and next year will be the first year of Kangxi. There will be a new beginning in the whole country."

Xuanye's reign title "Kangxi" (in Chinese characters "康熙") means "Peace and Prosperity". This reign title indicates his overall goal, to make China peaceful and prosperous. Historians use the reign title "Kangxi" to refer to him; thus, in this book, we'll be calling him Emperor Kangxi.

When Xuanye ascended the throne, he was only eight years old. Since he could not yet take up the reins of government, affairs were handled by Suony, Sukesaha, Ebilong and Aobai, the four regent ministers.

3. The Final Destruction of the South Ming Dynasty

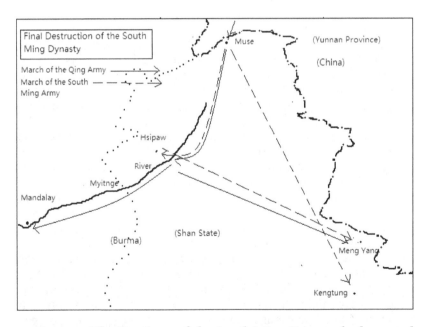

Emperor Zhu You Lang of the South Ming Dynasty had escaped to Mandalay, the Burmese capital. Wu San Gui, King of Pingxi, and Aixing'a, King of Dingxi, were ordered to carry out an expedition against the Kingdom of Burma. They commanded their troops to march to Burma. On 3 November 1661 they reached Muse (now

Muse, in the north part of Shan State, Burma), a town in the border between Burma and China. Li Ding Guo, King of Jin of the South Ming Dynasty, ran away to Kengtung (now in Burma). Bai Wen Xuan, King of Gongchang of the South Ming Dynasty, ran away to Hsipaw (in the northwest part of Shan State, Burma). He thought he and his troops could be protected by the Myitnge River. The Qing army marched from Muse for one hundred and fifty kilometers and reached the east bank of Myitnge River and was ready to cross the river to attack Hsipaw. Bai Wen Xuan ran away to the east. Wu San Gui and Aixing'a sent general Ma Ning to command a detachment to pursue Bai Wen Xuan. Wu San Gui and Aixing'a commanded the main force to march to Mandalay, the capital. Wu San Gui sent an envoy to see King of Burma to tell him that he should arrest Zhu You Lang and hand him over to the Qing army, otherwise he would regret it.

Wu San Gui and Aixing'a reached Mandalay on 1 December 1661. The King of Burma was very afraid. He arrested Emperor Zhu You Lang and sent some soldiers to escort Zhu You Lang, his mother and his wife to the Qing army. General Ma Ning commanded his troops to pursue Bai Wen Xuan. He caught up with Bai Wen Xuan in Meng Yang (now Meng Yang, in the east part of Burma). Bai Wen Xuan surrendered. On 10 December 1661 Wu San Gui and Aixing'a commanded the great army to return to Yunnan triumphantly. Wu San Gui and Aixing'a wrote a memorial to Emperor Kangxi to report their great victory. Having read the memorial, Kangxi issued an imperial edict to Wu San Gui and Aixing'a which read, "I have read your memorial. I am very glad to know that you have commanded the great army into Burma and have caught Zhu You Lang and all his family members. The troops sent by you have caught up with Bai Wen Xuan, four hundred and ninety-nine officials, three thousand eight hundred soldiers and seven thousand their family members in Meng Yang. All of them have surrendered. You have got many horses and elephants. You have done a good job in commanding this great action. All the officers and men in your army have fought hard and won this great victory. All the officers and men who have performed heroicly should be rewarded according to their contributions."

In April 1662 Wu San Gui took Zhu You Lang and his son from the jail and executed them. They were strangled to death with bowstrings. Then Wu San Gui sent some officials to escort Zhu You Lang's mother and wife to Beijing, the capital. On the way, Zhu You Lang's mother and wife committed suicide. Li Ding Guo was still in Kangtung (now Kangtung, in the east part of Burma). He often went to Mengla (now Mengla, in the south part of Yunnan Province) to observe the situation and collect information about Zhu You Lang.

Wu San Gui ordered General Zhang Yong to command ten thousand men to station in Puer (now Puer Hani Nationality and Yi Nationality Autonomous County, in the south part of Yunnan

Province) and Yuanjiang (now Yuanjiang Hani Nationality, Yi Nationality and Dai Nationality Autonomous County) to prepare for the attack by Li Ding Guo. But not long later, Li Ding Guo died in Kengtung (now in Burma). Wu San Gui sent envoys to Kengtung to persuade Li Ding Guo's son Li Si Xing to surrender. He promised to do so, and he led more than a thousand men to surrender. The South Ming Dynasty was thoroughly destroyed.

On 11 May 1662 Kangxi issued an imperial edict to the Ministry of Rites which read, "Wu San Gui, King of Pingxi, guarded Shaanxi Province and Sichuan Province, brought peace to Yunnan Province and Guizhou Province and exterminated the rebels. He has committed great deeds. Zhu You Lang claimed that he was a descendant of the Ming royal clan and instigated people to join him. He declared himself Emperor of the South Ming Dynasty. He seized one part of the country. For several years, government troops have been sent to carry out expeditions against him. The tranquility of the country was disturbed. King of Pingxi was ordered to lead a great army to cross the border to carry out an expedition against Zhu You Lang.

In December of the 18th year of Shunzhi, his army marched into the territory of Burma and caught Zhu You Lang and all his family members. Then he forced Bai Wen Xuan, King of Gongchang of the South Ming Dynasty, and all the offials and soldiers to surrender. King of Pingxi can accomplish this great task because he has been very devoted, astute and resourceful, and strategically minded. In this way the power of our country has reached far and wide. He has pacified all the rebels. He has performed heroicly. He should be rewarded handsomely so as to show my favor on him. I now grant him the title of Prince." The title of Prince was granted to the members of the royal clan. Wu San Gui was not a member of the royal clan. The fact that Kangxi granted the title of Prince to Wu San Gui showed that Kangxi had shown him a special favor. On 22 December 1662 Kangxi appointed Wu San Gui as Governor of Yunnan Province and Guizhou Province.

4. Zheng Jin Becomes Ruler of Taiwan

When Zheng Cheng Gong sailed from Jinmen to take Taiwan, he ordered General Chen Bao to command his troops to defend Nan'ao (now Nan'ao Island, in the east part of Guangdong Province), and ordered his eldest son Zheng Jin to defend Simimg (now Siming District, in the south end of Xiamen, Fujian Province). In March 1662 Zheng Cheng Gong believed Zhou Quan Bin's slanderous accusation against General Chen Bao and sent Zhou Quan Bin to lead a fleet to sail to Nan'ao to kill Chen Bao. When Chen Bao got the information, he led all the officers and men under him to go to Guangzhou (now Guangzhou, Guangdong Province) to surrender.

Zheng Jin committed adultery with the nanny employed to nurse his younger brother and the nanny gave birth to a son. Zheng Cheng Gong sent Zheng Tai, his cousin, to Siming to kill Zheng Jin and his mother Lady Dong. And there was the rumor that Zheng Cheng Gong would kill all the generals who had been appointed to defend Xiamen (now Xiamen, Fujian Province). At that time Zhou Quan Bin who had been sent by Zheng Cheng Gong to Nan'ao to kill Chen Bao sailed back to Xiamen. The generals in Xiamen caught him and put him in jail. Then they supported Zheng Jin as their head to rise in arms against Zheng Cheng Gong. At that time, Zheng Cheng Gong fell ill. When he got the information that his son Zheng Jin had risen in arms against him, he was very angry. He was so angry that he became mad. On 8 May 1662, he madly bit his fingers and died at the age of thirty-nine. After Zheng Cheng Gong died, the generals in Taiwan supported his younger brother Zheng Shi Xi as the Grand General. Zheng Shi Xi sent an envoy to inform Zheng Jin that his father had died. Zheng Jin released Zhou Quan Bin and made him a general. Zheng Jin and Zhou Quan Bin commanded a great army to attack Taiwan. They defeated the generals in Taiwan and entered Taiwan. Zheng Jin succeeded his father's title as King of Yanping. Zheng Shi Xi sailed to Quanzhou (now Quanzhou, Fujian Province) to surrender to the Qing Dynasty.

In 1663 Zheng Jin came back to Siming. Zheng Tai wrote a letter to the generals in Taiwan inducing them to rise against Zheng Jin. This was found out by Zheng Jin. Zheng Jin arrested Zheng Tai and killed him. Zheng Tai's younger brothers Zheng Ming Jun and Zheng Geng, and his son Zheng Zuan Xu went to Quanzhou to surrender to the Qing Dynasty. Generals Cai Ming Lei, Chen Hui, Chen Fu and He Yi led the troops under them to surrender. Zheng Jin's force became much weaker.

In October 1633 Geng Ji Mao, King of Jingnan, and Li Shuai Tai, Governor of Fujian Province, commanded a great army to march from Tong'an (now Tong'an District, Xiamen City, Fujian Province) which was situated to the north of Xiamen Island to attack Xiamen and Jinmen Island. General Ma De Gong commanded an army to march southward from Quanzhou (now Quanzhou, Fujian Province) to attack Xiamen. General Huang Wu and General Shi Lang who had been promoted as Commander-in-chief of the navy in Fujian commanded their troops to sail from Haicheng (now Haicheng Town, Longhai City, Fujian Province) to attack Xiamen and Jinmen Island. Zheng Jin ordered Zhou Quan Bin to lead the navy to meet Ma De Gong. The two hostile fleets met in Wusha in the sea outside Jinmen Island. Ma De Gong had three hundred warships and fourteen ships controlled by Hollanders. Zhou Quan Bin led only twenty warships to meet Ma De Gong's fleet. In the battle, Ma De Gong was killed. His fleet was defeated and turned back. The fleet commanded by Geng Ji Mao and Li Shuai Tai and the fleet commanded by Shi Lang successfully took Xiamen. Shi Lang commanded his fleet to sail further east and successfully took Jinmen Island and Wuyu Island (a small island situated six nautical miles south to Xiamen). Zheng Jin retreated to Tongshan (situated in Tongling Town, in the northeast part of Dongshan Island, in the southeast part of Fujian Province).

In 1664 Du Hui, a general under Zheng Jin, surrendered and presented Nan'ao Island (situated in the east part of Guangdong Province) to the Qing Dynasty. The army defending Tongshan had run short of food. Zhou Quan Bin left Tongshan to surrender. On 6 March, Geng Ji Mao, King of Jingnan, and Li Shuai Tai, the Governor of Fujian Province, commanded a great army to attack Bachimen (situated on the north point of Dongshan Island, Zhangzhou, Fujian Province). Weng Qiu Duo, a general under Zheng Jin, surrendered together with sixty thousand people and soldiers. On 14 March the troops under Geng Ji Mao and Li Shuai Tai took Tongshan. Zheng Jin ran away to Taiwan with only thirty ships. Kangxi made Shi Lang General of Jinghai and ordered him to command the navy to conquer Taiwan. But Shi Lang's fleet met with hurricane in the sea on their way to Taiwan. So they had to stop the action and turn back.

In 1665 the Qing court decided to stop military actions against Taiwan. Zheng Jin sent an envoy to their court, offering to be a vassal of the Qing Dynasty like the King of Korea. But Emperor Kangxi refused his offer. But anyway there was peace for both sides.

SECTION TWO: EMPEROR KANGXI ASSUMES THE REINS OF GOVERNMENT

1. The Four Regent Ministers

When Kangxi ascended the throne of the Qing Dynasty, he appointed Suony, Sukesaha, Ebilong and Aobai as the regent ministers.

Suony was a very senior official who had served three emperors of the Qing Dynasty, that is, Emperor Taizu (Nurhaci), Emperor Taizong (Huangtaiji), Emperor Shizu (Fulin), and now he was serving Kangxi. He had performed great work for the Qing Dynasty. This was the reason why his name was in the first place of the list of the four regent ministers.

When Emperor Huangtaiji died in August 1643, he did hot appoint any of his sons as crown prince to succeed to the throne of the Qing Dynasty. His brothers competed for the throne. It was Suony who insisted that only one of Emperor Huangtaiji's sons could succeed to the throne. At last Fulin, Emperor Huangtaiji's ninth son, was selected. During the reign of Shunzhi, Duoergun held all the power in his own hands. Many officials sided with Duoergun, but Suony did his best to assist the young emperor. When Shunzhi died, he appointed Suony, Sukesaha, Ebilong and Aobai as the regent ministers in his testamentary edict. Suony with Sukesaha, Ebilong and Aobai knelt down before the Kings and the late emperor'a brothers to beg them to attend to the state affairs. But the Kings and the brothers of the late emperor said, "The late emperor knew very well the four of you and entrusted the important task of administration of the government affairs to you. Who dares to interfere?" Then they made a vow of devotion to the young emperor before the late emperor's coffin and took up the task of administration of the government affairs.

Sukesaha established great military contributions during the reign of Emperor Huangtaiji. During the reign of Shunzhi, he was under the command of Duoergun. After Duoergun died, Sukesaha exposed Duoergun's conspiracy of rebellion. Duoergun's posthumous title of Emperor Yi and the temple title of Chengzong were deprived. Sukesaha fought very bravely in the battles to eliminate the remaining army forces of the fallen Ming Dynasty. When Kangxi ascended the throne, Sukesaha was appointed as a regent minister. His name was second on the list of the four regent ministers.

Ebilong established military contributions during the reign of Emperor Huangtaiji. In 1641 he followed Emperor Huangtaiji to carry out an expedition against the Ming Dynasty. He established military contributions in the battle of Songshan (now Songshan, situated to the south of Jinzhou, Liaoning Province). During the reign of Shunzhi, he commanded his troops to fight in the area of Wuchang (now Wuchang, Wuhan, Hubei Province) and killed Li Jin, Li Zi Cheng's nephew, in 1645. When Kangxi ascended the throne, Ebilong was appointed as a regent minister. His name was in the third place of the list of the four regent ministers.

Aobai was a tall and strongly built man and a brave fighter. In 1637 Emperor Huangtaiji ordered some high ranking generals to attack Pi Island (now Tan Island, North Korea) which was the Ming army base for threatening the (Later) Jin Dynasty. But they could not take it. Then Emperor Huangtaiji appointed Aobai as the commander of the vanguard army. Aobai and his troops crossed the sea to attack the island against the shells and cannon balls; he was the first one to land the island. He dashed into the enemy battle formation and killed many enemy soldiers. His troops followed him, defeated the Ming troops and took the island. Emperor Huangtaiji was very glad and granted Aobai the title of "Batulu" (meaning "hero" or "brave warrior"). In 1645 Aobai performed great deeds in taking Beijing, the Ming capital, and in destroying the Ming Dynasty. When Kangxi ascended the throne, Aobai was appointed as a regent minister. His name was in the last place of the list of the four regent ministers.

2. Aobai Arrogates All Powers to Himself

The four regent ministers all held grudges against Feiyanggu, the Commander-in-chief of Kangxi's imperial bodyguards, and he also resented them. Feiyanggu's son Wohe was one of the emperor's imperial bodyguards. When Wohe and Xizhu, Zheketu and Jueluosai'erbi, the other three imperial bodyguards, were attending the Emperor in court, they were disrespectful to the four regent ministers. In April 1664 Wohe attended Kangxi during a visit to Jingshan and Yingtai (the two imperial parks within the Forbidden City, Beijing). He rode the horse for the Emperor and used the Emperor's bow and arrows to shoot deer. On 7 April 1664 the four regent ministers accused Wohe of crimes, and for riding the horse for the Emperor and shooting deer with his bow and arrows, Wohe was condemned to death and beheaded. Then the four regent ministers accused Feiyanggu of complaining when he was sent to guard the late Emperor Shunzhi's mausoleum. Feiyanggu and his sons Nikan and Sahalian were all hanged to death. Feiyanggu's houses and all the properties were confiscated and given to Mulima, Aobai's younger brother.

When Duoergun led the Qing army into Shanhaiguan Pass and took Beijing in 1645, many Manchu people rushed into the Beijing area from Liaoning Province and settled down there. In order to provide the Manchu soldiers and people with land to grow crops so as to enable them to support themselves, the government of the Qing Dynasty issued an order to enclose land around Beijing and in Hebei Province, and distribute the land to the soldiers and people under the Eight Banners in accordance to the order of the Left Wing and the Right Wing. According to the original plan, the land in the east part of Beijing area should be given the army under the Yellow Banner with red color rims because the army under this banner was directly under the Emperor and was ranked number one of the Left Wing. But because Duoergun, who was the head of the army under the Pure White Banner, wanted to live in Yongping (now Lulong, Hebei Province) which was situated east to Beijing, so the land in this part was allocated to the army and people under the Pure White Banner. The army under the Yellow Banner with red color rims was given the land in what is now in the middle part of Hebei Province, in Baoding Prefecture, Hejian Prefecture and Zhuozhou, which were situated by the end of the Right Wing.

More than twenty years had passed since the allocation of land in different places to the armies of different banners. The soldiers and people of the different banners had settled down on the land allocated to them, and they lived and worked in peace and contentment.

In January 1666 there were disputes between Aobai and Sukesaha on many matters. Aobai belonged to the army of the Yellow Banner with red rims. Sukesaha belonged to the army of the Pure White Banner. The land which should have been allocated to the army and people under the Yellow Banner with red rimes were taken by the army and people under the Pure White Banner. Aobai was determined to change back. Suony hated Sukesaha too. Ebilong did not dare to hold different idea with Aobai and Suony. So he sided with them. So

Aobai instigated the heads of the armies under the eight banners to deliver applications to change land, using the excuse that their land was not arable anymore. Their applications were delivered to the Ministry of Revenue. Sunahai, the Minister of Revenue, presented a memorial to Kangxi which read, "The land was allocated long ago. In 1664 Your Majesty issued an order to forbid enclosing the land of the people. It is inappropriate to make any changes. We suggest that Your Majesty should reject all the applications." When the memorial was presented to Kangxi, Aobai, Suony and Ebilong intended to frame Sunahai. They suggested to Kangxi that all the kings and high ranking officials should gather together to discuss the memorial presented by Sunahai.

King Wenqi and other members of the royal clan were sent out to conduct an investigation on the land of the Eight Banners. They found that some parts of the land had been indeed been inundated and many parts of the land had been covered by sand. These parts of the land were not arable anymore. The condition of the land of the Yellow Banner with red rims was the worst. As for the land of the other banners, in some cases half of the land was arable; in some cases, less than half was arable; in some cases, all the land was not arable.

They reported what they had found to Kangxi in a memorial on 21 March 1666. The regent ministers said to Kangxi, "In the time of Taizu and Taizong, land and houses were allocated in the order of the Eight Banners. Later when Duoergun entered Beijing, he wanted to live in Yongping Prefecture. So he ordered to leave the land around Yongpin unenclosed. He wanted the army and people under his command to be near him; he ordered to give the land which should be allocated to the army and people under the Yellow Banner with red rims to the army and people under the Pure White Banner. The army and people under the Yellow Banner with red rims were given the land situated by the end of the Right Wing. According to the memorial presented by King Wenqi after his investigation, the situation of the land of the Yellow Banner with red rims was the worst. Now the boundaries of the land of the Eight Banners have been fixed. It will not be easy to change land. The land around Yongping has not been enclosed. It can be allocated to the army and people under the Yellow Banner with red rims. Emperor Shizu once said that everything should be done in accordance with the instructions of Emperor Taizu and Emperor Taizong. Now the allocation of land and houses should be done in the order of the Left Wing and Right Wing. So the land for the Yellow Banner with red rims should be on the head of the Left Wing. The land should be allocated in the order of the Eight Banners. As for how to make up for the land which is not arable and what to do with the land which the army and people of the Yellow Banner with red rims will leave, the officials of the Ministry of Revenue should discuss these matters and make decisions."

On 9 April 1666 the officials of the Ministry of Revenue presented a memorial to Kangxi to put up two suggestions for redistributing the land among the Eight Banners.

The first suggestion referred to the fact that the soldiers under the Yellow Banner with red rims had recently enclosed the land in four counties that are now part of Beijing; it was not necessary to make any further change to the land arrangements there; as for the land of the soldiers and people of the Yellow Banner with red rims in various parts of what is now Hebei Province, which were situated on the end of the Right Wing, these should be exchanged for the land situated to the north of the road from Tongzhou (now Tongzhou, Beijing) to Sanhe (now in Hebei Province) and to Fengrun (now Fengrun, in Hebei Province) which belonged to the soldiers and people under the Pure White Banner according to the original regulation. The land around Yongping (now Lulong, in the east part of Hebei Province) which had not been enclosed would be given to the soldiers and people of the Yellow Banner with red rims; if not enough, the land of the ordinary people situated to the north of the road from Zunhua (now Zunhua, in the east part of Hebei Province) to Yongping (now Lulong, in the east part of Hebei Province) would be enclosed and be given to the soldiers and people of the Yellow Banner with red rims; the soldiers and people of the Pure White Banner who would leave the land east to Tongzhou (now Tongzhou, Beijing) would be given the land around Yongping (now Lulong, in the east part of Hebei Province); if not enough, the land of the ordinary people to the north of Yongping, the land of the ordinary people in Luanzhou (now Luanxian, in the east part of Hebei Province) and Leting (now Leting, in the east part of Hebei Province) would be enclosed and be given to them. Whether the able-bodied men under the servants of the kings and dukes under the Yellow Banner with red rims and under the Pure White Banner should move from their land would be decided by the Emperor; as for the land of the soldiers and people under the other six banners, no change should be made to the land — half of which was arable and half of which was not arable. As for the land more than half of which was not arable or completely not arable, it would be changed for the unused land within the control of different banners, or changed for the land which had been returned by the soldiers and people of the Yellow Banner with red rims or of the Pure White Banners.

It was advised that all the actions suggested above should be taken after autumn harvest; by that time officials should be sent to make a survey of the land and make the plan for distribution.

Second, it was suggested that since the soldiers of the Yellow Banner with red rims had enclosed the land in parts of today's Beijing (Shunyi, Miyun, Huairou and Pinggu), the soldiers and people who would leave Zhuozhou should be given the land of the ordinary people enclosed in these four counties; the soldiers and people of the Yellow Banner with red rims who would leave the land in what is now Hebei Province (Xiongxian, Dacheng, Xin'an, Hejian, Renqiu, Suning and Rongcheng) would be given land in Jizhou (now Jixian, Tianjin) and Zunhua (now Zunhua, in the east part of Hebei Province) which originally belonged to the soldiers and people of the Pure White Banner; if this was not enough, the land of the ordinary people in these counties would be enclosed and be given to them; the land in Tongzhou (now Tongzhou, Beijing), Sanhe (now Sanhe, in the east part of Hebei Province), Yutian (now Yutian, in the east part of Hebei Province) and Fengrun (now Fengrun, in the east part of Hebei Province) which belonged the soldiers and people under the Pure White Banner would still belong to them. The remaining matters would be handled in the same way mentioned in the first suggestion.

When the memorial was presented to Kangxi, the regent ministers said to him, "The matter of moving the soldiers and people of the Yellow Banner with red rims in Zhuozhou to the land in the four counties of Shunyi, Miyun, Huairou and Pinggu should be handled in accordance with the second suggestion; as for the matter of giving the land to the north of the road from Tongzhou to Sanhe and east to Fengrun to the soldiers and people of the Yellow Banner with red rims and giving the land to the south of this road to the soldiers and people of the Pure White Banner mentioned in the first suggestion, it will be handled after autumn harvest; by that time officials will be sent out to measure the land for the Manchu people of the Pure White Banner, the land for the Han nationality serfs and the land for the royal clan; distribution of land will be made after we have got all the measurement. Other things will be reported to Your Majesty after the soldiers and people of the Yellow Banner with red rims have moved to new land distributed to them."

On 20 November 1666 Zhu Chang Zuo, the Viceroy of Zhili Province (now Hebei Province), Shandong Province (now Shandong Province) and Henan Province (now Henan Province), presented a memorial to Kangxi which read, "For the matter of changing land between the soldiers of the Yellow Banner with red rim and the soldiers of the Pure White Banner, Sunahai, the Minister of Revenue, Lei Hu, the Deputy Minister of Revenue, Wang Deng Lian, the Governor of Zhili Province, and I have got together to consider the matters of changing land and enclosing land. We have carried out the work of measuring land for a month. The officers and soldiers of the two banners have great arguments on whether the land is fertile or infertile. Over twenty years has passed since the distribution of land and houses to the soldiers of the different banners. Now the new land changed for them may not be better than the land they already have. They would rather live and work on the land which they already have than move to the new land although they do not say that. The people whose land has been enclosed have no land to work on. They have been thrown into great suffering. They are in desperation. If the order has been issued according to the policy of the court, I will not dare to exceed my power to report this to Your Majesty. But seeing that the people live in great difficulties, I have to report the true situation to Your Majesty. I hope Your Majesty will consider the true situation and issue the order to stop the changing of land and enclosing land." Wang Deng Lian, the Governor Zhili Province (now Hebei), presented a memorial to Kangxi which read, "The soldiers and people under different banners are not willing to change land. When they got the news that the land of the different banners will be changed and the land of the ordinary people will be enclosed, they all stop working in the fields. The fields are now bleak and desolate. I hope Your Majesty will issue an order to stop the changing of land and enclosing of land." When the two memorials had been presented to Kangxi, the regent ministers said to the Emperor, "The Viceroy and the Governor have their respective duties. They should carry out the matter of changing land in accordance with the order issued to them. Now they have interfered with the carrying out of the decisions made by the court and have presented memorials against the court decisions. This is a grave matter. The officials of the Ministry of Personnel and the officials of the Ministry of Defense should come together to discuss what punishment should be given to the officials concerned and they should report their decisions to the Emperor."

The regent ministers announced that Kangxi had issued the following order: "The Ministry of Personnel and the Ministry of Defense should know that the revenue officials of the Yellow Banner with red rims who had been sent to carry out the matter of changing land have all come back. Sunahai, the Revenue Minister, went with several officials to carry out the matter of changing land. More than one month has now passed but the task of changing land has not been fulfilled. The officials have come back without permission. The Personnel Ministry and the Defense Ministry should send officials to arrest the three high officers under the Yellow Banner with red rims who were responsible. Sunahai, the Revenue Minister, should be arrested and put in jail. Viceroy Zhu Chang Zuo and Governor Wang Deng Lian, too. The two ministries should hold a meeting to discuss what punishment should be given to the officials concerned."

The Personnel Ministry and the Ministry of Defense presented a report of the results of their discussion to the Emperor which read, "Sunahai, the Minister of Revenue, is the main official in charge of the matter of changing land. He did not send high ranking officials to carry out the job quickly. He said that it was very difficult to measure the land which had been distributed, and that the generals of the Yellow Banner with red rims would not accept the land which would be redistributed to them, and that the generals of the Pure White Banner would not point out the land boundary. Because Viceroy Zhu Chang Zuo and Governor Wang Deng Lian had presented memorials to Your Majesty, Sunahai waited for the result and delayed to carry out his work. He has not carried out the task entrusted by Your Majesty with all his heart. He should be dismissed from his post. The Ministry of Law should decide what punishment should be given to Sunahai. Viceroy Zhu Chang Zuo and Governor Wang Deng Lian did not carry out the matter which had been decided by Your Majesty and they have gone so far as to make comments on the matter. They should be dismissed from their posts. The Ministry of Law should decide what punishment should be given them. Emohui, the department head under the Ministry of Revenue, should be demoted for four grades and be retained in office. Officer Baka, Officer Lahe, and Officer Zuliangdong were the officials to accept land. When they saw that Sunahai delayed in giving land, they did not urge him to give land. They should be demoted for three grades and be retained in office. Baron Dalai came back to the capital from his work of changing land without permission. He should be punished by suspension of salary for one year. Bitieshi and Boshiku, who did not allow the officials to measure the land, should be handed over to the Ministry of Law."

The regent ministers declared that Emperor Kangxi had made the following decision, "Sunahai, Zhu Chang Zuo and Wang Deng Lian will all be dismissed from their posts and will be handed over to the Ministry of Law. The officials of the Ministry of Law should discuss what punishment will be given to them. Baka, Lahe and Zuliangdong will be dismissed from their posts. Emohui will be demoted for one grade and be retained in office."

On 20 December 1666 the officials of the Ministry of Law presented a report of their decision to Kangxi which read, "Sunahai delayed in giving land. Zhu Chang Zuo and Wang Deng Lian have presented memorials to Your Majesty and made comments on the matter of changing land. This is a grave crime. Sunahai, Zhu Chang Zuo and Wang Deng Lian should be punished by whipping 100 times. Their properties will be confiscated. Bitieshi and Boshiku, who did not allow the officials to measure the land, should be punished by whipping 100 times." When Kangxi had read the report, he knew that Aobai hated Sunahai because he would not please Aobai by doing what he wanted to do, and Aobai hated Zhu Chang Zuo and Wang Deng Lian because they had presented memorials to Kangxi stating that the soldiers of the Banners would not change land and enclose land. He knew that Aobai would put them to death. So Kangxi summoned the regent ministers to discuss the report of the Ministry of Law. Aobai, Suony and Ebilong said to Kangxi that Sunahai, Zhu Chang Zuo and Wang Deng Lian should be given serious punishment. Only Sukesaha did not say anything. Kangxi turned down Aobai's suggestion of giving serious punishment to Sunahai, Zhu Chang Zuo and Wang Deng Lian.

Aobai came out of the palace and declared a counterfeited imperial order, "Sunahai, Zhu Chang Zuo and Wang Deng Lian have committed serious crimes. They are condemned to death penalty by hanging. Their properties should be confiscated." On the same day Sunahai, Zhu Chang Zuo and Wang Deng Lian were executed.

Suony was already old. He saw that Aobai became more and more powerful and Aobai hated Sukesaha very much. He was very worried. So in March 1667 Suony and the other three regent ministers presented a memorial to Kangxi asking him to assume the reins of government. Kangxi did not give any reply to the memorial. In June 1667 Suony died of illness. On 3 July 1667 Kangxi issued a reply to the memorial which read, "I am still young and do not have the ability to handle the complicated affairs of the whole country. I wanted to wait for several more years. The regent ministers have presented memorials asking me to assume the reins of government. But I still did not agree. In their memorials the regent ministers said, 'Emperor Zhang assumed the reins of government at the age of fourteen. Now Your Majesty is also fourteen years old and has the ability to handle state affairs.' I went to see Grandma Empress with the regent ministers. Grandma Empress said, 'The Emperor is still young. If you regent ministers return the power, how can the Emperor handle the state affairs alone? This matter will be discussed again two years from now.' The regent minister presented a memorial again which read, 'Your Majesty personally attends to the state affairs. We shall assist Your Majesty.' Grandma Empress has at last agreed to let me assume the reins of government. I will choose a suitable date to assume reins of government." On 7 July 1667 Kangxi took charge of the government. A ceremony was held in Taihe Hall of the palace. Kangxi sat on the throne to accept congratulations chanted by the kings and officials.

A week later Sukesaha presented a memorial to Kangxi which read, "I am a person of mediocre ability with little learning. The late Emperor showed concern for me and appointed me as a regent minister. I have been always cautious and conscientious. I am afraid that I will fail to live up to the expectation of the late Emperor. When the late Emperor passed away, I really hoped that I could be buried alive with his remains so that all my troubles could be removed. But unexpectedly my name was listed as one of the regent ministers in the testamentary edict left by the late Emperor. I have done my best to fulfill the task entrusted by him. But in these two years I fell ill and cannot render my service for Your Majesty any more. This is a serious crime on my part. Now that Your Majesty has taken charge of the government, I hope Your Majesty will send me to guard the mausoleum of the late Emperor, so that I can keep my weak breath and have the chance to survive. In this way I can repay Your Majesty's kindness of letting me to survive."

Aobai and Ebilong came out to convey Kangxi's words: "You were appointed as regent ministers by the late Emperor in his testamentary edict. You have assisted me for seven years. I am considering how to repay your industrious service. But Sukesaha present a memorial to me asking me to let him to guard the mausoleum of the late Emperor.

In his memorial he says, 'I hope Your Majesty will send me to guard the mausoleum of the late Emperor, so that I can keep my weak breath and have the chance to survive.' I don't understand why he cannot survive when he stays here and why he can survive if I send him to guard the mausoleum of the late Emperor. Now the kings and the ministers should hold a meeting to discuss this matter and report your conclusion to me."

On 17 July 1667 the kings and the ministers reported their conclusion. In the memorial, Sukesaha was found to have committed 24 crimes. The main crimes were: Sukesaha said in his memorial to Kangxi that if he was sent to guard the mausoleum of the late Emperor he could keep his weak breath and have the chance to survive — this showed that he was not willing to let Kangxi take up the reins of government; Sukesaha was once ordered to escort the bow used by Kangxi and put it in Zhonghe Hall of the palace, but on the way he threw the bow up and down many times — this showed that he despised the Emperor; in the ceremony to celebrate Kangxi's assuming the reins of government, Kangxi issued an imperial edict of a general pardon of the criminals, but Sukesaha said that whether the general pardon of the criminals should be carried out should be discussed by the kings and ministers. — He was so bold as to comment on the imperial edict issued by the Emperor ... this showed that he look down upon the Emperor; when the late Emperor's coffin was carried to the mausoleum, Aobai walked by the side of the coffin and cried for more than two kilometers, but Sukesaha was late, he rode a horse to catch up with the team escorting the coffin, he should have come down from the horse and walked on foot and cried, but he was still on horseback and rode by the side of the coffin and cried, and very soon he turned back — this showed that he had abandoned the kindness shown to him by the late Emperor; Sukesaha once said to Banbulinshan that the Duke of Zhou assisted King Cheng of the Zhou Dynasty when King Cheng was fourteen years old and he returned the power to King Cheng when he was over twenty years old — this showed that he was unwilling to let Kangxi to assume reins of government.

With this record of slights, the kings and the ministers suggested that Sukesaha should be executed. Kangxi knew that Aobai was Sukesaha's diehard enemy and was eager to put Sukesaha to death at the least excuse. So he turned down the suggestion. But Aobai rolled up his sleeves and went before the Emperor in person and insisted that Sukesaha must be put to death. He did this several days in a row. And finally, Sukesaha was put to death by hanging.

3. Emperor Kangxi Arrests Aobai by a Clever Plan

Aobai had been very imperious and held the power of the court in his own hands. He did all kinds of bad things at his own will. Emperor

Kangxi knew this for a long time. But Aobai was a muscular man and it would be very difficult to subdue him and arrest him. So Kangxi selected some strong young men from his bodyguards and workmen in different offices and ordered them to be trained in wrestling. On 16 May 1669 Kangxi issued an imperial order to arrest Aobai which read, "Formerly the position of the Minister of Works was vacant. Aobai recommended Jishi, a man I have never known, to take the position. He said that Jishi was a capable man who was able to do the job. Aobai has colluded with Jishi to deceive me. He said that during the reign of Emperor Wen there were two Ministers of Revenue, so that one more Minister of Revenue should be appointed. Then he recommended Ma'ersai to the position for his personal interest. When he handles state affairs before me, he never cares whether what he has done is reasonable. He flies into a rage at the slightest discontent and shouts angrily at his subordinates. When a person is introduced to me, Aobai should talk with him with a calm voice. But instead, he has displayed his power and shouted questions at the person so loudly that the people present were all shocked. In the matters of personnel and administration Aobai arrogates all powers to himself and looks down upon me. He acts at his own will. All the civil officials and military officers are his followers. He appoints persons of his sworn followers to high ranking positions. Mulima, Saibende, Namo, Folun, Su'erma, Banbulinshan, Asiha, Gachuha, Jishi, Ma'ersai, Taibitu, Maiyinda, Wugesai, Budali and Aobai formed a clique. They discussed all the important state affairs at Aobai's home and then put them into practice without my permission. They often discussed the matters in the memorials presented to me by the Ministries and Government Offices at Aobai's home. As everyone knows, Aobai and his followers are extremely vicious. They disregard the laws. Aobai recommends and promotes his good friends and makes false charge against those he dislikes. I often think that Aobai is an old official and his name was listed in the names of the four regent ministers in the testamentary edict left by the late Emperor. I have bestowed much favor on him. I hoped that he would remove the evil and show repentance. But Aobai and his clique have acted even more viciously. He has gone against the great trust placed by the late Emperor and done great harm to the people. He has done a lot of evil things. Ebilong knows all these but he has kept his mouth shut. He has never revealed to me any of Aobai's evil doings. I have shown great favor to Alanda, but he has failed to live up to my expectation. In his memorials presented to me he praised Aobai as a sage. He should also be arrested and be interrogated."

On the same day Aobai came to have an audience with Kangxi. The Emperor ordered the young wrestlers to attack him; they held Aobai down and arrested him. Kangxi ordered the kings and officials to discuss his crimes.

On 28 May 1669 the kings and officials presented a memorial to Kangxi. Aobai was found to have committed 30 crimes. The main crimes were: Aobai was an important official who was entrusted by the late Emperor the task of assisting the Emperor, but he acted at his own will and disrespected the Emperor and arrogated all powers to himself, all the civil and military officials were Aobai's followers; Aobai and Mulima, Saibende, Namo, Folun, Su'erma, Banbulinshan, Asiha, Gachuha, Jishi, Ma'ersai, Taibitu, Maiyinda, Wugesai and Budali formed a clique, they discussed all the important state affairs at Aobai's home and then put them into practice without the Emperor's permission, they often discussed the matters in the memorials presented to the Emperor by the Ministries and Government Offices at Aobai's home; Aobai and the members of his clique usurp the power of the court and interfered the affairs of the court, Aobai recommends and promotes his good friends and makes false charge against those he dislikes, the Emperor had considered that Aobai had been a regent minister appointed by the late Emperor and shown great favor to him, but Aobai never showed any repentance and became even more evil; after the Emperor had assumed reins of government, Aobai acted beyond his authority and put Sukesaha and all his family members to death; Minister Sunahai, Viceroy Zhu Chang Zuo and Governor Wang Deng Lian were against Aobai's will and did not carry out the matter of changing land among the soldiers under the eight banners, Aobai put them to death without the Emperor's permission; Aobai arrogated all the power to himself, when the Emperor had assumed reins of government, he was still not willing to handover the power to the Emperor; he lied to the Emperor that Jishi was a capable man and appointed him to the position of the Minister of Works; he told the Emperor that there had been two Ministers of the Ministry of Revenue in the past and he appointed Ma'ersai, a member of his clique, to the important position. The kings and officials suggested to the Emperor that Aobai had committed serious crimes and deserved death penalty and all his family members should be executed.

Kangxi issued an imperial edict. "Aobai is stupid and ignorant. He really deserves death penalty. But considering that he has fought for the state for many years and has established many military contributions, I have decided to exempt him from death penalty. He should be kept in jail. All his properties should be confiscated." Aobai was thrown into jail. Not long later he died there. Many members of his clique such as Banbulinshan, Asiha, Gachuha, Jishi, Taibitu and Wugesai were executed.

SECTION THREE: EMPEROR KANGXI PUTS DOWN THE REVOLT OF THE THREE MILITARY GOVERNORS

1. The Three Military Governors

Wu San Gui defended Shanhaiguan Pass (in Qinhuangdao, in the northeast part of Hebei Province) for the Ming Dynasty against the army of the Qing Dynasty. In March 1645, Li Zi Cheng, the leader of the peasant uprising, took Beijing (now Beijing), the capital of the Ming Dynasty, and overthrew the Ming Dynasty. In April Li Zi Cheng commanded a great army to march to Shanhaiguan Pass. Wu San Gui asked Duo'ergun, the Prince Regent of Emperor Shunzhi of the Qing Dynasty, for help and let the Qing army under Duo'ergun to enter Shanhaiguan Pass. On 22 April 1645 a battle was fought by Shanhaiguan Pass. Li Zi Cheng's army was defeated by the united army of the Qing Dynasty and Wu San Gui. After the battle on that day Duo'ergun made Wu San Gui King of Pingxi (Pingxi means Pacification of the West) under the edict of Shunzhi. In September 1651 Shunzhi ordered Wu San Gui to carry out an expedition to Sichuan (now Sichuan Province). Wu San Gui succesffuly completed his task and took Sichuan Province in 1652. In February 1659 Wu San Gui commanded his troops to march to Kunming (now Kunming, the capital city of Yunnan Province) and took it. Then he marched his troops westward to take Yongchang (now Baoshan, in the west part of Yunnan Province) where Zhu You Lang, the Emperor of the South Ming Dynasty was. Zhu You Lang escaped to Burma. Wu San Gui commanded his troops to march into Burma and forced the King of Burma to hand over Zhu You Lang to him. Zhu You Lang was brought back to Yunnan and was executed. From then on the Ming Dynasty had completely fallen. For these great contributions, Emperor Kangxi granted him the title of Prince which had been only granted to the members of the royal clan. On 22 December 1662 Kangxi appointed Wu San Gui as the Military Governor of Yunnan Province and Guizhou Province.

Shang Ke Xi was a general of the army of the Ming Dynasty stationed in Guanglu Island (now in Liaoning Province). In March 1635 he led all the officers and men to surrender to the (Later) Jin Dynasty. In 1636 Huangtaiji, the Emperor of the (Later) Jin Dynasty, made him King of Zhishun (meaning Resourceful and Submissive). In 1645 Shang Ke Xi entered Shanhaiguan Pass with the Qing army to fight against Li Zi Cheng, the leader of the peasant uprising. He commanded his troops to fight against Li Zi Cheng's troops in the area of Shaanxi Province and in the area of Hubei Province. He performed great deeds in defeating Li Zi Cheng's army. In 1647 he was ordered to command his troops to take Hunan Province. On 20 May 1649 Shunzhi made Shang Ke Xi King of Pingnan (meaning "Pacifying the South"). Not long later Shunzhi ordered Shang Ke Xi to command 10,000 men to march south to take Guangdong Province. In February 1650 Shang Ke Xi commanded his troops to lay siege to Guangzhou, the capital city of Guangdong Province. The siege lasted for 10 months and at last the city was taken by the Qing army under Shang Ke Xi. In March 1659 Shunzhi ordered Shang Ke Xi to garrison Guangdong Province.

Geng Zhong Ming was a general of the army of the Ming Dynasty stationed in Northeast China. In March 1634 Geng Zhong Ming surrendered to the (Later) Jin Dynasty. In 1636 Emperor Huangtaiji made him King of Huaishun (meaning "Thankful and Submissive"). On 20 May 1649 Shunzhi made him King of Jingnan (Jingnan means "Tranquillizing the South") and ordered Shang Ke Xi and Geng Zhong Ming to carry out an expedition to Guangdong Province. When the army had started their march, the Ministry of Justice accused Chen Shao Zhong, a general under Geng Zhong Ming, of the crime of letting the officers and men to give refuge to the runaway people. Chen Shao Zhong deserved death penalty. Shunzhi ordered Geng Zhong Ming to carry out an investigation to the officers and men and find out those who had given refuge to the runaway people. After investigation, he found out three hundred of them. He arrested all of them and sent them to the Ministry of Justice. He presented a memorial to Shunzhi to admit his error and ask for punishment. The officials of the Ministry of Justice suggested to the Emperor that Geng Zhong Ming should be deprived his title of King of Jingnan. Shunzhi decided to pardon him and did not give him any punishment. The Emperor also pardoned General Chen Shao Zhong. But before the Emperor's order of pardon reached him, Geng Zhong Ming committed duiside in November 1649 in Ji'an (now Ji'an, Jiangxi Province). When Geng Zhong Ming died, his son Geng Ji Mao was a general in his army. Geng Ji Mao took command of his father's army. He asked Emperor Shunzhi for permission to succeed his father's title of King of Jingnan. At that time power was in the hands of Duo'ergun, the Regent Prince. He refused to give the permission. Geng Ji Mao commanded his troops to march to Guangdong Province together with the army under Shang Ke Xi.

In November 1650 Geng Ji Mao and Shang Ke Xi took Guangzhou, the capital city of Guangdong Province. In 1651 Shunzhi assumed the reins of government. He let Geng Ji Mao succeed his father's title of King of Jingnan. So there were two Kings in Guangzhou. Shang Ke Xi spent a lot of money and labor to build the residence and office of King of Pingnan, and Geng Ji Mao spent a lot of money and labor to build the residence and office of King of Jingnan. This caused great trouble to the people of Guangdong Province. An official of Guangdong Province presented a memorial to Shunzhi which read, "A province cannot tolerate two kings. It would be better if one of them is transferred to another Province." In March 1659 Geng Ji Mao was transferred to garrison Sichuan Province. In July 1660 Geng Ji Mao was transferred to garrison Fujian Province. At that time Zheng Cheng Gong, a general of the fallen Ming Dynasty, occupied Jinmen Island (now Jinmen Island situated in the southeast of Fujian Province). Geng Ji Mao defeated Zheng Cheng Gong. In 1662 Zheng Cheng Gong died. His son Zheng Jin took command of his army. Kangxi ordered Geng Ji Mao to suppress Zheng Jin's army. Geng Ji Mao wrote a report to the Emperor which read, "From 1661 to 1662, 290 officials and officers, 4,334 soldiers and 467 family members of Zheng Jin's army surrendered." Later Zheng Cheng Gong's younger brother Zheng Shi Xi, his elder brother's son Zheng Zuan Xu and

Governor Zheng Geng came to surrender. More than 700 generals and officers and 7,600 soldiers came with them. In October 1663 Geng Ji Mao commanded his troops to cross the sea and took Xiamen (now Xiamen, in the southeast part of Fujian Province) and then took Jinmen Island (now Jinmen Island, an island near Xiamen) which was a base of Zheng Jin's army. Zheng Jin ran away to Tongshan (now Tongshan Bay of Dongshan Island, in the southeast of Fujian Province). In March 1664 Geng Ji Mao commanded his army to attack Zheng Jin in Tongshan. Zheng Jin ran awy to Taiwan. When the news of the victory reached Kangxi, he rewarded Geng Ji Mao handsomely. In January 1671 Geng Ji Mao present a memorial to Kangxi in which he told the Emperor that he was seriously ill and he asked the Emperor's permission to allow his eldest son Geng Jing Zhong to succeed his title of King of Jingnan and be the Military Governor of Fujian Province. Kangxi gave his permission. In May 1671 Geng Ji Mao died. His son Geng Jing Zhong became King of Jingnan and Military Governor of Fujian Province.

2. Emperor Kangxi Deprives the Military Governors of Power

On 12 March 1673 Shang Ke Xi, the Military Governor of Guangdong Province, presented a memorial to Kangxi which read, "I am already 70 years old and have become weak. I hope I can be allowed to go back to Liaodong, my home place, to spend my old age. In the past I was granted land and houses in Liaodong. I hope that Your Majesty will grant the land and houses to me again. I will take some officers and soldiers and old people who have been under me, 4,394 households all together, to go back with me. There are 24,375 men and women in all. I hope the department concerned will provide food for all these people on their way to Liaodong." Having read his memorial, Kangxi gave him a reply which read, "Since you sailed from the island to submit to our dynasty, you have worked very hard and established great contributions. You have garrisoned in Guangdong Province for many years. I know from your memorial that you are already 70 years old. You want to go back to Liaodong. You are very sincere in your memorial. From this I can see that you are respectful and submissive and have the overall interest at heart. I am very pleased about that. Now Guangdong Province has been pacified. I will order the Kings in charge of government affairs, court officials and the officials of the Ministry of Revenue and the Ministry of Defense to discuss how to arrange the migration and settlement of the officers and men under you. I will let you know when they have made a decision."

On 21 March 1673 the officials of the Personnel Ministry presented a report of their discussion to Kangxi which read, "In the memorial presented by Shang Ke Xi to Your Majesty he says that he is already old and ill. He asked Your Majesty's permission to let his son Shang Zhi Xin to succeed his title of King of Pingnan. But now Shang Ke

Xi is still alive. There is no precedent that the son can succeed his father's title when his father is still alive. So it is not necessary to consider whether or not to allow his son to succeed his title." Kangxi agreed with their conclusion.

On 27 March 1673 the Kings in charge of government affairs and the court officials presented a memorial to Kangxi which read, "Shang Ke Xi, King of Pingnan, asked Your Majesty's permission to return to Liaodong. We suggest that Your Majesty should give the permission. But his son Shang Zhi Xin will still command the officers and men to stay in Guangdong. Then the father and son will be separated. The fathers and sons and brothers of the officers and men under the King of Pingnan will also be separated. Now Guangdong Province has been pacified. Since it has been decided that the officers and men under King of Pingnan should migrate back to Liaodong, then all the officers and men should migrate back to Liaodong. Only the Manchu troops of the left camp and the right camp of the army under the Pure Green Banner should still stay in Guangdong. The officials of the Ministry of Defense will make a decision as to how these two camps of the army shall be combined as one." Kangxi agreed with this suggestion.

On 3 July 1673 Wu San Gui, King of Pingxi, presented a memorial to Kangxi which read, "I have been ordered to garrison Yunnan Province. The family members of the officers and men under me began to migrate to Yunnan Province from 1662. In 1664 the migration was completed. Now the family members of the officers and men have stayed in Yunnan for 9 years. But I have stayed in the border area for 16 years. I have been granted so much favor by the Emperors that I cannot repay them even if I should die. The only way I can repay them is to exert to the utmost to defend the border area until my dying day. I have never thought of being relieved from my office. Now I hear that Shang Ke Xi, King of Pingnan, has presented a memorial to Your Majesty in which he has asked Your Majesty's permission to go back to Liaodong, and Your Majesty has granted him the permission to let all the officers and men under him to migrate back to Liaodong. I now ask Your Majesty's permission to let me and the officers and men under me to leave Yunnan Province and settle down in some place." Kangxi gave a reply to Wu San Gui which read, "Since you submitted to our dynasty, you have been very faithful and have carried out all the military activities. You have established great military contributions. You have garrisoned in the border area for many years. I have read your memorial in which you ask permission to let you and the officers and men under you to leave Yunnan Province and settle down in some place. You have been very respectful and cautious. Now Yunnan has been pacified. I will order the Kings in charge of government affairs and the officials of the Ministry of Defense and the Ministry of Revenue to discuss how to arrange the migration and settlement of the officers and men under you. I will let you know when they have made a decision."

On 9 July 1673 Geng Jing Zhong, King of Jingnan, presented a memorial to Kangxi which read, "Two years has passed since I succeeded my father's title of King of Jingnan. I have been longing to go back to the north. But there are still some troubles by the sea area. I dare not ask Your Majesty's permission to stop military actions by the sea area. Recently I hear that Shang Ke Xi, King of Pingnan, has presented a memorial to Your Majesty to ask permission to go back to Liaodong and Your Majesty has granted him the permission. I consider that the officers and men under me have carried out the southern expedition for more than 20 years. Now I sincerely ask Your Majesty's permission to let me and the officers and men under me to leave Fujian Province and settle down in my home place." Kangxi gave a reply which read, "Your grandfather and father were very devoted and fought very hard and established great military contributions. Since you succeeded the title of King of Jingnan and garrisoned Fujian, you have been working very hard in the border area. You have been very respectful and cautious. Now Fujian has been pacified. I will order the Kings in charge of government affairs and the officials of the Ministry of Defense and the Ministry of Revenue to discuss how to arrange the migration and settlement of the officers and men under you. I will let you know when they have made a decision."

On 28 July 1673 the Kings in charge of the government affairs presented a memorial to Kangxi which read, "Fujian Province has been pacified. There are local troops to defend the area of Fujian. King of Jingnan has asked Your Majesty's permission to move away from Fujian. We suggest that the King of Jingnan and all the family members of the officers and men under him should move away from Fujian." Kangxi agreed with their suggestion.

On 6 August 1673 the Kings in charge of government affairs presented a report of their discussion to Kangxi which read, "Wu San Gui, King of Pingxi, has asked Your Majesty's permission to move away from Yunnan and settle down in a place. We suggest that the king and all the family members of the officers and men under him should move away from Yunnan to a place outside Shanhaiguan Pass and settle down there. In Yunnan Province there are many chieftains of the people of the Miao Nationality. We should be on guard against them. Now King of Pingxi and the officers and men will move away, we should send Manchu troops to garrison Yunnan. The King of Pingxi and the officers and men will be able to move away only after the Manchu troops have arrived to garrison Yunnan. The Ministry of Defense should make a plan as to how the Manchu troops should be sent and how the Manchu troops should be combined with the four bands of the soldiers under the Pure Green Banner, and how much money and food should be provided for the migration of the officers and men under King of Pingxi." The Kings in charge of government affairs presented another suggestion to Kangxi which read, "Since Wu San Gui garrisoned Yunnan, the province has been in great peace and there have been no chaos. If the King of Pingxi moves away from Yunnan, Your Majesty has to send troops to garrison Yunnan. The marching of the Manchu troops to Yunnan and the migration of the King of Pingxi and the officers and men under him will cause great trouble to the people. The garrison troops sent to Yunnan may harass the local people. We suggest that Your Majesty should let Wu San Gui continue to garrison Yunnan." Kangxi gave a reply which read, "Wu San Gui has asked my permission to move away from Yunnan and settle down in a place. He has been very earnest. Now I order Wu San Gui to lead all the officers and men and their family members to move away from Yunnan. At present it is not necessary to send Manchu troops to Yunnan. If Manchu troops are really necessary, you should present a memorial to me when Wu San Gui and his officers and men are ready to start their migration. Then the Manchu troops will be sent. When the Manchu troops have arrived, it won't be too late for King of Pingxi to start moving."

On 9 August 1673 Kangxi gave an imperial edict to the Ministry of Revenue which read, "Wu San Gui, King of Pingxi, Shang Ke Xi, King of Pingnan, and Geng Jing Zhong, King of Jingnan, have asked my permission to move from the places where they were ordered to garrison and to settle down in their home places. I have granted them my permission. You should make preparation for the places in which the kings and the officers and men and their family members will settle down and the land and houses for them. You must make sure that when they arrive, they will have houses to live in peacefully, so that they will feel my great concern to them."

On 15 August Kangxi sent Zhe'erken, an assistant minister, and Fu Da Li, a Scholar of the Hanlin Academy, to Yunnan Province, Liang Qing Biao, a minister, to Guangdong Province, and Chen Yi Bing, an assistant minister, to Fujian Province, to handle the affairs of the moving of the three military governors.

On 24 August Kangxi granted Wu San Gui, King of Pingxi, an imperial edict which read, "Since ancient times emperors relied on the military officials to pacify the whole realm. When the whole realm had been pacified, the military officials would lead the army to return triumphantly and let their soldiers have a good rest. The emperors would let those military officials who had made major contributions spend their old age comfortably. The emperors would grant them handsome rewards and let them live a long life. You have been very faithful and courageous. You have defeated all the enemies. You have worked very hard to garrison in the border areas. With you garrisoning the south border areas, I don't need to worry about the safety of the south. This is one of your great contributions. You are now very old. You have commanded your officers and men to garrison in the bleak and wild border areas for many years. I am very concerned about you. Now the area of Yunnan has been pacified. You have asked for my permission to move away from Yunnan and settle down in your home place. Now I have sent Zhe'erken, the Deputy Minister of Rites, and Fu Da Li, a Scholar of the Hanlin Academy, to go to Yunnan to deliver my intention to you. You should lead all the officers and men under you to come to the north. I am now waiting for you here. When you have come, I will spend some happy days with you. You may enjoy your retired life. I have ordered the departments concerned to make well preparation for the settlement of all the officers and men under you. When you come, you will have comfortable houses to live in. So don't worry about it."

On 18 September 1673 Kangxi said to Xilantai, a high ranking official of the Ministry of Revenue, Dangwuli, a high ranking official of the Ministry of Defense, Samuha, a high ranking official of the Ministry of Revenue, and Xinzhu, a high ranking official of the Ministry of Defense, who were sent to Guizhow Province to arrange laborers, ships, and army provisions for the migration of Wu San Gui's officers and men, "Guizhou has always been a place of hardship. The people there live in great poverty. You should not disturb the life of the local people. If the officers and men under King of Pingxi reach the riverside, you must provide them with ships without any delay."

On 4 September 1673 Wu San Gui, King of Pingxi, presented a memorial to Kangxi which read, "The number of the family members of the officers and men under me has greatly increased for these 30 years. I earnestly ask Your Majesty to allocate a bigger piece of land than the land which had been allocated by the late Emperor in the area from Shanhaiguan Pass to Jinzhou. Then all the officers and men under me can enjoy the grace granted by Your Majesty." Kangxi gave a reply which read, "The family members of the officers and men under you will migrate from afar to the north. They should be settled properly. They will surely have good houses to live in. You should tell me exactly the places you want to let your officers and men to settle down as soon as possible."

3. Emperor Kangxi Suppresses the Military Governors' Rebellions

When Wu San Gui presented a memorial to Emperor Kangxi to ask his permission to leave Yunnan, he thought that the court officials would not give the permission and would persuade him to stay in Yunnan. In September 1673 Zhe'erken and Fu Da Li, the envoys sent by Kangxi to arrange the migration of Wu San Gui and the officers and men under him, arrived. This made him greatly disappointed. He planned a rebellion with his son Wu Ying Qi, Wu Guo Gui, Gao De Jie, the Deputy Commander, his son-in-law Xia Guo Xiang and Hu Guo Zhu. He deployed his trusted subordinates to defend strategic passes. People were allowed to go in the passes but were not allowed to go out of them. He planned to hold the rebellion on 24 September. On 21 September, Wu San Gui asked Zhu Guo Zhi, the Provincial Governor of Yunnan, to join in the rebellion, but he refused. So Wu

San Gui ordered his officers to kill Zhu Guo Zhi. Then he commanded all the generals under him to hold a rebellion. He named himself King of Zhou and Great Marshal of the Expedition Army. He ordered all the officers and men changed their hair style. The Qing government stipulated that all the men must have their hair shaved and only a small part of the hair remained to make a pig tail. Now all the men should let their hair grow. He ordered that all the flags must be white color. All the foot soldiers and cavalrymen wore white color hats. He arrested Zhe'erken and Fu Da Li, the two envoys sent by Kangxi to arrange the migration of Wu San Gui and the officers and men under him, Li Xing Yuan, the Provincial Supervisor, Gao Xian Chen and Liu Kun, two local officials. They would not submit to Wu San Gui. Wu San Gui kept them in a place in which there was communicable subtropical disease. Other local officials submitted themselves to Wu San Gui. Wu San Gui sent envoys to take letters to Shang Ke Xi, King of Pingnan, Geng Jing Zhong, King of Jingnan, the generals and officials in Guizhou Province, Sichuan Province, Hunan Province and Guangxi Province asking them to respond to his rebellion. He sent General Ma Bao to command troops as the vanguards to march to Guiyang, the capital city of Guizhou Province. Li Ben Shen, the Commander-in-chief of the army stationed in Guizhou Province, planned to respond to Wu San Gui's rebellion. Gan Wen Kun, the Governor of Yunnan Province and Guizhou Province, sent an envoy to ride very quickly to report to Cai Yu Rong, the Governor of Sichuan Province and Hunan Province, that Wu San Gui had rebelled. He urged Zhe'erken, Dangwuli, an official under Fu Da Li, Samuha, Xinzhu and Sa'ertu to go quickly back to the capital to report to Kangxi that Wu San Gui had rebelled. Wu San Gui sent cavalrymen to run after them. Xinzhu and Sa'ertu were caught and killed. Gan Wen Kun led several cavalrymen to ride to Zhenyuan (in the east part of Guizhou Province), a place very close to Hunan Province. Jiang Yi, the Deputy Commander of the army stationed in Zhenyuan, who had already got the letter sent by Wu San Gui, sent troops to surround Gan Wen Kun. Gan Wen Kun and all his followers died. When General Ma Bao commanded his troops to Guizhou, Cao Shen Ji, the Governor of Guizhou Province, and Wang Yong Qing, the Commander-in-chief of the army stationed in Guizhou Province, surrendered.

On 21 December Dangwuli and Samuha, who had been sent to Guizhou to arrange the laborers, ships and food supplies for the migration of Wu San Gui and his officers and men, rode back to Beijing, the capital, and presented a memorial to Kangxi which read, "Gan Wen Kun, the Governor of Yunnan Province and Guizhou Province, told us that Wu San Gui had killed Zhu Zhi Guo, the Governor of Yunnan Province, and held a rebellion on 21 September. Zhe'erken, who had been sent to arrange the migration of Wu San Gui and his family members, has been detained. We have ridden day and night back to the capital to report the situation." Kangxi summoned the kings in charge of government affairs and the court officials to the palace and said to them, "Now Wu San Gui has held a rebellion. Jingzhou is a place of critical importance. Now I order General Shuodai to command the imperial guards to march there at double speed and defend Jingzhou resolutely. Some troops should be sent to march forward to Changde so as to stop the advance of the rebels. In order to avoid delay by feeding horses, capable officials should be sent to prepare food for the horses in places in which the troops will stop for the night. You should hold a discussion to make a decision as to where the great army should be sent to suppress the rebels and report your decision to me as soon as possible."

On 22 December 1673 Cai Yu Rong, the Governor of Sichuan Province, Hunan Province and Guangxi Province, presented a memorial to Kangxi which read, "Wu San Gui has rebelled. He proclaimed himself to be Great Marshal of the Expedition Army. He has decided that next year will be the first year of King of Zhou. Li Ben Shen, the Governor of Guizhou, has responded to his rebellion. Xinzhu, the official of the Ministry of Defense, and Sa'ertu, who were sent to Guizhou to make preparation for the migration of Wu San Gui and his officers and men, could not get away. They were caught. They would not surrender and were killed. Gan Wen Kun, the Governor of Yunnan Province and Guizhou Province, left Guiyang in a great hurry with some cavalrymen when he got the information that Wu San Gui has held a rebellion. On 8 December he reached Zhenyuan. But the General of the Army defending Zhenyuan has already responded to Wu San Gui's rebellion. He commanded some troops to surround Gan Wen Kun and his followers. Gan Wen Kun saw that it was impossible for him to make his escape. He killed his son and then killed himself. All his followers also killed themselves. Cao Shen Ji, the Governor of Guizhou Province has surrendered to the rebel army."

Cai Yu Rong presented another memorial to Kangxi which read, "Gan Wen Kun, the Governor of Yunnan Province and Guizhou Province, sent me a letter in which he secretly told me that Wu San Gui had rebelled. Then I sent Cui Shi Lu, the Commander-in-chief of the army stationed in Yuanzhou to march quickly to Guizhou Province to resist Wu San Gui's army. I ordered Xu Zhi Du, the Commander-in-chief of the army stationed in Yiling, and Li Zhi Lan, the Commander-in-chief of the army stationed in Yongzhou, to command the troops under them to march to Guizhou. Later I worried that the defense of Hunan Province was weak. Then I sent a letter to Zhou Bang Ning, the Commander-in-chief of the army stationed in Runan, to come to Hunan Province to strengthen the defense of Hunan." When Kangxi got the memorial, he notified the Ministry of Defense about this.

On 22 December Kangxi ordered to stop the moving of King of Pingnan from Guangdong Province and King of Jingnan from

Fujian Province. He recalled Liang Qing Biao who had been sent to Guangdong to arrange the migration of Shang Ke Xi, King of Pingnan, and Chen Yi Bing, who had been sent to Fujiang to arrange the migration of Geng Jing Zhong, King of Jingnan, back to Beijing. He issued an order to the Ministry of Defense which read, "Sang'er, the Governor of Yunnan Province, should be transferred as the Governor of Hunan Province and Guangxi Province. Eshan, the Commander-in-chief of the army stationed in Hunan Province and Guangxi Province, will remain in his present position. He should cooperate with Cai Yu Rong, the Governor of Sichuan Province, Hunan Province and Guangxi Province, to do their best to resist and suppress Wu San Gui's rebellion and stabilize the three provinces." Kangxi considered that Guangxi Province bordered Guizhou, he granted Sun Yan Ling, the general garrisoning Guangxi Province, the title of General of Pacifying the Barbarians. He appointed Xian Guo An as Commander-in-chief of the army stationed in Guangxi Province. He ordered them to strengthen the defense there.

On 22 December Kangxi ordered General Wa'erka, the Commander-in-chief of the army stationed in Xi'an (now Xi'an, Shaanxi Province), to command his troops to march into Sichuan Province. He said in his imperial order, "Sichuan Province borders Yunnan Province. Now Wu San Gui has rebelled. You may command the generals and men to hurry into Sichuan Province. You should deploy generals to defend all the critical passes from which Wu San Gui's troops may enter Sichuan Province from Yunnan Province. I will send large number of forces to suppress the rebellion in Yunnan. When our troops reach Yunnan, Wu San Gui has to send his troops to cope with our troops. In this way his forces will be dispersed and weakened. When opportunity comes, you and the generals under you must seize the opportunity to march forward to suppress the rebellion. As for the defense of Xi'an, I will send the imperial guard army to march to Xi'an and station there."

A man named Yang Qi Long claimed that he was the Third Crown Prince of the royal clan of the Ming Dynasty. He gathered together some people to plan a rebellion. They planned to set fire to the houses in Beijing and outside Beijing and start the rebellion. Huang Cai Feng, a workman in the house of Lang Ting Shu, an official under the Yellow Banner with red rims, and Chen Yi, a workman in the house of Zhou Gong Zhi, an official under Pure Yellow Banner, took part in Yang Qi Long's gang. On 22 December, Lang Ting Shu found out the scheme. He arrested Huang Cai Feng and other three men and took them to the government office to reveal the scheme. Zhou Gong Zhi also went to the government office to report to the official that there were more than thirty vicious men hiding in his home. Tuhai, a general under the Pure Yellow Banner, commanded the officers and men under him to surround Zhou Gong Zhi's house. Jihali, a general under the Yellow

Banner with red rims, also commanded the officers and men under him to go to Zhou Gong Zhi's house to catch the rebels. Chen Yi and the other rebels set fire to the house and resisted arrest. The government officers and men rushed into the house and arrested Chen Yi and the other rebels. Then the government officers and men began to search in the city and arrested those people who were involved in the rebellion. Several hundred rebels were arrested. Yang Qi Long ran away. All the arrested rebels were brought to the office of the Ministry of Justice to be investigated. Kangxi issued an imperial edict to tell the people that the rebellion in Beijing had been suppressed, and those innocent people who were not involved in the rebellion would not be punished and they should not run away.

On 23 December Kangxi gave an instruction to the Personnel Ministry and the Ministry of Defense which read, "Wu San Gui has rebelled. Many military officers and civil officials in Hebei Province and other provinces were originally under Wu San Gui. Now that Wu San Gui has rebelled, they are now afraid that they would be under suspicion of being involved in his rebellion and would be arrested. I have been magnanimous to all my people. You are the officials and people under my reign. You have not been involved in the rebellion. Although your fathers, sons or brothers are now in Yunnan, you will not be involved in the case of Wu San Gui's rebellion and you will not be punished. From now on, you should be at ease and work hard to fulfill your duty. There is nothing to be worried about."

On 25 December Kangxi appointed Le'erjin as Grand General of Tranquilizing the South and Pacifying the Rebels to command the generals to pacify Wu San Gui's rebellion. King Chani, Generals Jueluo Zhuman, Enei, Boyilibu, Jueluo Ba'erbu, Yi'erduqi, Esitai, and Shuodai were appointed as military advisors. Fandali, Wang Guo Zhao, Luxibatulu, Tuodai and Mushuhun would go with Le'erjin.

On the same day Wu Ying Xiong, Wu San Gui's son, was arrested and put in jail. He was deprived of all his titles. An imperial edict was issued to notify the military officers, civil officials, soldiers and ordinary people in Yunnan Province and Guizhou Province that: "Wu San Gui submitted to our dynasty when he was at the end of his resources. My father Emperor Shizu, considering that Wu San Gui had sincerely submitted and had established military contributions, granted him the title of King of Pingxi. He promoted the generals and officers under Wu San Gui to high ranking positions and granted them handsome rewards. He ordered Wu San Gui to garrison Yunnan Province and placed great confidence on him. When I succeeded to the throne, I granted him the title of Prince. I entrusted him with the responsibility of defending the border area. I have granted him many graces. But Wu San Gui is a treacherous man. He is very proud of himself and has gone so far as to start a rebellion. In July this year, he presented a memorial to me in which he asked my permission to move away from Yunnan Province. I thought that Wu San Gui was sincere in asking my permission. I considered that he was already old and weak and had stayed in the border area for a long time. So I granted him my permission and let him retire. I ordered the departments concerned to make proper preparation for the settlement of Wu San Gui and his officers and men so that they would be satisfied. I also sent officials to Yunnan to convey my concern for them. I have shown great kindness to Wu San Gui. Recently Cai Yu Rong, the Governor of Sichuan Province and Hunan Province, presented a memorial to me in which he told me that Wu San Gui had rebelled. He has betrayed me and the court officials who have been very kind to him all these years. He has held the rebellion at his own will. He is now on a rampage and the people have been plunged into an abyss of suffering. This is not allowed by law. What he has done has aroused the hatred of the people. Now I have stripped him of all his titles. I have sent the Grand General of Tranquilizing the South and Pacifying the Rebels to command the Imperial Guard Army to suppress the rebellion. When the great army reaches there, the rebellion will soon be put down.

"But what worries me is that the local officials and people who are in the area controlled by the rebels, and who are still devoted to the court, could not help themselves. Some of them have been forced by the rebels to join in the rebellion. When the great army comes, the rebels and those who are forced to join in the rebellion will be destroyed indiscriminately. I am not hard hearted enough to do that. Now I declare, all of you should observe the law and keep away from the rebellion. Don't let the rebels seduce you into joining in the rebellion. As for those who have joined in the rebellion, if they show repentance and surrender, they will not be censured for their past misdeeds. If your fathers, sons or brothers are now officials in Hebei Province or other provinces, you should not worry about them. I have issued an imperial order to ask them to be at ease and work hard to fulfill their tasks. They will not be involved in the case of Wu San Gui's rebellion. So your worries can be removed. Anyone who can catch Wu San Gui and present his head to our army will be granted the titles which had been granted to Wu San Gui. Those who can kill or catch the generals under Wu San Gui, or get them to surrender with all the officers and men under them and the cities, will be granted rewards according to their contributions. I will keep all my promises. All of you are my people. I am sure you are devoted to me and dutiful to your father and mother. You must think very carefully before you make your decision. If you join in the rebellion, you will end up in disaster; if you submit to us, you will be granted handsome rewards. Don't make any wrong decision that will you will regret all your life. The local officials should announce my policies and carry out all of them."

In December Wu San Gui's army took Qinglangwei (now Qingxi, in the east part of Guizhou Province). Cai Yu Rong, the Governor of

Sichuan Province and Hunan Province, sent Commander Cui Shi Lu to defend Yuanzhou (now Zhijiang Dong Nationality Autonomous County, in the west part of Hunan Province). On 15 January 1674 when Wu San Gui's army reached Yuanzhou, Cui Shi Lu surrendered and handed the city over to Wu San Gui's army. Then the rebel army marched forward and took Chenzhou (now Yuanling, Hunan Province).

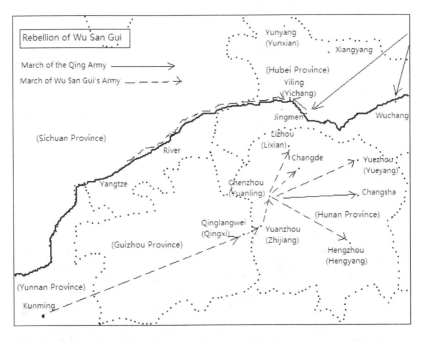

In January 1674 Wu San Gui deployed his generals to take Hunan Province. He sent Yang Bao Yin to take Changde, Xia Guo Xiang to take Lizhou (now Lixian), Zhang Guo Zhu to take Hengzhou (now Hengyang), and Wu Ying Qi to take Yuezhou (now Yueyang). Lu Zhen, the Governor of Changsha, gave up the city and ran away to Yuezhou. Huan Zheng Qing and Chen Wu Heng, two generals under Lu Zhen, surrendered and handed over the city of Changsha to Wu San Gui's army. Yang Lai Jia, the Commander-in-chief of the army stationed in Xiangyan (in the north part of Hubei Province) led the officers and men under him in a rebellion. Hong Fu, the Deputy Commander-in-chief of the army stationed in Yunyang (now Yunxian, in the northwest part of Hubei Province) commanded his soldiers to attack Tong Guo Yao, the Governor of Yunyang. Tong Guo Yao defeated Hong Fu. Hong Fu retreated to a mountain fortress and responded to Wu San Gui's rebellion. Wu San Gui went to Changde (in Hunan Province) from Yunnan Province.

On 22 January 1674 Kuasai, an imperial guard, rode back from Jingzhou (in Hubei Province). He reported to Kangxi that Lu Zhen had given up Changsha and run away. Kangxi ordered General Jueluo Zhuman to march quickly to Wuchang (in Hubei Province). Kangxi said to him, "Wuchang is a strategically important city. It must be defended carefully. If the rebels come, you must defend the city resolutely. If there are many enemy troops, you should not fight them. If enemy troops do not come, you should command your troops to the north of Yuezhou and station your troops by the Yangtze River."

On the same day, Kangxi granted an imperial edict to Le'erjin, the Grand General of Tranquilizing the South Pacifying the Rebels, who was on his way to carry out an expedition against Wu San Gui. He said, "I hear that Lu Zhen has run away to Yuezhou. I have ordered Jueluo Zhuman to take his troops and rush to Wuchang and defend the city. You may command your troops to march to Wuchang before Jueluo Zhuman arrives. When your troops reach Wuchang and find that Wuchang is safe, you may take Jueluo Zhuman's troops under your command."

On 11 February Kangxi wrote to Commander Jueluo Ba'erbu, Commander Yi'erduqi, Commander Esitai and Suodai, the commander of the vanguard army, saying, "Changde is a critical point situated by the lake. It must be defended. Before the great army commanded by Grand General Le'erjin arrives, you should command your troops and Suodai should command the vanguard army to march to Changde and defend it resolutely. Ba'erbu and the other commanders station their troops in Jingzhou. When Grand General Le'erjin arrives, they should also march to Changde and station themselves there. When Ba'erbu reaches Changde, the commanders who have come to Changde beforehand should go to Changsha and station there, and join forces with the troops under Jueluo Zhuman. All of them should put themselves under the command of Grand General Le'erjin. I have made this arrangement in accordance to my understanding of the situation from afar. You are now in the places concerned; if you find that it is difficult to carry out my order, you should make proper adjustment. You will not be accused of going against my order."

Kangxi issued another edict to Commander Jueluo Zhuman, Deputy Commander A'jintai and Kenqitai which read, "Before I ordered you to defend Wuchang and Yuezhou. Now I consider that Changsha is a strategic passage to Wuchang. It leads to Wugang and Baoqing, to the west part of Guangdong Province. If you march to Changsha, you are actually holding a strategic place which can lead to other places by water and by land and can strengthen the defense of Guangdong Province. When Grand General Le'erjin reaches Jingzhou, he should send a commander with troops to help you to defend Changsha. On the day you start your march, inform Ba'erbu and the generals, commanders and officials in Guangxi Province that you have reached Changsha and will defend Hunan Province resolutely.

I am considering the situation from afar and make this arrangement. If it is difficult to carry out my order due to the real situation in your place, you may make proper adjustment. You don't need to stick to my order."

On 13 February Cai Yu Rong, the Governor of Hunan Province and Guangdong Province, presented a memorial to Kangxi. "Wu San Gui sent his general Yang Bao Ying to attack Changde. Yang Bao Ying's father is Yang Yu Ming who was originally the Governor of Guangdong Province. Yang Yu Ming has retired and is now in Changde. He has collaborated from within the city of Changde with his son. Weng Ying Zhao, the Governor of Changde, has surrendered to the rebels. Changde has been taken by the rebels." Kangxi granted Cai Yu Rong an imperial edict which read, "You should send an envoy to go to General Niyahan in Anqing and order him to select capable cavalrymen in his troops, and order the commanders in Jiangning to command 2,000 soldiers to Wuchang and Changsha. You should discuss this matter with Commander Jueluo Zhuman before you send the troops to Wuchang and Changsha. Niyahan will command the main force to go. Deputy Commander Xibu will command the remaining troops still to station in Anqing. Niyahan should take some ships to Wuchang."

On 18 February, Governor Cai Yu Rong sent a memorial to Kangxi. He reported that on 8 February Wu San Gui's troops had reached Lizhou (now Lixian, in the north part of Hunan Province); the officers and men defending Lizhou rebelled and handed over the city of Lizhou to Wu San Gui's troops; Sang'e, the governor, and Zhou Bang Ning, the Commander, came back to the outskirt of Lizhou from Changde (in Hunan Province); but their troops were isolated and weak and could not fight with the enemy, so they had to withdraw to Jingzhou (in Hubei Province).

Two days later, Cai Yu Rong reported that Huang Zheng Qing and Chen Wu Heng, the two generals defending Changsha (the capital of Hunan Province), had rebelled and handed over the city to Wu San Gui's army. Kangxi granted an imperial edict to Grand General Le'erjin, Commander Jueluo Ba'erbu, Commander Yi'erduqi and Commander Esitai which read, "When you led your troops to Jingzhou, Changde and Lizhou were still in the hands of our army. At that time you should have hurried to Changde and Lizhou after a short rest. But you had a long delay and Changde and Lizhou fell into the hands of the enemy in succession. Now Changsha has also fallen. When the troops commanded by Commander Enei reach Jingzhou, you may order Commander Enei defend Jingzhou area. You may order Commander Jueluo Ba'erbu to march to Changde and attack the city. Xiangyang is a vital strategic point for our army. The rebels in Sichuan Province will surely plan to attack it. You may assign some commanders under you to defend Xiangyang." Kangxi granted Grand General Le'erjin another imperial edict which read, "Recently I got the information that the troops in Changde have rebelled and turned to Wu San Gui. The rebels in Kuizhou of Sichuan Province are very strong. Although the troops under Commander Jueluo Ba'erbu also strong, they cannot carry out the expedition against the enemies on two sides. You should send more troops to reinforce Commander Jueluo Ba'erbu's troops. You should select brave cavalrymen and strong horses to Jingzhou to join forces with Jueluo Ba'erbu's troops."

On 25 February Grand General Le'erjin reported, "Changde has fallen into the hands of Wu San Gui's army. The rebels may march to the east part of Hubei Province from Sichuan Province. I am afraid that Xiangyang is in danger. I plan to order Commander Enei and two deputy commanders to command the troops under them to go quickly to Xiangyang and station there. Now I have got Your Majesty's instruction. I will order Commander Enei to go quickly to Xiangyang. I will send scouts to find out the situation in Yunyang. If Yunyang is safe, I will order the two deputy commanders to lead the troops under them to Jingzhou to join forces with Commander Ba'erbu's troops." Kangxi replied, "Yang Lai Jia, the Commander-in-chief of the army in Xiangyang, submitted to us from the sea. He is a mediocre person. The officers and men under him look down upon him. In order to prevent an unforeseen event, you may let the officers and men of the Han Nationality continue to station in Xiangyang. You may tell my intention to Yang Lai Jia secretly. You don't need to guard against him too carefully. Otherwise you will speed up his rebellion."

On 27 February Kangxi wrote to the Ministry of Revenue and the Ministry of Defense, "Wu San Gui is a wicked person. He is as wicked as a poisonous snake. He has repaid my kindness shown to him with enmity. He has rebelled. What he has done has thrown the people into suffering. By the end of the Ming Dynasty Li Zi Cheng commanded the uprising army to take Beijing. Wu San Gui turned to our dynasty at the end of his resources. Considering that he had submitted, my father Emperor Zhang granted him the title of King of Pingxi and entrusted him with important tasks. When our army had taken Guizhou Province and Yunnan Province, and the border areas were pacified, he was ordered to garrison the border areas. He was given the power to handle all the affairs in the border areas. Since I succeeded to the throne, I have trusted him all the more. I granted him the power to select officials to the positions of the two provinces. I have provided food and military supplies to the officers and men under him. I hope that he would repay my kindness shown to him with gratitude. I granted him the title of Prince. I put him on the top position. Last year he presented a memorial to me asking my permission to let him go back to his home place. Considering that he had been in the border areas for a long time and he is already old and weak, I granted him my permission to let him move back to his home place so that he could reunite with his sons and grandsons. I ordered the departments concerned to prepare land and houses for Wu San

Gui and all the officers and men under him and provide food for them on their way home. I have done all I could. But he harbored evil intentions and planned a rebellion. He gave a date for his movement. But suddenly he commanded his troops to hold a rebellion. He has thrown the people in great sufferings. He occupied cities. He issued official communiqués. He did his best to expand his influence. Now many people in the nearby prefectures and counties who do not know his true intention were instigated to join in his rebellion. He spread rumors to agitate ignorant people against the government.

All his schemes are against the law and heavenly principles. I have sent great armies to suppress his rebellion. I have told the generals that I pay great attention to the ordinary people, and I have instructed them that they should not cause the slightest trouble to the people. My purpose is to save the people from suffering and tranquilize the areas. Now Grand General Le'erjin and other generals have commanded their troops to carry out an expedition against Wu San Gui's rebellion. The rebellion will soon be suppressed. The rebels will be punished. Wu San Gui is a treacherous man. He is not devoted to his monarch and he is not dutiful. At present he is the head of the rebellion, and he will leave a name that will stink to eternity. When he is captured, his head will be cut down and kept in a cage to show to all the people so as to give vent to the pent-up anger of the people. I am afraid that the people do not know the reason why I should carry out an expedition against Wu San Gui's rebellion and will feel surprised and bewildered. They cannot see through Wu San Gui's true intention and believe in Wu San Gui. If they make a wrong decision, they will fall into a trap. A wrong decision made by a person will bring disaster to him. A right decision made by a person will bring good fortune to him. This decision is of vital importance. I am not hardhearted enough to see my people to go against the laws and be punished. The Ministry of Revenue and the Ministry of Defense should send letters to the governors of Hebei Province and the other provinces to instruct them to put up official notices in all the prefectures and counties under their jurisdictions to tell the people to live and work in peace and not to believe rumors. They should convey my concern to the people."

Jin Guang Zu, the Governor of Guangdong and Guangxi Provinces, reported to Kangxi that Sun Yan Ling, the general in Guangxi Province, had rebelled. He had killed Commander Wang Yong Nian and Deputy Commander Meng Yi Mao, and he had arrested Ma Xiong Zhen, the Governor of Guangxi Province, and put him in jail.

On 4 March 1674 Wu San Gui sent Liu Zhi Fu, Wang Hui and Tao Ji Zhi to command 10,000 naval troops on 700 ships to sail along the Yangtze River from Sichuan Province to attack Yiling (now Yiling District, Yichang, in the west part of Hubei Province). When they reached Yiling, they established five camps on each bank of the river. At that time, Grand General Le'erjin stationed his army in Jingzhou (in Hubei Province). He sent Commander Esitai to command troops of the Manchu Nationality and Han Nationality to fight with Wu San Gui's troops on land and on the river and defeated them. The enemy troops ran away.

Two days later Kangxi appointed Huashan as the General of Tranquilizing the South to command an army to garrison Jingkou (now Jingkou District, Zhenjiang, Jiangsu Province) situated on the southern bank of the Yangtze River. Deputy Commanders Ma Si Wen and Yang Feng Xiang, and Sahai, a Scholar, would go there with him. Before they left for Jingkou, Kangxi said to them, "I consider that Jingkou is a place of vital importance. This is the reason why I am sending you to garrison there. If there are rebellions in the places near Jingkou, you should command troops to suppress the rebellions in these places. You should discipline the officers and men under you when your troops are on the march or they station in a place. They must not bring trouble to the people. As far as I know, some troops brought trouble to the people when they were marching through places before. It should be taken as a warning for you. Otherwise you will be punished if you commit such mistakes."

Then Kangxi wrote to Grand General Le'erjin to say, "I have read the memorials presented by Commander Jueluo Ba'erbu, Commander Yi'erduqi, Esitai and Commander Suodai. They all told me that they would march forward to recover the area of Yunnan Province and Guizhou Province in August this year. I think that it is not yet time to recover these two provinces. We should recover these two provinces only after Sichuan Province has been pacified. Now what is more important is Hunan Province. This province borders with the west part of Guangdong Province in the south; it connects the lower reach of the Yangtze River in the east. Recently the deputy commander of the army stationed in Changsha surrendered to the rebels. The rebels have got all the soldiers and ships in Changsha. Now what we should do is to take Changde when chance comes so as to cut the enemy's communication lines to the rear, so that the rebels cannot reinforce each other. General Niyahan and Commander Jueluo Zhuman should command the troops under them to press to Changsha. The rebels in Changsha will have to surrender or give up the city of Changsha and run away. Then the rebels will be disheartened and the people may come back to till their land. This will provide great help to the troops which are ready to march to Guizhou Province and Yunnan Province.

"If we do not carry out this plan, the force of the rebels will grow rapidly and the people will not be able to go back to till their land. If we do not pacify Hunan Province first, when our troops go deep into the areas controlled by the rebels, it will be very difficult for us to transport food and military supplies to our troops. This is my suggestion for the actions of our army. The troops are more than 500 kilometers away from me. I cannot issue instructions to every movement of the troops. Now the common aspiration of the people is unstable. Now we cannot get much information about Guangxi

Province. If there are rebellions in Jiangxi Province, we will have to send troops to suppress the rebellions there. Then we have to transport a lot of food and military supplies to the troops. And I am afraid that the common aspiration of the people will waver again.

"Before you left the capital with the great army, you told me that you would march to Guizhou Province and Yunnan Province not later than August this year. But now the commanders defending Changsha, Lizhou and Changde have turned over to Wu San Gui although Wu San Gui has not yet come. It seems that these places will be recovered in August. If rebellions break out in other places, will you dispatch troops to suppress the rebellions? If you do so, your main force will be weakened. If you suppress them one by one, your troops will be very tired. The only thing you should do now is to take Changde and Changsha first so as to terrify the rebels. This is the way to win victory. Before you take any action, you should listen to the opinions of the generals under you." Kangxi granted another imperial edict to Grand General Le'erjin which read, "I have got the information that Wu San Gui is now in Changde. The troops under you should march to Changde and Lizhou after a short rest. Wu San Gui may take a chance to attack Yuezhou and Wuchang. Before your troops march to Changde and Lizhou, you should secretly order General Niyahan and Commander Jueluo Zhuman that they should act cooperatively with each other so as to ensure safety. Jingzhou and Wuchang are both important places. You should pay more attention to the protection of Wuchang. You should take action in accordance with the situation."

Geng Jing Zhong, the King of Jingnan, led a rebellion in Fujian Province on 16 March. He arrested Fan Cheng Mo, the Governor of the Province, and put him in jail. Liu Bing Zheng, the Inspector of Fujian, surrendered. Geng Jing Zhong declared himself to be Grand General of All the Armies. He appointed Zeng Yang Xing, Bai Xian Zhong and Jiang Yuan Xun as generals. Very soon they took Yanping (now Yanping District, Nanping, Fujian Province), Shaowu (in the northwest part of Fujian Province), Funing (now Xiapu, in the northeast part of Fujian Province), Jianning (in the west part of Fujian Province) and Tingzhou (now Changting, in the southwest part of Fujian Province). Geng Jing Zhong made an agreement with Wu San Gui that both of them should send troops to attack Jiangxi Province. He instigated Liu Jin Zhong, the Commander-in-chief of the army in Chaozhou (in the east part of Guangdong Province), to cause chaos in Guangdong Province. He sent an envoy to Taiwan to ask Zheng Jin to send troops to take the prefectures and counties along the coast of the sea so as to support his rebellion. When Li Zhi Fang, the Govenor of Zhejiang Province, got the information that Geng Jing Zhong had rebelled in Fujian Province, he sent troops to station in Quzhou (in the southwest part of Zhejiang Province). He sent General Wang Ting Mei and other generals to command their troops to get ready to resist the attack by Geng Jing Zhong's troops.

Kangxi sent General Laita to command troops to Zhejiang Province, and sent General Xi'ergen to command troops to Jiangxi Province to resist the attacks by Geng Jing Zhong's troops. Geng Jing Zhong sent Zeng Yang Xing, Lin Chong, Xu Shang Chao and Feng Gong Fu to command more than 10,000 men to go pass Xianxiaguan Pass (situated in Bao'an, in Zhejiang Province) and took Jiangshan and Pingyang (both in Zhejiang Province). Then Geng Jing Zhong's troops attacked Wenzhou (also in Zhejiang). Zu Hong Xun, the commander of the army defending Wenzhou surrendered and presented the city of Wenzhou to Geng Jing Zhong's army. Geng Jing Zhong made Zu Hong Xun general. Geng Jing Zhong's army grew into an army of more than 100,000 men. Then Geng Jing Zhong's troops took Yueqing (in the southeast part of Zhejiang Province), Tiantai, Xianju and Chengxian. Bandits rose in Ninghai, Xiangshan, Xinchang and Yuyao. Zeng Yang Xing commanded the rebel troops to threaten Shaoxing and Ningpo, and then they took Huangyan. Geng Jing Zhong sent a detachment to attack Jinhua. Geng Jing Zhong and his generals Zhou Lie, Wang Fei Shi and Shang Ming commanded their troops to march into Jiangxi Province and took Guangxin (now Shangrao), Jianchang and Raozhou (now Poyang) . Geng Jing Zhong's troops also took Kaihua (in Zhejiang Province), Shouchang (in the west part of Zhejiang Province), and Chun'an (in the west part of Zhejiang Province). A detachment of Geng Jing Zhong's army took Huizhou (now Huixian, in the southeast part of Anhui Province), Wuyuan (in the northeast part of Jiangxi Province) and Qimen (in the south part of Anhui Province).

On 19 March Hong Fu, the Deputy Commander of the troops stationed in Xunyang (now Xunxian, in the west part of Hubei Province), rebelled. Tong Guo Yao, the Governor of Xunyang, defeated him. On 28 March Yang Lai Jia, the Commander-in-chief of the army in Xiangyang (in Hubei province), held a rebellion in Gucheng (in Hubei Province).

On 2 April 1674 General Niyahan presented a memorial to Kangxi. "Zhe'erken, the Deputy Minister of Rites, and Fu Da Li, the Scholar of Hanlin Academy, who were appointed by Your Majesty as envoys to go to Yunnan to handle the matter of Wu San Gui's migration, have come back to Wuchang. They have brought a memorial written by Wu San Gui." Kangxi Emperor replied, "I think, Wu San Gui is very crafty. I suspect that he is now playing a trick. If Wu San Gui pleads guilty and begs to surrender, you and the other generals may accept his surrender. But you have to be very careful and on guard against his tricks. If Wu San Gui truly surrenders, you may accept his surrender with due politeness. You should take strict precautions against any actions taken by the generals and officers under Wu San Gui. You should not divert your forces. It is not necessary for you to march forward now. You must consider the situation before you take any action."

Places Taken by Geng Jing Zhong

Some time before, Shang Ke Xi, King of Pingnan, had writtend to Emperor Kangxi, "Now Geng Jing Zhong has held a rebellion in Fujian Province. I am closely related with Geng Jing Zhong because my son Shang Zhi Xin's wife is Geng Jing Zhong's younger sister. Now that Geng Jing Zhong has held a rebellion, people will suspect that I have been involved in it. I have been granted the title of King of Pingnan. I am now over 70 years old. Although I am not wise, I will never submit to the rebels so as to pursue wealth and rank. I will do my best to defend Guangdong Province even at the sacrifice of my life so as to show my devotion to Your Majesty." On 10 April Kangxi gave him a reply which read, "You have performed heroically for the state. I know very well that you are a devoted person. Recently you have adopted measures to consolidate the defense of the border areas. This is your great contribution. I have read your memorial. Although you are old, you are still concerned about the situation of the whole country. I highly praise your devotion. Now you should do your best to prepare for the attack by the enemy and for the suppression of the rebellions. I rely heavily on your service. I hope you will not let me down." Then Kangxi issued an imperial edict to the Ministry of Defense which read, "Shang Ke Xi, King of Pingnan, has presented me a memorial asking me to send more troops to defend the border areas. He has been very devoted and should be highly praised. All the military arrangements and the defense of the local places in Guangdong Province and Guangxi Province will be handled by Shang Ke Xi and Governor Jin Guang Zu. I hope they will cooperate closely to fulfill their task."

On 11 April Shang Ke Xi, King of Pingnan, wrote to Kangxi to recommend his second son Commander Shang Zhi Xiao. He said, "This son can restrain himself and be cautious. He is kind to his subordinates. He can succeed to my titles. As for the military affairs, although I am old, I still have the ability to command the troops. I will not make any mistakes in defending the border areas." Kangxi wrote back, saying, "Now I give my permission to let Shang Zhi Xiao succeed to the title of King of Pingnan."

On 13 April Kangxi issued an imperial edict to the Ministry of Defense and the Ministry of Justice which read, "Wu San Gui first turned to the side of Li Zi Cheng by the end of the Ming Dynasty. But later his father was killed by Li Zi Cheng and he turned to our side. My father Emperor Zhang considered that he had surrendered and had established some contributions. So he made Wu San Gui King of Pingxi. He let him command a great army and entrusted him with great military power. My father showed him special kindness. When I succeeded to the throne, I granted him the title of Prince and took him as a trusted follower. I granted him with much more kindness. I expected that he would be grateful and devoted to me and do his best to repay my kindness. But unexpectedly Wu San Gui engaged in a rebellion. He first asked my permission to move from the border areas to his home place. But very soon he carried out his rebellion. He has thrown the people into suffering. He is extremely vicious. What he has done has aroused indignation from the people. I have sent great armies to suppress his rebellion. His rebellion will be finally suppressed. The kings and the officials suggested that Wu San Gui's son and grandsons should all be executed so as to uphold the state law. They presented this suggestion several times. But I hoped that he would reform and surrender. So I was not hardhearted enough to kill his son and grandsons. Recently I read the memorial presented by Wu San Gui. He used impolite words and raised unreasonable requirements in the memorial. The kings and the officials all think that Wu San Gui has committed a serious crime and will not reform. His son and grandsons should all be executed. They should not be spared. I think Wu San Gui has held a rebellion and has committed a serious crime. He should be punished in accordance with the law. The kings and the officials have suggested that his son and grandsons should all be executed as a punishment to Wu San Gui for his crimes. I cannot turn down their suggestion and spare the lives of his son and grandsons. I should agree with the suggestion presented by the kings and the officials to put Wu Ying Xiong, his son Wu Shi Lin and other sons to death by dismembering their bodies. But considering that Wu Ying Xiong has attended upon me for a long time, I am not hardhearted enough to put them all to death. Now I have decided to put Wu Ying Xiong and his son Wu Shi Lin to death by hanging. Wu Ying Xion's other young sons will be spared and just put in jail. Other criminals who deserve death penalty will be executed. All the persons involved who have not committed serious crimes can be pardoned and released so as to show our leniency. You should publicly notify this to all the people so that they will understand my intention." On that day Wu Ying Xiong and his son Wu Shi Lin were executed.

When Wu San Gui rebelled in Yunnan in December 1673, Kangxi was a young man of twenty years old. Wu San Gui thought that Kangxi was a greenhorn and would be easy to deal with. But very soon he found that Kangxi dispatched his armies to put down the rebellion successfully. Wu San Gui began to feel that his rebellion was not justifiable and he regretted that he had done it. When he reached Lizhou (now Lixian, in the north part of Hunan Province), he hesitated. When the news reached him that his son Wu Ying Xion and his grandson had been executed, he was having his meal. He stood up and exclaimed, "The young emperor is so capable! I am doomed to fail."

When Geng Jing Zhong rebelled in Fujian Province, Kangxi issued an imperial edict to Echu, the general of the troops stationed in Jiangning (in the south part of Jiangsu Province), and Axixi, the Governor of Jiangning, which read, "Zhejiang Province is in danger and needs to be defended. If the general defending Zhejiang Province asks you to send troops, you may send a commander with 1,000 cavalrymen by land and by the river to reinforce the troops there. If your troops are going to Zhejiang Province, you may transfer the troops in Anqing of Anhui Province to defend Jiangning." At the same time Kangxi ordered Tula, the general of the troops stationed in Hangzhou (the capital city of Zhejiang Province), Li Zhi Fang, the Governor of Hangzhou, and Commander Saibaili to "Take some troops of Manchu and Han Nationality to get ready to resist attacks by the rebels. I have instructed the troops stationed in Jiangning to get ready to reinforce Hangzhou. If you need Manchu troops, you may transfer the troops from Jiangning to Hangzhou."

Very soon Fujian Province fell into the hands of the rebels. Kangxi ordered Deputy Commander Hutu and Deputy Commander Mahada wwith the troops in Jiangning to march quickly to Hangzhou. When they reached Hangzhou, they should cooperate with General Tula to defend Hangzhou. Kangxi also ordered General Huashan to choose 500 soldiers under him to hurry to Hangzhou to put them under the commander of General Tula. Kangxi ordered the troops stationed in Anqing (now Anqing, Anhui Province) to go to Jiangning. When they reached Jiangning, General Huashan ordered them to go to Jingkou (now Jingkou District, Zhenjiang, Jiangsu Province) quickly.

Kangxi told the Minister of Defense, "Sun Yan Ling was originally the son of a low-ranking officer under Kong You De, King of Dingnan. He was not a capable man and has not established outstanding contributions. Kong You De led the troops of the Ming Dynasty under him to submit to our dynasty from the sea. He commanded his troops to fight very bravely and at last laid down his life in the battle field. My father Emperor Zhang highly praised his loyalty. He would not disband the officers and soldiers under him. He gathered together all the officers and soldiers and appointed a commander originally under him to command these officers and soldiers. He showed great concern to them. Sun Yan Ling married Kong You De's daughter. So Emperor Zhang promoted him to the rank of a general and let him command all the officers and men originally under Kong You De to garrison Guangxi Province. He should be scrupulous in this position and exert his best to fulfill his task so as to repay the kindness of Emperor Zhang shown on him. But since he took the position of commander-in-chief of the army in Guangxi, he has made many mistakes. The officials of the Ministry of Justice suggested that he should be punished. By I pardoned him because his father-in-law had performed great deeds and still let him command his troops as before. Recently I granted him the seal of General of Pacifying the Southerners. I have shown him great grace. But Sun Yan Ling harbored evil intention. He has been devoid of gratitude. He colluded with Wu San Gui and held a rebellion. He has caused trouble in the local area. He deserves death penalty. Now I have deprived him of the title of general. I will send great armies to Guangxi Province to suppress his rebellion. He will end up in failure and be punished by law. As for the officers and men under him, they were originally under Kong You De, King of Dingnan. They were granted favors and rewards by the emperors of our dynasty. They have been loyal and righteous. They will not join in his rebellion willingly. They are not willing to follow him at the sacrifice of their past contributions. If anyone in Guangxi can catch Sun Yan Ling and kill him, he will be granted handsome rewards and enjoy high rank. Those who will surrender with all the subordinates or cities will be granted rewards in accordance with their contributions. Anyone who will come to surrender will be exempted from punishment and be recruited in our army. As for the fathers and brothers of the officers and men under Sun Yan Ling who are in the capital, in Hebei Province and other provinces, they will not be involved in the case of Sun Yuan Ling's rebellion. They should not have any doubts about our policies. Otherwise they will act against the law. My purpose is to save them from destruction. Your ministry should let all the people know about this as soon as possible."

Shang Ke Xi, King of Pingnan, sent a memorial to Kangxi to report to him that Wu San Gui had sent an envoy to bring a letter to him asking him to join in his rebellion; he had arrested the envoy and had sent a group of soldiers to escort the envoy with the letter to the capital. Kangxi highly praised Shang Ke Xi for his loyalty.

Shang Ke Xi reported to Kangxi that Wu San Gui had sent 20,000 troops to station in Huangshahe (now Huangshahe Town, Quanzhou, in the northeast part of Guangxi Zhuang Autonomous Region); if they joined forces with Sun Yan Ling's troops, the enemy forces would become very powerful. He asked Kangxi to send troops from nearby provinces to Guangdong Province to join forces with his troops to suppress Sun Yan Ling's rebellion. On 24 April Kangxi appointed Commander Gente as General of Pingkou (Pingkou means "Pacifying the Rebels") and ordered him to command troops to Guangxi Province to suppress Sun Yan Ling's rebellion. He should cooperate with Shang Ke Xi to take military actions against Sun Yan Ling.

On 27 April Emperor Kangxi issued an imperial edict to the Ministry of Defense which read, "Geng Jing Zhong is a person of mediocre ability. He does not have much knowledge. He could hold the position of the Military Governor of Fujian Province only because his grandfather Geng Zhong Ming, a general of the Ming Dynasty, came to submit to our dynasty from the sea with his troops. My grandfather Emperor Taizong granted him the title of King of Huaishun as an award for his submission. When my father Emperor Zhang had taken Beijing, he ordered Geng Zhong Ming to command his troops to take Guangdong Province. But he died on the way. His son Geng Ji Mao succeeded his title. He first garrisoned in Guangdong Province and then was transferred to garrison Fujian Province. He did his best in his job. I granted him great favor. When he died of illness, I sent special envoys to attend to his funeral. I let Geng Jing Zhong succeed his father's title of King of Jingnan. His grandfather, father and he enjoyed the favor granted by my grandfather, father and me for more than 40 years. He now enjoys high rank and wealth only because his grandfather and father had made great contributions. He should have been grateful and do his best to repay my kindness shown on him. But he harbored evil intentions and planned a rebellion secretly. He held a rebellion after Wu San Gui had rebelled. He agitated the local people by demagogy. He has committed a serious crime. He will be punished by law. Now I have decided to deprive his title of King of Jingnan. I will send great armies to suppress his rebellion. I understand that his officers and men and the local officials and people are forced to take part in the rebellion by Geng Jing Zhong. Although they are still loyal to the court, they cannot show that they are innocent. When my great troops arrive, all of them will be destroyed indiscriminately. Anyone who can catch and kill Geng Jing Zhong and present his head to our troops will be granted high rank and wealth. As for those who will surrender with his subordinates or with the cities will be granted handsome rewords in accordance to their contributions. Anyone who will come to surrender will be exempted from punishment and be recruited in our army. Those officials or officers in Hebei Province and other provinces who were once under Geng Jing Zhong will not be involved in the case of Geng Jing Zhong's rebellion. The officials and officers whose fathers or sons or brothers are now in Fujian Province will not be involved in the case of Geng Jing Zhong's rebellion. They should not have any doubts about our policies. Otherwise they will act against the law. My purpose is to save them from destruction. Your ministry should let all the people know about this as soon as possible."

On 29 April Shang Ke Xi, King of Pingnan, presented a memorial to Kangxi asking him to send troops to suppress the rebellions and suggested that naval troops should be send along the Yangtze River to withstand the attack by the rebels. Kangxi ordered the Ministry of Defense to tell Shang Ke Xi the deployments which had been made to deal with the rebels: Grand General Le'erjin and the other kings would command the main forces to go to pacify Yunnan Province and Guizhou Province through Changde (in Hunan Province) and Lizhou (now Lixian, Hunan Province); Ya'erhan, the General of Tranquilizing the South, Commander Jueluo Zhuman and Commander Ba'erbu would command the troops under them to go from Wuchang (now Wuchang, Hubei Province) to take Yuezhou (now Yueyang, Hunan Province) and Changsha (the capital city of Hunan Province) on land and by the Yangtze River, then they would march to Guangxi Province; Commander Yilibu would station his troops in Yiling (now Yiling District, Yingchang, Hubei Province); Commander Fandali and Deputy Commander Deyeli stationed the troops under them in Yunyang (now Yunxian, Hubei Province); Heye, General of Anxi, Deputy Commander Hulibu, and Wa'erka, General of Xi'an, would command the troops under them to take Sichuan Province from Hanzhong (in the southwest part of Shaanxi Province); Deputy Commander Kuang'erkun and Wu Guo Zhen had stationed their troops in Hanzhong; Xibuchen, General of Zhenxi, commanded his troops to station in Xi'an (now Xi'an, Shaanxi Province); Minister

Mo Luo had been sent to govern Shaanxi Province; Lahada, General of Zhendong, would command his troops to station in Yanzhou (in Shandong Province), and other places of strategic importance in Henan Province and in the south of the Yangtze River; Hashan, General of Annan, and Wang Zhi Ding, General of Zhenhai, would command the troops under them to station in Jingkou (now Jingkou District, Zhenjiang, Jiangsu Province); Amida, General of Yangwei, and Echu, General of Jiangning, commanded their toops to station in Jiangning, Anqing and other places of strategic importance along the Yangtze River; Laita, General of Pingnan, would command his troops to pacify Fujian Province from Zhejiang Province; Gente, General of Pingkou, and Xibu would command the troops under them to go to Guangdong Province to cooperate with Shang Ke Xi to suppress the rebellions.

Kangxi urged Shangshan to attack Yuezhou (now Yueyang, Hunan Province). Wu San Gui sent Wu Ying Lin, Liao Jin Zhong, Ma Bao, Zhang Guo Zhu, Ke Ze and Gao Qi Long to command their troops to resist the attack. He also sent some troops to march into Jiangxi Province. They reached Nankang (in the southwest part of Jiangxi Province), then they marched northward and took Duchang (in the north part of Jiangxi Province). Wu San Gui sent troops to march from Changsha (in Hunan Province) to Yuanzhou (now Yuanzhou District, Yichun, in the west part of Jiangxi Province). They took Pingxiang (in the west part of Jiangxi Province), Anfu (in the west part of Jiangxi Province), Shanggao (in the northwest part of Jiangxi Province) and Xinchang (in the northwest part of Jiangxi Province). Kangxi made Prince Yuele Grand General of Dingyuan Pingkou (Dingyuan means "pacifying the faraway places", Pingkou means "suppressing the rebels") and ordered him to command his troops to march into Jiangxi Province to resist the attacks by Wu San Gui's troops. Kangxi made Prince Labu Grand General of Yangwei (Yangwei means "showing great military strength") and ordered him to command his troops to guard the south part of the Yangtze River. At that time Wang Fu Chen was already the commander-in-chief of the army in Shaanxi Province and Gansu Province. He responded to Wu San Gui and held a rebellion in Ningqian (in the southwest part of Shaanxi Province). Moluo, the Governor of Shaanxi Province, tried to suppress the rebellion, but was killed in battle. Wu San Gui sent his general Wang Ping Fan to march into Sichuan Province. Wang Ping Fan joined forces with Wu Zhi Mao, the original commander-in-chief of the army in Sichuan Province, who had held a rebellion. Kangxi again urged Shangshan to attack Yuezhou. But Shangshan asked Kangxi to send him more troops and did not take any action to attack Yuezhou.

Battles in Jiangxi, Hunan and Hubei

In January 1675 Emperor Kangxi ordered Yuele, Grand General of Dingyuan Pingkou, to take Changsha (in Hunan Province) from Yuanzhou (now Yichun, in the west part of Jiangxi Province). Yuele marched his great army to Nanchang (now Nanchang, the capital city of Jiangxi Province). He sent troops to attack Shanggao (in the northwest part of Jiangxi Province), Xinchang (in the northwest part of Jiangxi Province), Dongxiang (in Jiangxi Province), Wannian (in Jiangxi Province), Anren (in the west part of Hunan Province) and Xincheng (in the southwest part of Jiangxi Province). His troops took all these places. Then he commanded his troops to recover Guangxin (now Shangrao, Jiangxi Province) and Raozhou (now Boyang, Jiangxi Province). Yuele's troops attacked Pingxiang (in the west part of Jiangxi Province). Wu San Gui's general Xia Guo Xiang defended Pingxiang resolutely. Yuele's troops could not take it. Kangxi ordered Yuele to command his troops to march to Hunan Province. He ordered Prince Labu to garrison Nanchang (now Nanchang, the capital city of Jiangxi Province). Wu San Gui sent a general to lead 70,000 men to defend Liling (now Liling, in the east part of Hunan Province). They built wooden fortresses to defend the city of Liling.

Wu San Gui ordered the troops in Yuezhou (now Yueyang, Hunan Province) to dig three deep ditches around the city of Yuezhou and made many traps with bamboo trees. He ordered troops to plant big woods in the narrow entrance of Dongting Lake (in the north part of Hunan Province) to prevent the enemy naval army from entering Dongting Lake from the Yangtze River. He ordered land troops to build many fortresses with barricades of felled trees before them to prevent the enemy cavalrymen from getting close to the fortresses. Wu San Gui went to Songzi (in the south part of Hubei Province) from Changde (in the north part of Hunan Province). He ordered his naval troops to sail along Hudu River (in the south part of Hubei Province) to Hudukou (now in Taipingkou, in the south part of Hubei province) where Hudu River joined the Yangtze River so as to stop the communication between the troops under Grand General Le'erjin and the troops under Shangshan. Wu San Gui declared that his troops would cross the Yangtze River to attack Jingzhou (in the south part of Hubei Province) and break the dike of the Yangtze River to lead water of the river to immerse the city of Jingzhou. He sent some of his troops in Yuezhou to march to Jingshan Mountain (situated in the west part of Hubei Province). He ordered his generals Wang Hui, Yang Lai Jia and Hong Fu to command their troops to attack Gucheng (in the west part of Hubei Province) and they took it. Ma Hu Bei, the commander of the army defending Gucheng, was captured. Then they attacked Yunyang (now Yunxian, in the northwest part of Hubei Province), Junzhou (now Danjiangkou, in the northwest part of Hubei Province), and Nanzhang (in Hubei Province). Grand General Le'erjin sent King Chani to defend Yiling (now Yiling District, Yichang, Hubei Province). King Chani should cooperate with Commander Yilibu to prepare to resist the attack by Wu San Gui's troops. Grand General Le'erjin asked Kangxi to send more troops to reinforce him. But Kangxi reproached him for his delay in taking actions and refused to send more troops to him.

In spring 1676 Wu San Gui sent troops to attack Guangdong Province. He made Shang Zhi Xin, Shang Ke Xi's son, Grand General. At that time Shang Ke Xi was seriously ill. So Shang Zhi Xin surrendered to Wu San Gui. Shang Zhi Xin sent soldiers to guard Shang Ke Xi's residence and not to let anyone go into the residence to report anything to Shang Ke Xi. He took away the military power from Shang Zhi Xiao and let him attend to Shang Ke Xi. Shang Ke Xi was so worried and so angery that he died. In December 1676 Shang Zhi Xin regretted that he had surrendered to Wu San Gui, then he sent an envoy to see Labu in Jiangxi Province to convey his intention to surrender and do good deeds to atone for his crimes. Kangxi accepted his surrender and granted him a letter to comfort him.

In the same year Sun Yan Ling also regretted that he had held a rebellion and intended to surrender. But Wu San Gui's general Wu

Shi Zong occupied Guilin (in the northeast part of Guangxi Zhuang Autonomous Region) and killed Sun Yan Ling.

Wu San Gui sent his generals Han Da Ren and Gao Da Jie to command over 30,000 men to attack Ji'an (in the west part of Jiangxi Province) and they took it. Kangxi ordered Prince Labu to defend Raozhou (now Boyang, Jiangxi Province). Yuele commanded his troops to attack Pingxiang (in the west part of Jiangxi Province) fiercely. His troops destroyed 12 enemy fortresses and killed more than 10,000 enemy soldiers. Xia Xiang Guo, Wu San Gui's general defending Pingxiang, ran away with his troops. So Yuele took Pingxiang. Yuele commanded his troops to attack Liling (in the east part of Hunan Province) and Liuyang (in the northeast part of Hunan Province). They took them all. Then Yuele commanded his troops to attack Changsha (the capital city of Hunan Province). Wu San Gui sent Hu Guo Zhu to defend Changsha. Ma Bao and Gao Qi Long, two generals under Wu San Gui, commanded their troops from Yuezhou (now Yueyang, Hunan Province) to join in the defense of Changsha. Wu San Gui commanded the main force to march from Songzi (in the south part of Hubei Province) to Yuelu Mountain (situated in the west part of Changsha City on the west bank of Xiang River) and was ready to reinforce Changsha. He ordered Han Da Ren and Gao Da Jie to attack Xingan (in Jiangxi Province) from Ji'an. After they took Xingan, they marched to Taihe. Then they again took Pingxiang and Liling so as to cut off the retreat of Yuele's troops.

Kangxi strictly urged Labu to reinforce Yuele. Labu commanded his troops to march from Raozhou (now Boyang, Jiangxi Province) to Yugan and Jinxi. Then they attacked Ji'an. Gao Da Jie led 4,000 men to resist the attack by Labu's army. The two hostile armies fought in Dayuesi (in Ji'an). Gao Da Jie sent 100 cavalrymen to attack the battle formation of Labu's army and destroyed the battle formation. Labu stationed his troops in Luozishan Mountain (situated in the northeast of Ji'an). Gao Da Jie sent some troops to attack the camps of Labu's army. Labu and Xi'ergen, the deputy commander of the army, gave up the camps and ran away. Labu's troops were seriously defeated.

It happened that Han Da Ren did not get along with Gao Da Jie. Gao Da Jie was so unhappy that he died. Then Labu again sent troops to lay siege to Ji'an. Han Da Ren did not dare to go out to fight.

Seeing that Wu San Gui had left Songzi, Grand General Le'erjin led his army to cross the Yangtze River from Jingzhou and took Shishou (in the south part of Hubei Province). He sent King Chani to attack the fortresses of Wu San Gui's army in Taipingjie (a place in Lixian, Hunan Province) but King Chani's troops were defeated and they retreated back to Jingzhou. Kangxi ordered General Muzhan to command the troops in Shaanxi Province to go to Jingzhou.

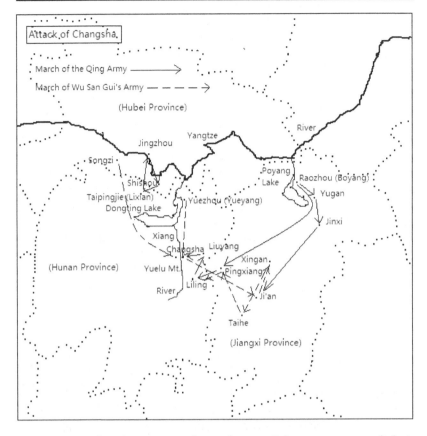

Kangxi ordered Prince Jieshu and King Fulata to command their troops to go to Zhejiang Province. They fought with Geng Jing Zhong's rebel troops and recovered many prefectures and counties in Zhejiang Province. In spring 1676 King Fulata led his troops to attack Wenzhou (in the southeast part of Zhejiang Province) from Huangyan (in the southeast part of Zhejiang Province). They fought fiercely and took many enemy fortresses. Zeng Yang Xing, a general under Geng Jing Zhong defended the city resolutely. Fulata's troops attacked the city for a month but could not take it. Kangxi urged Jieshu to lead his troops to march from Jinhua to Quzhou (in Zhejiang Province) then march into Fujian Province. In August the troops under Jieshu and Laita marched past Quzhou and took Jiangshan (in the southwest part of Zhejiang Province). Jieshu sent an envoy to Xianxiaguan Pass (situated to the south of Jiangshan, Zhejiang Province) to demand Jin Ying Hu, the commander defending the pass, to surrender. Jin Ying Hu handed over the pass to Jieshu. Then Jieshu commanded his troops to go through the pass and entered into Fujian Province. They took Pucheng (in the northwest part of Fujian Province). Zheng Jin, who had come to Fujian Province from Taiwan, reached Xinghua Bay and was about to attack Fuzhou (now Fuzhou, the capital city of Fujian Province). Geng Jing Zhong was at the end of his resources. He planned to surrender. Jieshu commanded his troops to march to Jianyang. Jieshu sent a letter to Geng Jing Zhong demanding him to surrender. Geng Jing Zhong gave Jieshu a reply letter asking him to beg Kangxi to pardon him. Jieshu's army marched to Yanping (now Yanping District, Nanping, Fujian Province). Jieshu sent an envoy to Fuzhou to read out Kangxi's order to pardon him. Then Geng Jing Zhong surrendered. He asked Kangxi's permission to lead his army to attack Zheng Jin's army so as to atone for his crime. Kangxi gave his permission and allowed him to resume his title of King of Jingnan. Geng Jing Zhong led his army to meet Zheng Jin's army. They defeated Zheng Jin and he ran back to Taiwan.

In 1677 Shangshan sent solders to take 3,000 horses to Yuele's army, but all the horses were robbed by Wu San Gui's troops on the way. Wu San Gui sent troops to reinforce his army in Ji'an. Wu San Gui's army and the army commanded by Labu were locked in a stalemate in Ji'an. General Muzhan marched his army from Yuezhou (now Yueyang, Hunan Province) to joined forces with the army commanded by Yuele to attack Changsha. They successfully took Changsha. The troops sent by Wu San Gui to reinforce Ji'an all retreated. Han Da Ren gave up the city of Ji'an and ran away. Then Ji'an was taken. Wu San Gui left Yuelu Mountain and went to Hengzhou (now Heyang, Hunan Province). He sent troops to attack Nan'an (now Ganzhou, Jiangxi Province) and Shaozhou (now Shaoguan, in the north part of Guangdong Province). In 1678 Yuele's troops recovered Pingjiang (in Hunan Province) and Xiangyin (in Hunan Province). Lin Xing Zhu, Wu San Gui's general defending Xiangyin, led his naval troops to surrender. Muzhan commanded his troops to attack Yongxing (in the south part of Hunan Province) and they took it. Then they took 12 cities in the southeast part of Hunan Province including Chaling, Youxian, Lingxian, Anren, Xingning, Chenzhou, Yizhang, Linwu, Lanshan, Jiahe, Guiyang and Guidong. Labu commanded his troops to pursue Han Da Ren who had given up Ji'an and they caught up with him in Ningdu (in Jiangxi Province).

After a battle, Han Dan Ren was defeated. He ran away to Fujian Province and went to Jieshu's army and surrendered. Wu San Gui sent Ma Bao and Hu Guo Zhu to command the troops under them to attack Yongxing (in the southeast part of Hunan Province). Commander Yilibu and Commander Hakeshan came out of the city to fight. Both of them were killed in battle. Muzhan and Shuodai defended the city resolutely.

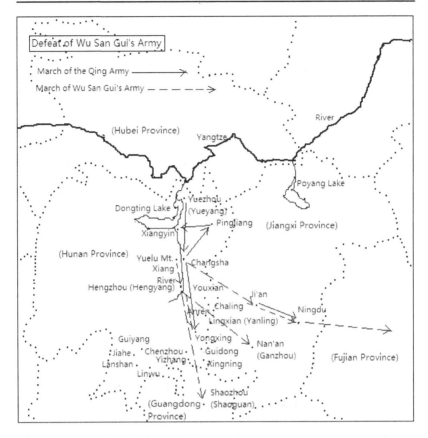

In that year Wu San Gui was 67 years old. Six years had passed since he rose up in rebellion. The area he occupied was greatly reduced. His army was greatly weakened. He wanted to ascend the throne of an emperor so as to make himself happier. His subordinates made formal appeals to him to declare himself emperor. So he ascended the throne of the Zhou Dynasty in March. He decided that the title of his reign was Zhaowu (meaning "demonstrating great military power"). He made Hengzhou (now Hengyang, Hunan Province) the capital of the Zhou Dynasty. He appointed court officials. He made his generals dukes, marquises and earls. He held examinations in Yunnan Province, Guizhou Province, Sichuan Province and Hunan Province to select officials. He named the house in which he lived the Palace. He did not have time to change all the tiers of his house into yellow tiers, so he had workmen paint all the tiers yellow. He ordered workmen to build big houses as the court. An altar was built on Hengsahn Mountain (in the outskirts of Hengyang) for the ceremony of his ascension to the throne. All the generals and officials would go there to express their congratulations.

But on the day of the ceremony there was a great wind and heavy rain, so the ceremony had to be ended hastily. Not long later, he choked on his food while he was eating. In August he suffered from dysentery. He was so seriously ill that he could not speak. He summoned his grandson Wu Shi Fan to Hengzhou from Yunnan Province. On 11 September Wu San Gui died — before Wu Shi Fan arrived. At that time Ma Bao and Hu Guo Zhu were fiercely attacking Yongxing (in Hunan Province). When they heard that Wu San Gui had died, they burned their fortresses and led their troops back to Hengzhou.

Wu Shi Fan was hurrying from Yunnan to Hengzhou. When he reached Guiyang (the capital city of Guizhou Province), his subordinates supported him in ascending the throne. He decided that the title of his reign was Honghua.

At that time Shangshan, Grand General of Anyuan Jingkou, died. Kangxi made King Chani Grand General of Anyuan Jingkou, and ordered him to attack Yuezhou (now Yueyang, Hunan Province). Wu San Gui's son Wu Ying Qi defended Yuezhou resolutely. Chani's troops attacked Yuezhou for a long time but could not take it. Kangxi issued an imperial edict that he would take command of the expedition. But very soon the news of Wu San Gui's death came. Then Kangxi gave up the idea of personally commanding the expedition. He urged the troops to march forward. Chani cut all the supply routes to Yuezhou and Hengzhou (now Hengyang, Hunan Province). Soon Wu Ying Qi's troops in Yuezhou ran out of food. They tried to make a breakthrough but they were defeated. More than half of Wu Ying Qi's men were killed.

Wu Ying Qi commanded 5,000 men to attack Lushi (a place in Hubei Province). General Ena and Commander Hangqi commanded their troops to defeat Wu Ying Qi. Wu Ying Qi ran away to Changsha. Chani took Yuezhou. Then his troops recovered Huarong, Anxiang, Xiangtan and Hengshan in Hunan Province.

When Grand General Le'erjin got the news that Wu San Gui had died, he commanded his troops to cross the Yangtze River from Jingzhou. Wu San Gui's naval force in the upper reaches of the Yangtze River and the land force stationed in Jingshan Mountain (in the northwest part of Hubei Province) all fled in disorder. Le'erjin's troops took Songzi, Zhijiang, Yidu, Shimen (these four counties are in Hubei Province), Cili (in Hunan Province) and Lizhou (now Lixian, Hunan Province).

In what is now Hunan Province, Le'erjin's troops also took Changde. Labu's troops took Hengzhou (now Hengyang), Qiyang, Laiyang, and Baoqing (now Shaoyang). At the same time, also in Hunan Province, Wu San Gui's generals Wu Guo Gui and Ma Bao retreated from Hengzhou to Wugang (in the southwest part of the province). Wu Ying Qi retreated from Yuezhou (now Yueyang) to Chenzhou (now Yuanling, in the west part of the province). Hu Guo Zhu retreated from Changsha to Chenlongguan (in Yuanling). The troops under Muzhan took Yongming (now Jiangyong, in the southwest part of Hunan), Jianghua (now Jianghua Yao Nationality Autonomous County), Dong'an, Daozhou (now Daoxian) and Yongzhou.

Yuele's troops marched from Hengzhou to recover Changning (in Hunan). Then they attacked Wugang. Wu Guo Gui commanded 20,000 men in a stout defense of Wugang. Yuele's troops attacked the city fiercely. Wu Guo Gui was killed in battle. His troops collapsed. Yuele's troops gave a hot pursuit and took Wugang.

In that year General Mangyitu commanded his troops to march into Guangxi Province. Wu San Gui's general Wu Shi Zong was defeated and ran away. But very soon he was killed in battle.

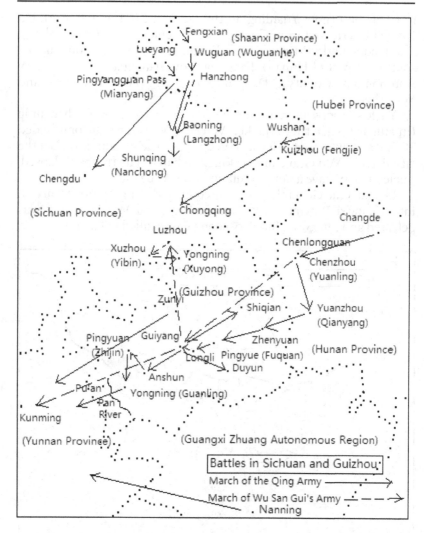

Fengxian (Shaanxi Province)
Lüeyang Wuguan (Wuguanhe)
Pingyangguan Pass Hanzhong
(Mianyang)
(Hubei Province)
Baoning Wushan
(Langzhong) Kuizhou (Fengjie)
Shunqing
(Nanchong)
Chengdu
(Sichuan Province) Chongqing
Changde
Luzhou
Xuzhou Yongning Chenlongguan
(Yibin) (Xuyong) Chenzhou
(Yuanling)
(Guizhou Province)
Zunyi Shiqian Yuanzhou
(Qianyang)
Pingyuan Guiyang Zhenyuan
(Zhijin) Longli Pingyue (Fuquan) (Hunan Province)
Anshun Duyun
Pu'an Yongning (Guanling)
Pan
Kunming River
(Yunnan Province) (Guangxi Zhuang Autonomous Region)

Battles in Sichuan and Guizhou
March of the Qing Army ⎯⎯⎯⟶
March of Wu San Gui's Army ⎯·⎯ ⎯ ⟶
Nanning

In spring 1680 General Zhao Niang Dong took Pingyangguan Pass (situated in the northwest of Mianxian, in the southwest part of Shaanxi Province) from Lüeyang (in the southwest part of Shaanxi Province). Then he commanded his troops to march into Sichuan Province and took Chengdu. Wang Jin Bao took Wuguan (in the southwest part of Shaanxi Province) from Fengxian (in the southwest part of Shaanxi Province). Then he marched his troops southward and took Hanzhong (in the southwest part of Shaanxi Province). Wu San Gui's general Wang Ping Shan retreated to Baoning (now Langzhong, Sichuan Province). Wang Jin Bao commanded his troops to pursue Wang Ping Shan to Baoning. A battle was fought in Jingping Mountain (situated in the south of the city of Langzhong). Seeing that the city was going to fall, Wang Ping Shan killed himself with his own sword.

Wang Jin Bao took Baoning. Then Wang Jin Bao marched his troops southward and took Shunqing (now Nanchong, Sichuan Province). General Wu Dan and Commander Xu Zi Du marched their troops from Wushan (in the east part of Sichuan Province) to take Kuizhou (now Fengjie, in the east part of Sichuan Province) and Chongqing (in Sichuan Province). Yang Lai Jia and Tan Hong surrendered. Chani commanded his troops to attack Chenlongguan (in Yuanling, Hunan Province) from Changde (in the north part of Hunan Province). His troops marched through a bypath and took Chenlongguan. Then they took Chenzhou (now Yuanling, Hunan Province). Wu San Gui's generals Yang Bao Yin and Cui Shi Lu surrendered. General Zhangtai's troops took Yuanzhou (in the area around Qianyang, in the west part of Hunan Province). Wu Ying Qi and Hu Guo Zhu ran away from Chenzhou (now Yuanling, Hunan Province) to Guiyang (the capital city of Guizhou Province). Emperor Kangxi recalled Le'erjin and Chani back to Beijing, the capital. He urged Zhangtai, Muzhan and Cai Yu Rong in Yuanzhou (now Qianyang, Hunan Province), Labu in Nanning (the capital city of Guangxi Zhuang Autonomous Region), Wu Dan and Zhao Niang Dong in Zunyi (in Guizhou Province), to march into Yunnan Province in three routes. Wu Shi Fan ordered Wu Ying Qi, Wang Hui, Gao Qi Long and Xia Xiang Guo to march into Sichuan Province from Guiyang. They took Luzhou, Xuzhou (now Yibin), and Yongning (now Xuyong) in Sichuan Province. Tan Hong who had surrendered rebelled again and took Kuizhou (now Fengjie, in the east part of Sichuan Province). Kangxi again urged Zhangtao to march to Guiyang (in Guangxi Zhuang Autonomous Region) quickly. He appointed Laita as the supervisor of all the troops in Guangxi. When Wu Ying Qi attacked Yongning, Wu Dan did not send any reinforcement from Chongqing. Kangxi dismissed him from his post. He appointed Zhao Niang Dong as the supervisor of all the troops in Sichuan Province. Then the three routes of the troops marched into Yunnan Province. Wu Shi Fan summoned Wang Hui, Gao Qi Long and Xia Guo Xiang to reinforce Guiyang (in Guizhou Province) from Sichuan Province. He ordered Ma Bao and Hu Guo Zhu to attack Sichuan Province.

In October the troops under Zhangtai took Zhenyuan (in Guizhou Province) from Yuanzhou (now Qianyang, Hunan Province). Wu Shi Fan's general Zhang Zu Fa was defeated and ran away. Then Zhangtai's troops took Pingyue (now Fuquan, Guizhou Province) and Longli. Then Zhangtai's troops attacked Guiyang. Wu Shi Fan and Wu Ying Qi ran back to Yunnan Province. Zhangtai's troops took Guiyang, Anshun, Shiqian and Duyun in Guizhou Province. Wu Shi Fan's officials Guo Chang, Qiu Yuan, Zang Shi Yuan, Qi Pin Jin and Wen Tai led more than 100 officials and 1,300 soldiers to Zhangtai's army to surrender. Zhangtai's troops continued to march forward. Wu Shi Fan's officials Cai Guo Chang and Zheng Kai Shu surrendered and handed over the city of Pingyuan (now Zhijin, Guizhou Province) to Zhangtai's army. Then Zhangtai's troops marched southward to Yongning (now Guanling). Wu Shi Fan's troops burned away the chain bridge over Pan River (now Bei Pan River, in the southwest part of Guizhou Province) and ran away. Long Tian Gu, the chieftain of the native people in Pu'an and Sha Qi Long, the chieftain of the native people in Yongning, led the people under them to build a floating bridge over the river to let the troops under Zhangtai cross the river.

In spring 1681 Wu Shi Fan appointed Gao Qi Long as Grand General and ordered him and Xia Guo Xiang, Wang Hui, Wang Yong Qing and Zhang Zu Fa to command 20,000 men to resist Zhangtai's army. They attacked Pingyuan (now Zhijin, Guizhou Province) and took it. They stationed their troops on the mountain in the southwest of the city. Muzhan and Commander Zhao Lai Jin commanded their troops to march from Yongning (now Guanling, in the southwest part of Guizhou Province) and attack the enemy troops on the mountain and defeated them. Gao Qi Long ran away. Wang Hui surrendered. Then Zhangtai's troops recovered Pingyuan.

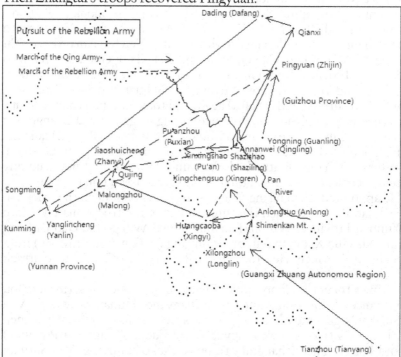

Zhangtai's troops marched to Annanwei (now Qinglong, in the southwest part of Guizhou Province). Wu Shai Fan's generals Xian Yu, Ba Yang Yuan, Zheng Wang and Li Ji Ye stationed their troops of 10,000 men on the west bank of Pan River. When Zhangtai's troops attacked the enemy troops, they were defeated by the enemy troops.

Two days later Zhangtai ordered Commander Bai Cheng Gong to lead his troops to attack the enemy troops. A battle was fought in Shazishao (now Shaziling, in the southwest part of Guizhou Province). The battle lasted from noon to evening. Commander Bai Cheng Gong's troops fought very bravely. Xian Yu, Zheng Wang and Li Ji Ye retreated to Jiaoshuicheng (to the north of Zhanyi, in the east part of Yunnan Province). Zhangtai's troops took Xinxingsuo (now Pu'an, in the southwest part of Guizhou Province), Pu'anzhou (now Panxian, in the southwest part of Guizhou Province), Qianxi (in Guizhou Province), and Dading (now Dafang, Guizhou Province). Laita's troops marched from Tianzhou (now Tianyang, Guangxi Zhuang Autonomous Region) to Xilongzhou (now Longlin, in the west part of Guangxi Zhuang Autonomous Region).

Wu Shi Fan's general He Ji Zu went with a force of 10,000 men to defend the narrow pass of Shimenkan Mountain (to the south of Anlong, Guizhou Province). Laita ordered his troops to attack the pass and they took it. Then they took Anlongsuo (now Anlong, in the southwest part of Guizhou Province). He Ji Zu retreated to Xinchengsuo (now Xingren, Guizhou Province). His troops joined forces with the troops under Zhan Yang and Wang You Gong. There were 20,000 men in all. They were stationed in Huangcaoba (in Xingyi, in the southwest part of Guizhou Province). Laita ordered his troops to march forward.

After a battle Laita's troops took 22 strongholds and captured Zhan Yang and Wang You Gong. They captured more than 1,000 enemy soldiers. Then they marched forward and took Qujing (in the east part of Yunnan Province) and Jiaoshuicheng (now Zhanyi, situated to the north of Qujing). Xian Yu ran away. Then Laita's troops took Marlongzhou (now Malong, Yunnan Province) and Yanglincheng (now Yanglin, Yunnan Province). At that time the troops under Zhangtai also arrived. The troops under Laita and the troops under Zhangtai joined forces in Songming (in Yunnan Province).

In February 1681 the troops under Zhangtai and Laita attacked Kunming, the capital city of Yunnan Province. The troops stationed in Guihua Temple (in the southeast part of Kunming). Wu Shi Fan sent his general Hu Guo Bing to command 10,000 men to resist the attack. Zhangtai and Laita ordered their troops to attack and they defeated the enemy troops. Hu Guo Bing and nine commanders under him were killed. 600 soldiers were captured. The troops under Zhangtai and Laita pursued the enemy troops and they reached the city of Kunming. Wu Shi Fan's generals Zhang Guo Zhu and Li Fa Mei surrendered. The troops under Zhangtai and Laita took the prefectures of Lin'an (now Jianshui, in the south part of Yunnan Province), Yao'an, Dali, Heqing and Lijiang. Wu Shi Fan summoned Ma Bao, Hu Guo Zhu and Wu Xiang Guo back to save Yunnan Province. Kangxi ordered

Zhao Liang Dong to send troops to attack the troops under Ma Bao. Ma Bao led his troops from Xundian to Chuxiong. His troops were defeated there. Then Ma Bao and Ba Yang Yuan, Zhao Guo Zuo, Zheng Wang, Li Ji Ye and Lang Ying Bi went to Yao'an to surrender. Hu Guo Zhu came from Lijiang through Heqing to Yunlong. He found that there was no future for him. Then he committed suicide by hanging himself to death. Xia Guo Xiang went to Guangxi after he was defeated in Pingyue (now Fuquan, Guizhou Province). Li Guo Liang, Commander-in-chief of the army in Guangxi, sent troops to surround his troops. Then Xia Guo Xiang, Wang Yong Qing and Jiang Yi surrendered. From then on there were no reinforcements for Wu Shi Fan. The troops under Zhao Liang Dong marched from Jiajiang (in the south part of Sichuan Province) and took Yazhou (now Ya'an, Sichuan Province) and Jianchang (now Xichang, in the south part of Sichuan Province). They crossed Jinsha River and reached Wuding (in Yunnan Province). In September they marched forward and joined forces with the troops under Zhangtai and Laita.

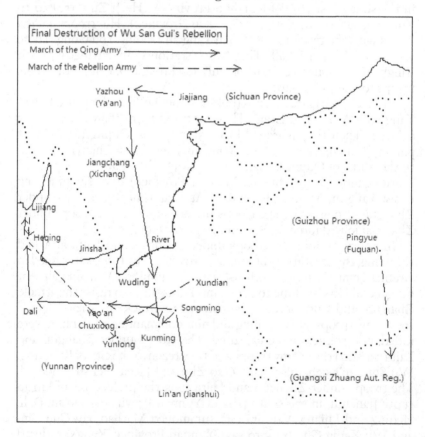

By that time, the troops under Zhangtai and Laita had laid siege to Kunming for several months but could not take it. Zhao Liang Dong suggested that they should cut Wu Shi Fan's supply route on Kunming Lake and then start a fierce attack on the city. His suggestion was accepted. Then they commanded their troops to storm the city. Xian Yu and others planned to arrested Wu Shi Fan and Guo Zhuang Tu and hand them over to Zhangtai and surrender. Wu Shi Fan and Guo Zhuang Tu found out their plan and they committed suicide. In October Xian Yu and others surrendered and handed the city of Kunming to Zhangtai's army. Muzhan and Commander Ma Qi entered the city first and arrested the high officials of the Zhou Dynasty. They cut the head of Wu Shi Fan's dead body down and sent it to the capital. From then on Yunnan Province, Guizhou Province, Hunan Province and Guangxi Province had been pacified. Kangxi ordered his officials to declare the great victory to all the people.

Historians highly praise Kangxi for putting down the rebellions of the three military governors. They write, "When Kangxi first assumed the reins of government, the first thing he had to deal with was the three military governors. When Shang Ke Xi asked permission to go back home to spend his old age, he did not mean to give up the power of a military governor.

"It was Kangxi who made the decision to strip the fiefdoms of the three military governors. When Wu San Gui held a rebellion, Geng Jing Zhong, Sun Yan Ling and Shang Zhi Xin responded to his rebellion and they rebelled too. Six provinces fell into the hands of the rebels. Kangxi first sent troops to defend Jingzhou (in the south part of Hubei Province) to stop the rebels from marching to the north. He stationed troops in Taiyuan (the capital city of Shanxi Province), Yanzhou (in Shandong Province), Jiangning (in Jiangsu Province) and Nanchang (the capital city of Jiangxi Province), so that they could reinforce one another when necessary. These troops marched forward in good order and discipline. The troops did not feel tired although they marched for a long distance to fight.

"Wu San Gui staged a rebellion when he was already very old. He thought that Kangxi, being young and without the guidance of the kings and generals who had helped to found the Qing Dynasty, who had already died, would be at a loss as to what to do. But when Wu San Gui learned that Kangxi was leading his armies calmly and confidently and all the generals obeyed his orders, he exclaimed that he had never expected that Kangxi was so capable. Kangxi made plans for the victory in court and his armies won great victories in the battlefields. If Wu San Gui had obeyed Kangxi's order to move away from the areas he had garrisoned, Kangxi would have spared him. It was a pity that Wu San Gui had not understood Kangxi's intension."

1. The Situation in Taiwan

In 1674 Geng Jing Zhong planned to respond to Wu San Gui and hold a rebellion in Fujian Province. He sent an envoy to Taiwan to ask Zheng Jin to help him. In 1674 Geng Jing Zhong held a rebellion. Zheng Jin appointed a general to stay to defend Taiwan. Then he and several generals crossed the sea and sailed westward to Fujian. They landed in Siming (now Siming District, in the south part of Xiamen, in the southeast part of Fujian Province). Then they took Tong'an (now Tong'an District, in the north part of Xiamen). Then he commanded his troops to march northward to attack Quanzhou, which was defended by Geng Jing Zhong's army. The soldiers defending Quanzhou rebelled. The general sent by Geng Jing Zhong made a breakthrough and ran away. Zheng Jin's army entered Quanzhou. Zheng Jin's army marched southward and took Zhangzhou. Geng Jing Zhong sent troops to lay siege to Chaozhou (in the east part of Guangdong Province). Liu Jin Zhong, the commander-in-chief of the troops in Chaozhou, surrendered to Zheng Jin. Zheng Jin sent his general Zhao De Sheng to Chaozhou and defeated Geng Jing Zhong's troops. Zheng Jin and Geng Jing Zhong became enemies.

In 1675 Geng Jing Zhong made peace with Zheng Jin and they colluded with each other again.

In 1676 Prince Jieshu commanded a great army to Fujian. Geng Jing Zhong surrendered. Jieshu's troops took Quanzhou. Zheng Jin's general Liu Guo Xuan commanded his troops to lay siege to Quanzhou again. The siege lasted for two months but they could not take it. Li Guang Di, an official who had gone back to Fujian to see his parents, led some troops to relieve Quanzhou. Commanders Lin Xian, Huang Gao and Pu Zi Wei commanded their naval troops to relieve Quanzhou. Liu Guo Xuan raised the siege to Quanzhou and retreated to Changtai (in the southeast part of Fujian Province). The troops under Jieshu attacked Liu Guo Xuan's troops. Liu Guo Xuan was defeated. He gave up Changtai and ran away. Zheng Jin sent Xu Hui to command 20,000 men to attack Fuzhou (the capital city of Fujian Province). Xu Hui stationed his troops in Wulongjiang (now Wulongjiang Street, Minhou County). Prince Jieshu sent Deputy Commander Lahada to command his troops to cross Min River to attack the camps of Xu Hui's troops in Wulongjiang. Xu Hui's troops were defeated. Lahada's troops pursued the enemy for 20 kilometers and recovered Quanzhou, Tingzhou (Changting) and Zhangzhou. In 1677 Jieshu's troops took Haicheng (in the southeast part of Fujian Province). But very soon it was taken by Zheng Jin's troops again. Then Zheng Jin's troops laid siege to Quanzhou again. Deputy Commander Muhelin's troops took Taining, Jianning, Ninghua, Changting, Qingliu, Guihua (now Mingxi), Liancheng, Shanghang,

Wuping and Yongding, 10 counties in all. Lahada's troops forced the enemy to raise the siege to Quanzhou. Zheng Jin led his troops to retreat to Siming. In 1678 Prince Jieshu sent an envoy to demand Zheng Jin to surrender. But Zheng Jin refused.

Liu Guo Xuan retreated from Changtai to Shuitou (a town in Nan'an, in the southeast part of Fujian Province). Then he sent troops to attack Jiangdong Bridge (in Zhangzhou) and Shima (in Longhai). Zheng Jin sent his generals Lin Yao and Lin Ying to lead their troops to attack Quanzhou. Commander Duan Ying Ju defeated them and caught Lin Yao. Then Duan Ying Ju and Muhelin commanded their troops to attack Liu Guo Xuan, but they were defeated. Duan Ying Ju and Muhelin were killed in battle. Liu Guo Xuan took Pinghe, Zhangpin and Haicheng. Liu Guo Xuan led his troops to march to Quanzhou and laid siege to the city. Emperor Kangxi urged his generals to command their troops to attack Liu Guo Xuan. General Lahada, General Laita, Governor Yao Qi Sheng, Inspector Wu Xing Zuo and Commander-in-chief Yang Jie commanded the troops under them to march forward. They took Pinghe, Zhangping and Hui'an. Then they forced Liu Guo Xuan to raise the siege to Quanzhou. The troops under Yao Qi Sheng and Laita chased Liu Guo Xuan to Changtai. They caught up with him in Wugong Mountain (situated in Zhangzhou). Liu Guo Xuan's troops were seriously defeated. More than 4,000 soldiers were killed. Zheng Jin led his troops to retreat to Siming (Siming District, Xiamen).

Kangxi sent naval troops to Fujian to prepare to attack Jinmen. In February 1680 Wu Xing Zuo's troops came from Tong'an and joined forces with the troops under Yao Qi Sheng and Yang Jie. Then they march towards Jinmen Island. Commander Wan Zheng Se commanded the naval troops to attack Haitan Island. 16 ships of Zheng Jin's army were destroyed. More than 3,000 soldiers were drowned. Zheng Jin's general Zhu Tian Gui led his troops to retreat. Wan Zheng Se commanded his troops to pursue the enemy. Meizhou Island, Nanri Island, Pinghai County and Chongwu County were taken. Deputy Commander Woshen defeated Zheng Jin's generals Lin Ying and Zheng Zhi and marched his troops towards Yuzhou (in Xiamen). Liu Guo Xuan ran back to Siming. Wu Xing Zuo and Lahada commanded their troops to pursue Zheng Jin's troops to Xunwei (a village in Jimei, Xiamen). Then they took Jinmen Island. Zheng Jin ran back to Taiwan. On 27 January 1681 Zheng Jin died.

Zheng Jin's eldest son Zheng Ke Zang stayed in Taiwan when Zheng Jin commanded his troops to attack Fujian. He was appointed as Supervisor of the State. He had some grudges with Feng Xi Fan, the head of the bodyguards. When Zheng Jin died, he colluded with Zheng Cong, Zheng Jin's younger brother, and killed Zheng Ke Zang. They supported Zheng Ke Shuang, Zheng Jin's second son, as King of Yanping. Zheng Ke Shuang was young and weak. Power was actually in Feng Xi Fan's hands. Fu Wei Lin, a general, planned to unite with other generals to kill Feng Xi Fan. But his plan was found out. Feng Xi Fan arrested him and killed him.

2. Preparations for Taking Taiwan

In June 1681 Yao Qi Sheng, Governor of Fujian Province, presented a memorial to Kangxi which read, "Zheng Jin already died on 27 January. His eldest son was killed. Feng Xi Fan, the head of the bodyguards, supported Zheng Jin's second son Zheng Ke Shuang as the master of Taiwan. Zheng Ke Shuang is Feng Xi Fan's son-in-law." Kangxi gave Yao Qi Sheng a reply which read, "Now that Zheng Jin is dead, there will surely be disturbance among the enemy officials. We must take this chance to take Penghu Islands and Taiwan. Governor Yao Qi Sheng, Inspector Wu Xing Zuo, Commander-in-chief Nuomai and Commander-in-chief Wan Zheng Se should cooperate with General Lahada and Vice Minister Wu Nu Chun to command the naval army to sail forward to take Penghu Islands and Taiwan. You must apply the policy of attacking the enemies by military force and offering amnesty to the enemies and enlist their services so as to pacify Jinmen Islands and Taiwan."

In August 1681 Yao Qi Sheng, Governor of Fujian Province, presented a memorial to Kangxi which read, "The naval troops under me are former subordinates of Zhu Tian Gui, Commander-in-chief of the army in Pingyang of Zhejiang Province. If these naval troops are commanded by another person, they may not submit to his command. Zhu Tian Gui is so famous that the rebels in Penghu and Taiwan are very afraid of him. When he came over, he became a diehard enemy of the rebels in Penghu and Taiwan. If Your Majesty let him command the troops originally under him, he will surely do his best to repay Your Majesty's kindness. I hope Your Majesty will order the Governor of Zhejiang Province to send Zhu Tian Gui with his 300 picked troops to Fujian to help to take Penghu and Taiwan." Kangxi accepted his suggestion and ordered the Governor of Zhejiang Province to send Zhu Tian Gui and his 300 picked troops to Fujian Province.

Li Guang Di said to Kangxi, "Zheng Jin is already dead. His son Zheng Ke Shuang is young and weak. His subordinates are striving for power and there are conflicts among them. It is the right time to take Taiwan." He recommended Shi Lang to command the naval troops to take Taiwan because Shi Lang knew sea warfare very well. Kangxi accepted his suggestion and appointed Shi Lang as the Fujian Provincial Commander-in-chief of the Naval Force. When Shi Lang arrived in Fujian to take his position, he presented a memorial to Kangxi which read, "The enemies have anchored their ships in Penghu Islands for a long time. They will do all they can to defend Penghu Islands. In winter and spring times hurricanes rise very often. It will be very difficult for our ships to cross the sea. Now I am training the naval troops for sea battles. I have sent spies to get contact with my former subordinates in Penghu and Taiwan to let them cooperate from within when I attack from without. We can wait till March and April next year when the wind is favorable for us to sail to Penghu and Taiwan. We shall surely win."

Shi Lang had promised to start the attack of Penghu and Taiwan in March or April of 1682. In April 1682 Shi Lang presented a memorial to Kangxi which read, "Summer has come. The strong south wind blows continuously. We cannot sail to Penghu and Taiwan in such weather. Please allow us to postpone the attack till October." Kangxi gave him a reply which read, "Attacking the enemy in Penghu and Taiwan is an important matter. Governor Yao Qi Sheng and Commander-in-chief Shi Lang are now in Fujian Province. You should observe the changes of the sea and the situation of the enemy. If the chance comes, you should cooperate with each other and take actions to destroy the enemy."

Sun Hui, an advisor, proposed to Emperor Kangxi to postpone the attack of Taiwan. In July 1682 a comet appeared. Liang Qing Biao, the Minister of Revenue said to Kangxi that it was an unlucky sign and the attack of Taiwan should be postponed. Kangxi then issued an order to postpone the attack of Taiwan. Shi Lang presented a memorial to Kangxi which read, "I have chosen 20,000 crack troops. I have 300 warships. My army is strong enough to destroy the enemies in Penghu and Taiwan. I hope Your Majesty will urge the Governor to provide sufficient provisions and funds for the troops. When there is favorable wind, my troops will sail out to attack Penghu and Taiwan." Kangxi agreed with him.

In May 1682 Yao Qi Sheng, the Governor of Fujian Province, presented a memorial to Kangxi which read, "Liu Guo Xuan sent Huang Xue, an official under him, to take a letter to me. He asks Your Majesty to allow Taiwan to be a vassal state and provide tributes to the government like the Ryukyu Islands and Korea. The people in Penghu and Taiwan will not shave their hair and will not leave Penghu and Taiwan. We are waiting for Your Majesty's instruction whether his request can be accepted." Kangxi said, "The rebels in Taiwan are actually people of Fujian Province. Their situation is not the same as the people in the Ryukyu Islands and Korea. If they show repentance, they should shave their hair and come out to surrender. The Governor of Fujian Province should choose capable officials and send them to Taiwan to persuade the rebels to surrender. It is possible that the rebels know that our great army is going to attack Taiwan and they play this trick to delay the advance of our army. You must find out their true intension. If there is an opportunity to take advantage of, you may order Commander-in-chief Shi Lang to command the troops to attack Penghu and Taiwan." Then Yao Qi Sheng sent Deputy Commander Huang Chao to persuade Liu Guo Xuan to surrender. But Liu Guo Xuan insisted on his former suggestion. Then Kangxi urged Shi Lang to take action.

3. Reunification of Taiwan

Liu Guo Xuan knew that Shi Lang would attack Penghu and Taiwan taking the advantage of the south wind. So he commanded a great army from Taiwan to Penghu Islands and defended the islands resolutely. He ordered his soldiers to build walls along the seashore where the ships could reach and the men could land on shore. Behind the walls there were canons.

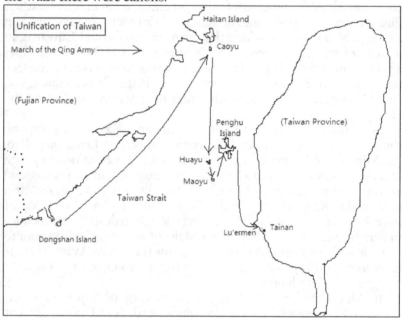

In June 1683 Shi Lang commanded his naval troops to sail from Tongshan (in Dongshan Island, Fujian Province) and took Caoyu (an island situated to the south of Haitan Island, Fujian Province), Huayu (an island situated to the southwest of Penghu Islands) and Maoyu (an island situated to the southwest of Penghu Islands). On 16 June Shi Lang sent Commander Lan Li to command his troops on small boats to attack Penghu Islands. At that time it was high tide. The enemy ships surrounded the small boats. Shi Lang took a big warship to break into the enemy warships. Suddenly a strayed arrow hit one of his eyes and blood spilt out. But he did not retreat and he continued to command the battle. Commander Wu Ying followed Shi Lang and his troops killed 3,000 enemy soldiers. On 18 June Shi Lang's troops took Hujing Island (situated to the southwest of Penghu Island, one of the main islands of Penghu Islands) and Tongpanyu (also situated to the southwest of Penghu Island). On 22 June Shi Lang sent Commander Chen Mang and Commander Wei Ming to lead their troops in 50 warships to sail eastward to Jilongyu (situated to the west of Penghu Island) and Sijiaoshan. He sent Commander Dong Yi and Commander Kang Yu to lead their troops in 50 warships to sail westward to Niuxinwan Bay to attract the attention of the enemy. Shi Lang himself commanded the troops in 56 warships in the center. The 56 warships were divided in 8 teams. There were 7 warships in each team. He assigned troops in 80 warships to stay behind as the reinforcement. Then they started a fierce attack on Penghu Island. All the enemy ships sailed out to fight. Zhu Tian Gui took the lead to enter the enemy battle formation and fought very bravely. But unfortunately he was killed in battle. The battle lasted from seven in the morning till five in the afternoon. Shi Lang's troops fought very fiercely regardless of their personal safety. In this battle 194 enemy warships were destroyed, more than 300 officers and officials and more than 12,000 enemy soldiers were killed. Seeing that he was going to lose the battle, Liu Guo Xuan took a speed boat and escaped back to Taiwan. 165 enemy generals and officials led more than 4,800 soldiers to surrender. Shi Lang successfully took Penghu Island in seven days.

On 15 July Zheng Ke Shuang sent Zheng Ping Ying and Feng Xi Gui, Liu Guo Xuan sent his younger brother Liu Guo Chang and Feng Xi Fan sent his younger brother Feng Xi Han to the army under Shi Lang in Penghu Island to deliver their letters of surrender to Commander-in-chief Shi Lang. They asked permission to hand over their seals and lead their subordinates to leave Taiwan and come back to the mainland. They asked to be put in suitable positions. Shi Lang asked Governor Yao Qi Sheng to pass their letters of surrender and their requirements to Kangxi. Kangxi issued an imperial edict to Zheng Ke Shuang, Liu Guo Xuan and Feng Xi Fan which read, "An emperor is in charge of protecting the whole territory and granting benevolence to all his people. He hopes that even the people in the faraway places will enjoy peace and prosperity. Your grandfather Zheng Cheng Gong occupied Taiwan by the end of the Ming Dynasty. After our dynasty pacified Fujian Province, your grandfather stayed in Taiwan and would not obey the rule of our dynasty. When your father Zheng Jin was in power, he used Taiwan as a base. He colluded with the rebels in the mainland and invaded Fujian Province. We defeated him many times and did our best to persuade him to surrender. But he obstinately stuck to his wrong course till he died. Then you succeeded your father in young age. You were fooled by your subordinates and wanted to follow the examples of your grandfather and father. You thought that Taiwan is far away from the mainland and protected by the sea, and you used it as your base and sent troops to harass the coastal areas. I consider that the people in the mainland and the people in the islands are all my people. I will save them from suffering. So I ordered Shi Lang to train the troops and warships were built. Then Shi Lang commanded the great naval troops to sail across the sea. Very soon he reported that he had won a great victory and took Penghu. Those who dared to resist our great army were all destroyed.

The remaining ones have run back to Taiwan. Now our troops are ready to attack Taiwan and I expect that they will take Taiwan very soon. Recently Governor Yao Qi Sheng reported to me that you had sent envoys to beg me to spare you. I have always shown benevolence and mercy to all the people. Now I have issued this imperial edict. Envoys will be sent to convey my intension to you. If you really admit your mistakes and repent and decide to surrender, you should lead all the officials and people to leave Taiwan and come to the mainland. I will spare all your crimes of resisting my army. I will appoint you to suitable positions. I have made this promise. I will not go back on my words. If you still suspect my kindness and delay in obeying my orders, when my army starts the attack, you will all be destroyed. Then it will be too late for you to regret. Think carefully and do the right thing to save yourselves."

On 11 August Shi Lang led all his officers and men to sail towards Taiwan. On 13 August they reached Lu'ermen (situated outside the port in the northwest of Annan District, Tainan City). Then Shi Lang and his troops landed on Taiwan. On 18 August Zheng Ke Shuang and all his officers and officials had their hair shaved. Then Shi Lang read out Kangxi's imperial edict to them. After they had heard the imperial edict, they cheered happily. They all faced the direction of Beijing, knelt down and touched their heads to the ground to pay their respect to Kangxi. Zheng Ke Shuang handed over the gold seal of King of Yanping to Shi Lang. Taiwan was pacified. When the report of the great victory reached Kangxi, he granted Shi Lang the title of General of Jinghai (Jinghai means "Pacifying the Sea") and made him Marquis of Jinghai.

Zheng Ke Shuang, Liu Guo Xuan, Feng Xi Fan and their family members and relatives, 17 persons in all, were escorted to Beijing, the capital of the Qing Dynasty. Kangxi granted Zheng Ke Shuang the title of Duke of Haicheng (Haicheng means "the sea has become limpid"). He made Liu Guo Xuan and Feng Xi Fan earls. He appointed Liu Guo Xuan as the Commander-in-chief of the army in Tianjin (in Hebei Province).

SECTION FIVE: EMPEROR KANGXI FORCES THE RUSSIANS TO LEAVE THE CHINESE BORDER AREA

1. The Russians Take Yakesa (Albazino) and Nibuchu (Nerchinsk)

By the end of the Ming Dynasty the Russians took the chance that China was in great chaos and sent troops to take Yakesa (now Albanzino, Russia) and Nibuchu (now Nerchinsk, Russia) which were situated within the territory of China. Yakesa was situated in the north part of Heilongjiang Province on the east bank of the place where Emuer River and Heilong River joined. The people of Dawoer

Nationality lived in this place. Yakesa was the home place of A'erbaxi, the head of the tribe of Dawoer Nationality. Nibuchu was the place where the people of Maoming'an tribe lived. Maoming'an tribe was a sub-tribe of Mongolian Ke'erqin tribe. The Russians caused great sufferings to the people in Yakesa and Nibuchu. They burned the houses of the people. They killed the Chinese people and looted the people.

The authorities of the Qing Dynasty did not have the time to take care of this matter because after the Qing troops entered Shanhaiguan Pass, they had to concentrate on the pacification of the whole China. After Emperor Kangxi had assumed the reins of government, he had to concentrate on the pacification of the rebellions of the three military governors and reunification of Taiwan. So he did not have the time to take care of this matter.

2. Battles to Recover Yakesa

In December 1682 Emperor Kangxi sent Deputy Commander Langtan with several officers to go to collect information about the Russians in the area along Heilong River. Langtan went as far as to the north part of Heilongjiang Province where the people of Dawoer Nationality and Ewenki Nationality lived. He came back and reported the information about the Russians there to Kangxi. Kangxi said to the kings and officials in charge of the government affairs, "According to the report by Langtan, it will be easy for us to defeat the Russians. 3,000 troops will be enough. I agree with him. It is not a good idea to carry out war against the Russians now. We should postpone the attack of the Russians. Now I order to send 1,500 troops from Ningguta and have warships built. They should be equipped with cannons and firelocks. They should establish wooden fortresses in Heilongjiang City and Humaer and get ready to fight with the Russians. The food supplies will be provided by the people of Ke'erqin and from the places where the people of Xibo Nationality live. We may collect 33,000 Bushels of grains. This amount of food may be enough for the troops for 3 years. And when the troops reach there, they should immediately till the land and grow crops. Then they will have enough food supplies. Heilongjiang City is not far from the villages where the people of Ewenki Nationality live. It will take 5 days to get there. A post station may be established between them. When our troops are going to march to Zeya River, we will order the people of Ewenki Nationality to provide cows and sheep to our troops. In this way the Russians will not be able to accept the run-aways from our side. And their run-aways will come to our side. Then the Russians will not be able to stay there for long." Then Kangxi ordered Bahai, the general of the troops in Ningguta (now Hailin, Heilongjiang Province), and Deputy Commander-in-chief Sabusu to command the troops in Ningguta to Heilongjiang City (now Heihe,

Heilongjiang Province) situated by Heilong River where Zeya River joined Heilong River, and to Humaer (now Huma, in the north part of Heilongjiang Province).

In July 1683 Boke, a commander in the north part of Helongjiang Province, captured more than 30 Russian soldiers. He selected five of them and sent soldiers to escort them to Beijing, the capital. The other 26 Russian soldiers remained in the place where the people of Ewenki Nationality and Dawoer Nationality lived. The place was near the place where the Russian main force was in. So officials there suggested that all of the 26 captured Russian soldiers should also be escorted to the capital. The kings and officials suggested to Kangxi, "Yifan and Mihailuomoluo, the two Russians captured by Boke, should be granted hats and clothes. They should be escorted to the place where General Sabusu is and let them go back to the Russians. The Ministry of Minority Affairs should write a letter and let Yifan take the letter to the commander of the Russians. The letter should be as follows, 'Before we sent Mengede and other officials to make an agreement with you that neither side should accept the run-aways of the other side. You should send Gentemuer, who ran away to your side last year, back to our side. But you broke the agreement. You sent troops to invade our border area. You looted and killed the people of Dawoer Nationality. You burned the people of Feiyaka Nationality. This is the reason why we have sent troops to station in Wusuli. If you leave our border area and return the land to us and send back the run-aways from our side, then it will be all right. Otherwise we will accept the run-aways from your side. We shall arrest and kill the people from your side.'" Kangxi agreed with their suggestion.

On 9 November 1683, Kangxi said to Amuhulang, the Minister of Minority Affairs, "I have unified the whole country. All the people in this country, no matter they are Chinese or foreigners, are my people. I care all of them and hop they live and work in peace and contentment. The Russians from Russia have invaded our border area where the people of Ewenki Nationality and Dawoer Nationality live without any reason. They looted and killed the local people. They accept the run-aways such as Gentemuer, the head of the Dawoer Tribe. They have committed a lot of crimes. But I was not hardhearted enough to send troops to annihilate them. I have demanded them explicitly to give up their wrong doings and go back to their own country. I have also instructed them to send the run-aways to us. I have given explicit instructions to the envoy sent by the Russians. But the Russians insisted on their wrong doings. They sent soldiers to the places where the people of Feiyaka Tribe and Qileer Tribe live. They burned the houses and killed the people there. They seduced the people of Ewenki Nationality, Dawoer Nationality and Elunchun Nationality, 20 persons in all, into a house, and then they set fire to the house and burned all of them to death. We have warned them many times, but still they insisted on their wrong doings. So I have ordered generals to lead troops to station in Heilongjiang City and Huma'er. Their task is to stop the willful doings of the Russians. Recently some Russian soldiers went pass the area in Heilongjiang City. They met with our troops. Our troops forced more than 30 Russian soldiers to surrender. They have sent me a report about this. I show lenience to the captives. None of them has been killed. We have provided food and clothing to them. If the Russians in Yakesa and Nibuchu give up their eveil acts, send the run-aways such as Gentemuer to us and go back to their own country, then the two countries will be at peace. This is a good choice for the Russians. If they persist in their wrong doings and stay in our border area, I will carry out an expedition against them. Then they will be seriously punished. Those Russians who think that they are too far away from home and are willing to surrender will be accepted. I will show grace on them. The Ministry of Minority Affairs should follow my instruction and write a letter to demand the Russians to surrender. You should let Yifan and Mihailuomoluo take the letter back to the Russians. If the Russians have any reply, Yifan and Mihailuomoluo should inform us immediately."

Deputy Commander-in-chief Sabusu presented a memorial to Kangxi which read, "If we attack Yakesa in winter, there will be great difficulties in transporting the cannons and food supplies. If there is heavy snow, it will be unfavorable for military actions. We suggest that our troops may station in Wusuli for the winter. In April next year, the ice on Heilong River will melt. Then we will go forward to attack Yakesa." Kangxi ordered the kings and officials in charge of government affairs to discuss the memorial presented by Sabusu. Not long later they gave a result of their discussion to Kangxi which read, "Before Your Majesty suggested to postpone the attack of Yakesa and to take military action when chance comes. Sabusu has suggested attacking Yakesa in April next year. We agree with his suggestion." Kangxi instructed, "Since our troops are ordered to station in Wusuli, 600 soldiers in Ningguta and 500 soldiers of Dawoer Nationality with their family members should be sent there in the coming autumn. A general, a deputy commander-in-chief and officers should be appointed to garrison Wusuli. Next year food supplies should be transported from the place where the people of Sibe Nationality live to Wusuli. Sabusu has sent soldiers to transport the food supplies for the troops enough to support them to June next year. Now that the military action will be postponed, we should order Sabusu to send sailors to go to the place where the people of Sibe Nationality live by land. Next year when ice in Heilong River is melted, they will transport food supplies on ships along the river. Langtan should hurry to the place where Sabusu is and make a decision with him whether the transportation of food supplies can be carried out this way." Not long later Sabusu presented a memorial to Kangxi which read, "In July this year it already began to snow and there was a hard frost. If the soldiers in Ningguta with their family members move to

Wusuli next autumn, I am afraid they will not be able to get enough food because it is very cold in autumn in Wusuli. I suggest that in spring next year 500 soldiers of Dawoer nationality in nearby place should be sent to Wusuli and they should till the land and grow crops there. Their family members should go to Wusuli after autumn when crops have been harvested. The 3,000 soldiers in Ningguta should be divided in three groups. These three groups of soldiers should be led by commanders and take turns stationing in Wusuli." The kings and officials in charge of government affairs discussed Sabusu's memorial and agreed with his suggestion. Kangxi gave a reply to the kings and officials in charge of government affairs which read, "If we follow Sabusu's suggestion and let the three groups of soldiers take turns stationing in Wusuli, they will be very tired. This is not a long term plan. The best way is to build a strong city in Heilongjing City and let the troops to station there permanently. They should be equipped with cannons and warships. Scouts should be sent to Huma'er to collect information about the Russians. Ten post stations should be established from Heilingjiang City to Wula in Jilin Province. There should be 50 men in each post station. If there is an emergency, envoys should ride Mongolian horses to go to Wula as quickly as possible. As for ordinary matters, envoys can go by the ten post stations. Food supplies can be transported on boats along Heilong River and stored in Heilongjiang City. When the soldiers reach there, they will stay there for two years. Generals and commanders will be appointed to command these soldiers. If the Russians come down the Heilong River by warships, our naval troops may follow them and attack them. Heilongjiang Province is a vast province. Ten post stations should be established. The family members of the soldiers will be properly accommodated in the same place where the soldiers are. When these measures have been put into practice, the Russians will be at the end of their resources. Eersai, the Deputy Minister of Minority Affairs, should go to Heilongjiang to discuss with Sabusu and make decisions. He should report the results of their discussion to me." By the end of September, Sabusu presented a memorial to Kangxi which read, "Your Majesty has made very clear instructions for the matters of stationing troops in Heilongjiang permanently. We shall carry out your instructions resolutely. But next year, some soldiers will move away and the remaining soldiers will have to work hard to build the city and grow crops at the same time. I am afraid that they will not be able to sustain for long. I hope Your Majesty will send 500 soldiers from Ningguta to help us to build the city. When the building of the city is completed, I will send them back to Ningguta." Kangxi gave a reply to Sabusu which read, "The soldiers in Ningguta have been sent to other places. I will order Deputy Commander-in-chief Mutai to lead 600 soldiers in Shenyang to go to your place in March next year. They will take all the tools for city building with them."

In November 1683 the people of Qileer Nationality and Xilugenu Nationality who live by Niuman River (now Bureya River, Russia) killed more than ten Russian soldiers. They came to submit to the Qing army with their wives and children. Zhuerkengge, the head of a tribe of Elunchun Nationality, killed five Russian soldiers by Zeya River. He reported this to the Qing officials and presented the firelocks they captured to the officials. The people of Feiyaka Nationality killed many Russian soldiers. On 16 November General Sabusu reported all these to Kangxi. He suggested to Kangxi, "We should offer official positions to Jiliguoli, Efonaxi and Makeximu, the Russian soldiers who recently surrendered to us. Yifan, Egefan and Xituban, the three Russian soldiers who surrendered before, have been working hard to do their services for us. We should also offer official positions to them." Kangxi gave him a reply which read, "We have offered Yifan the rank of field officer of cavalry. We shall offer Jiliguoli, Efonaxi and Makeximu, who surrendered recently, the official positions of rank seven. Efonaxi and Feilipu, the two Russian soldiers who surrendered recently, will be sent to the troops under Sabusu. Their task is to bring the Russian soldiers to negotiated surrender. Now it is very cold. They should be granted fur coats and hats."

Yisang'a, the Personnel Minister, present a report to Kangxi which read, "We have discussed the matter of transporting food supplies to Heilongjiang in accordance with the instructions of Your Majesty. We suggest that 50 ships should be built in Wula. Apart from the 150 sailors sent by Sabusu, 200 more soldiers in Wula and 400 hunters should be sent. When the ice melts next year, the grains in Yitong and Sibe will be transported. Each ship will carry 137.5 Bushels of grains. The food supplies for the troops under Deputy Commander-in-chief Mutai for three months will also be transported. All the food supplies will be transported to Heilongjiang. The food supplies planned to be transported in 1865 will be transported by the sailors sent by Sabusu and the 600 hundred soldiers sent from Wula." Kangxi gave him a reply which read, "You should increase the numbers of ships to transport the food supplies for 1865. Then it will not be necessary to transport food supplies in 1685. You should discuss this matter and make a decision and report your decision to me." Not long later Yisang'a reported their decision to Kangxi which read, "50 ships will not be enough to transport all the food supplies for two years. 30 more ships should be built. 15 persons are needed in each ship. 1,200 persons are needed for all the ships. A part from the 150 sailors sent by Sabusu, 690 hunters in Wula and 360 soldiers in Ningguta are needed. Some capable officers should be selected to supervise the food transportation to Heilongjiang." Kangxi agreed with their decision. He also told them, "Many hunters will be sent to do the transportation work. Now I order Commander Xiteke to command them to go. The soldiers, hunters and sailors should be given pay for one more month."

A team of Russian soldiers from Niuman River (now Bureya River, Russia) reached Hengggun River (now Ergun River, flowing through the border between Inner Monglolian Autonomous Region, China and Siberia, Russia). They joined forces with the Russian soldiers from Beihai (now Lake Baikal, in Siberia, Russia). They fought with the people of Feiyaka Nationality. The people of Feiyka Nationality had to move to Hezhou (now Aohan Qi, Inner Mongolian Autonomous Region, China). On 19 January 1684 Sabusu, the General of Heilongjiang, presented a memorial to Kangxi to report this fact and suggested to Kangxi Emperor, "We must wipe out these Russian soldiers or offer amnesty to them as soon as possible. Otherwise they will slaughter everyone there who is of Hezhe, Feiyaka and Qileer nationality. I am afraid that more Russian soldiers will come. I suggest that in April when ice melts two high ranking officers with 300 officers and soldiers should be sent there. They should take four cannons with them. The people of Feiyaka near Henggun River may be guides for these troops. When they reach the place where the Russian soldiers are, we should first offer amnesty to them. If they do not surrender, we shall annihilate them. If the Russian soldiers run away, we should pacify the people in this area." Kangxi agreed with his suggestion.

Sabusu presented a memorial to Kangxi, "On 11 January this year, Officer Eluoshun reached the place where the Russian soldiers were. He sent Yifan to persuade the Russians to surrender. 21 Russian soldiers headed by Mihailuo surrendered." Kangxi ordered to escort them to the capital and to deliver them to the Ministry of Revenue for settlement.

In May 1683 Commander Mala presented a memorial to Kangxi which read, "I went to the place where the Ewenki people live to collect information about the Russians from the local people. They told me that there are about 600 Russian soldiers in each of Yakesa and Nibuchu. They built houses in about 10 places from Ergun River to Yakesa. They till the land and grow crops to support themselves. They also hunt for martens to make valuable fur coats. This is the reason why they can occupy Yakesa and Nibuchu for so many years. Although the fields in the area of Nibuchu do not produce crops, the Russians take the tributes presented by the people of Ewenki Nationality. The Mongolians of Kalka Nationality and Baerhu Nationality sometimes drive their livestock to Nibuchu to trade. The Russians in Nibuchu use the fur of martens they catch to trade with the Mongolians for the livestock. In this way they can exist. We may send envoys to the King of Chechen Tribe of the Khalkha Mongolians to ask him to prohibit his people near Nibuchu from doing business with the Russians in Nibuchu. General Sabusu should send his troops to go towards Yakesa both on land and by Heilong River to show to the Russians that they are going to attack Yakesa. His troops should cut all the crops near Yakesa. Then the Russians will be in a difficult position. In that case we may send cavalrymen to suppress the Russians in Yakesa." Kangxi gave an instruction to the Ministry of Defense which read, "Mala suggests that if we cut all the crops grown by the Russians, then the Russians will be in a very difficult position. And Body Guard Guanbao reported to me that General Sabusu also thinks that it is a good strategy to cut the crops grown by the Russians. Then the Russians will not be able to sustain for long. Now I order Sabusu to send troops to go to Yakasa on land or both on land and on ships by Heilong River to cut all the crops grown by the Russians. If they go only on land, they should throw all the crops they cut into Heilong River. If they go both on land and on ships by Heilong River, they should put all the crops they cut into the ships and take them back on ships. Before the troops go, envoys should be sent to warn the Russians that they have occupied Yakesa and Nibuchu for many years and we have demanded them to leave many times; but they would not leave and accepted the run-aways from our side and they have looted and killed our people in the border area. Now our troops will go on land and by Heilong River to suppress the Russians, they should go back to Russia so as to save themselves. And we should also send envoys to King of Chechen Tribe of the Khalkha Mongolians to ask him to prohibit his people near Nibuchu from doing business with the Russians in Nibuchu."

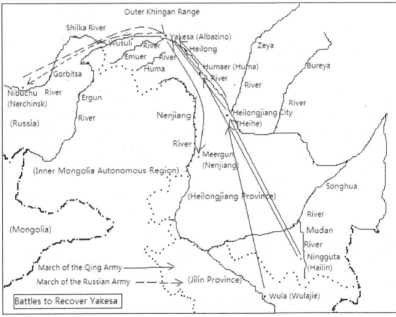

In April 1685 Kangxi sent Guanbao, his bodyguard, to Heilongjiang to convey his instructions to Commander Pengchun and General Sabusu, "Arms are a curse, and war is a dread thing. I rule over the whole realm with benevolence. I never like killings. Our troops are all very good fighters. They are equipped with good weapons. The Russians will not be able to resist our crack troops. They will surely surrender and hand over the land of Yakesa back to us. By that time you should not kill any of the Russians. You should send them back to Russia, their home place. Then they will disseminate my kindness to the people of Russia."

In May 1685, Commander Pengchun and General Sabusu commanded their troops to march to Yakesa on land and on ships by Heilong River. On 22 May they reached Yakesa. They followed Kangxi's instructions and sent an envoy with a letter to tell the Russians that Kangxi would not kill them and demanded the Russians to leave Yakesa and go back to Russia. But the Russians thought that the city of Yakesa was strong and they refused to leave. On 23 May the troops under Pengchun and Sabusu built camps on land and by Heilong River. At night 24 May they moved the cannons to the front of their camps. At dawn 25 May they started a fierce attack. The Russians in the city were all very scared. Elikeshe, the head of the Russian soldiers defending the city of Yakesa, found that they could not resist such fierce attack. He went to the troops under Pengchun and Sabusu to beg to surrender. Pengchun and Sabusu again told them that Kangxi was lenient to them and would not kill them. Elikeshe and all the officers and soldiers were all moved to tears. They all bowed in the direction of Beijing and paid their respects to Kangxi. Then Pengchun and Sabusu sent all the Russian soldiers and all the women and children back to Russia and they recovered Yakesa in accordance with the instructions of Kangxi.

When the victory was reported to Kangxi, he said, "Others thought that Yakesa was far away and it was very difficult to suppress the Russians there. But I made the decision to send troops to suppress them. Now Heaven has shown grace on us and we have recovered Yakesa. I am very happy about this." All the kings and officials came to express their congratulations. Kangxi said to them, "The strategy of governing the country is to bring long term peace and stability to the country. It seems that the battle against the Russians in Yakesa is a minor matter. But actually it is a very important act. The Russians invaded the areas of Heilong River and Songhua River for more than 30 years. The places they occupied are close to the place of origin of our ancestors. If we do not suppress them, I am afraid that the people in the border areas cannot live in peace. So after I assumed the reins of government, I began to pay attention to this matter. I sent officers to collect information about topography of those areas and the roads leading to them, and about the people who live in those areas. I also considered the proper ways of sending troops and transportation of food supplies to the troops. I made up my mind to order the troops to march forward to suppress the Russians. Now Yakesa has been recovered. I feel very happy. The most important thing to pacify the

Russians is to make them submitted. It is not necessary to give them heavy military blows. I sent my bodyguard Guanbao to tell Pengchun and Sabusu not to kill the Russians so as to show my benevolence to them; when they surrender, they should be sent back to Russia, their home place. I am very glad that Pengchun and Sabusu carried our all my instructions and recovered Yakesa."

After the 600 Russian soldiers headed by Elikeshe left, the troops under Pengchun and Sabusu destroyed the city of Yakesa. 45 households of the Russians soldiers who would not go back to Russia were brought to Shengjing (now Shenyang, Liaoning Province) and settled down there. The people of Ewenki Nationality and Dawoer Nationality who had been captured by the Russians were sent back to the places where they lived. The Khalkha Mongolians who were in Yakesa were sent back to their masters.

After the battle of Yakesa Emperor Kangxi ordered Sabusu to lead his troops to move to Meergen (now Nenjiang, Heilongjiang Province) and station there. They built a city there to prevent the Russians from coming back from Nibuchu (now Nerchinsk, Russia).

In January 1686 Sabusu sent Shuogese, an officer of the cavalrymen, with several cavalrymen to collect information about the Russians. They did not reach Yakesa because their horses were very tired. But they met with some local people. They told them that the Russians had come back and had built strongholds in Yakesa. Shuogese came back to Meergen and reported what they had heard to Sabusu. Then Sabusu reported this information to Kangxi and said that he would command his troops to attack Yakesa when the ice melted. Kangxi thought that the information about the Russians was based on what the soldiers had heard from the local people but not based on what they had seen with their own eyes. So he ordered Sabusu and Manpi, the Deputy Minister of Minority Affairs, to get credible information about the Russians. Then Sabusu and Manpi sent Wumubulindai, the deputy head of the tribe of Dawoer Nationality, with some people under him to Yakesa. They went to Yakesa and caught Ekesuomuguo, a Russian soldier. They interrogated him. He told them that last year Yifan, the head of the Russian troops in Nibuchu, ordered Elikeshe, the head of the Russian soldiers in Yakesa, who had been released and sent back to Russia by Pengchun and Sabusu, to lead 500 Russian soldiers to go back to Yakesa and build strongholds to occupy it. When he was asked how many months the food supplies they stored could support them, he told them that the food supplies were enough for them for two years. Then Manpi and Sabusu reported this reliable information to Kangxi. Kangxi thought that if the Russians in Yakesa were not suppressed as soon as possible, they would surely store much more food supplies and defend Yakesa resolutely; by that time it would very difficult to defeat them. He ordered Sabusu to have all the warships repaired and command the troops from Wula (now Wulajie, Jilin Province) and from Ningguta (now Hailin, Heilongjiang

Province) to march to Heilongjian City (now Heihe, Heilongjiang Province). When they reached Heilongjiang City, Sabusu ordered the troops from Shengjing (now Shenyang, Liaoning Province) to defend the city. He commanded 2,000 troops to march to Yakesa. Kangxi ordered Lin Xing Zhu to command 400 troops from Fujian Province who were equipped with rattan shields to go to attack the Russians in Yakesa.

3. The Treaty of Nibuchu (Nerchinsk)

In March 1688 Chahan Khan (Peter Alexeyevich, the emperor of Russia) sent Feiyueduoluo and some others as his envoys to a place by Selenga River (in Mongolia). He expected that the government of the Qing Dynasty would also sent envoys there to negotiate the boundary between Russia and China. Emperor Kangxi appointed Suoetu, Commander-in-chief of the Imperial Bodyguards, Tong Guo Gang, Kangxi's maternal uncle, Alani, a prime minister, Ma Qi, Minister of Justice, and Commander Mala to represent the government of the Qing Dynasty to negotiate with the Russians. He sent 800 soldiers to escort them.

On 2 May 1688 Kangxi said to Suoetu and the other representatives, "The Russians have invaded our border areas. Battles took place in the areas of Heilong River, Songhua River and Huma River. They have occupied Nibuchu and Yakesa. They accepted Gentemuer and other run-aways. Then our troops built strongholds in Heilongjiang City. We attacked Yakesa twice. Now we have laid siege to Yakesa. This is the reason why we are fighting with the Russians. The areas along Heilong River are the most important places. A ship may sail from Heilong River to Songhua River, then from Songhua River to Nenjiang River; it can sail further south to Mudan River. Then they can reach Wula, Ningguta, and places where the people of Sibe Nationality, Horqin Mongolians, Ewenki Nationality and Dawoer Nationality live. If they sail down the Heilong River, they can reach the sea. Ergun River, Bureya River and Zeya River all join Heilong River. Our people of Elunchun Nationality, Qileer Nationality, Bilaer Nationality, Hezhe Nationality and Feiyaka Nationality live on the left bank and the right bank of Heilong River. If we don't take back all these areas, the people in the border areas will not be able to live in peace. I think, Nibuchu, Yakesa, the upper reach and lower reach of Heilong River and all the rivers and streams which join with Heilong River are all our territory. They cannot be given to the Russians. We should demand the Russians to deliver Gentemuer and the other run-aways to us. If they follow our instructions, we shall return all their run-aways to them. Then we may negotiate with them and delimit the boundaries. We may allow them to come to do business. Otherwise you should stop negotiating with them and come back immediately." On that day Suoetu and the other representatives started their journey. Not long later, war broke out between the Khalkha Mongolians and Elute Mongolians in Mongolia. When the news of the war was reported to Kangxi, he sent his bodyguards Kuasai and Guanbao to catch up with Suoetu and the other representatives and ordered them to turn back to a place where the Qing troops were stationed. In accordance with the instruction of Kangxi, Suoetu wrote a letter to tell the Russian representative for the negotiation the reason why they could not get to the place for the negotiation. He sent Suoluoxi, an officer of the troops escorting them, to take the letter to the Russian representative. The Russian representative gave them a reply letter telling them that some Russians had been sent from Nibuchu to Beijing. Suoluoxi took the reply letter to Kangxi. Then Kangxi summoned Suoetu and the other representatives back to Beijing.

On 6 April 1689 the emperor of Russia sent Feiyaoduoluo and some others to Nibuchu as his representatives to negotiate the delimitation of the boundaries of Russia and China. Kangxi sent Suoetu and the other representatives to Nibuchu to negotiate with the representatives of the emperor of Russia. Before he left, Suoetu presented a memorial to Kangxi which read, "Nibuchu and Yakesa are a part of our territory. I suggest that Nibuchu should be the boundary. The places within Nibuchu belong to us." Kangxi said, "If we take Nibuchu as the boundary, the envoys and business men of Russia will have no place to stay. It will be difficult for them to do business with us. At the beginning of the negotiation, you may propose to take Nibuchu as the boundary. If the Russian representative request in real earnest to give Nibuchu to Russia, Ergun River may be the boundary."

Suoetu and the other representatives went to Nibuchu. They held meetings with Feiyaoduoluo and Elikexie, the representatives of Russia. The representatives of Russia argued that Nibuchu and Yakesa were the places opened up by the Russians and should belong to Russia. Suoetu told the representatives of Russia that Nibuchu was the living place of the people of Maoming'an Tribe of China and Yakesa was the home place of A'erbaxi, the head of the tribe of Dawoer Nationality; but these two places were illegally occupied by the Russians. He cited these facts to denounce the invasion acts of the Russians. Then he told the Russian negotiators that Kangxi had been very lenient to the captured Russian soldiers and would not kill any of them. Then Feiyaoduoluo and the other Russian negotiators cheered and were completely convinced. They spread out the maps and began to negotiate the delimitation of the boundaries. The Russian negotiators and the Chinese negotiators swore that the two countries would be in peace forever. Suoetu wrote a memorial to report the progress of the negotiation to Kangxi. Kangxi ordered the kings and officials in charge of government affairs to discuss the memorial presented by Suoetu. After discussion they wrote a memorial to Kangxi which read, "The Russians illegally occupied Yakesa and other places for more than thirty years. They looted and killed our people there. Your Majesty has been lenient to them and was not hardhearted to send a great army to annihilate them. Your Majesty just sent troops to station in places along Heilong River and waited for them to repent themselves. But the Russians insisted on their wrong doings. Then Your Majesty issued the order to attack Yakesa. Your Majesty ordered to release all the captured Russian soldiers. But not long later the Russians occupied Yakesa again and they built strongholds there. Your Majesty sent troops to lay siege to the city of Yakesa. The Russian troops were at the end of their resources. At this time the emperor of Russia sent envoys to ask for peace. Your Majesty issued an order to lift the siege. Your Majesty sent officials to convince the Russians by reasoning and justice and they were deeply grateful to Your Majesty. The officials should follow Your Majesty's instruction to delimit the boundaries. Boundary tablets should be set up in places along Gorbitsa River. Manchu characters, Chinese characters, Russian characters and Mongolian characters should be carved on the boundary tablets. Although the boundaries between Russia and China have been delimited, all the troops should still station in the places they have been sent. Troops should be sent to station in Moergen and along Heilong River." Then officials were sent to set up boundary tablets. On the tablets the following information was carved: "This is the tablet for the boundary delimited through negotiation between the representatives of Russia and the representatives of the Qing Dynasty."

The main points of the Treaty of Nibuchu (Nerchinsk) were: 1. Gorbitsa River (the upper reach of Shilka River) which flows into Heilong River from the north will be the boundary; the boundary is from the upper reach of this river to Outer Khingan Range to the sea; all the rivers and streams which flow into Heilong River in the south of the Outer Khingan Range belong to China; all the rivers and streams in the north of the Outer Khingan Range belong to Russia; 2. Ergun River which flows into Heilong River will be the boundary; the areas on the south bank of this river belong to China; the areas on the north bank belong to Russia; the houses of the Russians in the area of estuary of Meileerke River which is situated to the south bank of Ergun River should be moved to the north bank of Ergun River; 3. All the strongholds and houses built by the Russians in Yakesa should be destroyed; all the Russian people who live in Yakesa should go back to the places under the jurisdiction of the emperor of Russia taking all their belongings with them; 4. Hunters are not allowed to go across the boundary; if one or two hunters go across the boundary to hunt animals or commit crimes of stealing, they will be arrested and sent to the officials in charge of the place; they will be punished according to their crimes; if ten or fifteen hunters go across the boundary carrying weapons and if they kill or loot the local people, they will be arrested, after the incident has been reported to the emperor of Russia or China, they will be executed; amity should be maintained between Russia and China and it should not be affected by minor matters; conflicts should be avoided; 5. All the past events will not be discussed again; all the Chinese people living in Russia and all the Russian people living in China may stay in the place where they are and will not be sent back to China or Russia; 6. Since the treaty has been concluded, China and Russia will be friendly with each other forever; traders of either country holding passports are allowed to do their business in the other country; 7. After the conclusion of the treaty neither country should accept run-aways from the other country; any person of one country who runs away to the other country should be sent back to his country immediately.

SECTION SIX: EMPEROR KANGXI DEFEATS GALDAN, KHAN OF DZUNGAR KHANATE

1. Galdan Becomes Khan of the Dzungar Khanate

In the vast areas of Qinghai (now Qinghai Province) there lived the Mongolian people of Elute Tribe. Xining, the most important city of Qinghai, was 2,500 kilometers away from Beijing, the capital of the Qing Dynasty. Qinghai bordered Gansu Province in the east and the north; it bordered Western Region (now Xinjiang Uygur Autonomous Region) in the northwest and the west; it bordered Tibet (now Tibet Autonomous Region) in the west and the south; it bordered Sichuan (now Sichuan Province) in the south. It had an area of 720,000 square kilometers. It was divided into two parts: the left and the right. The left part: the distance from the east point Dongkeer Temple (in Huangyuan, Qinghai Province) to the west point Taolai River (now Tulai River, Qinghai Province) was 400 km; the distance from the south point Boluochongkeke River (now the upper reach of Huang Shui River, in the northeast part of Qinghai Province) to the north point Xilatala (now Wuwei, Gansu Province) was 200 km; the distance from the southeast point Lala Mountains (now Laji Mountains, in Guide, Qinghai Province) to the northwest point Ejina River (now Hei River, which flows from Gansu Province to Qinghai Province) was 400 km; the distance from the northeast point Yongchang (in Gansu Province) to the west point Bulongjier River (now Shule River, which flows from the northwest part of Gansu Province into the north part of Qinghai Province) was 1,500 km. The right part: the distance from the east point Dongkeer Temple to the west point Gasi Lake (now Gas Hure Lake, in the northwest part of Qinghai Province) was 1,250 km; the distance from the south point Zhangla Mountain (in Zhangla, in the north part of Sichuan Province) to the north point Boluochongkeke River was 750 km; the distance from the southeast point Daerji Mountains (in Lintan, in the southeast part of Gansu Province) to the northwest point Xiergalajin

River (now Dang River, in the northwest part of Gansu Province) was 1,000 km; the distance from northeast point Ketengkuteer (situated to the west of Xining, Qinghai Province) to the southwest point Muluwusu River (now Togtun River, in the southwest part of Qinghai Province) was 750 km.

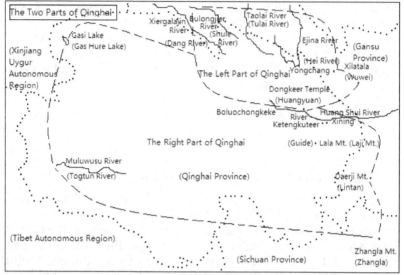

There were four subtribes in the Elute Tribe: 1. Heshuote Tribe, 2. Dzungar Tribe, 3. Duerbote Tribe, 4. Tuerhute Tribe. Each tribe had its tribe head. These four tribes were generally known as Elute. Apart from these four tribes, there was a small Mongolian tribe called Huite Tribe in Qinghai. At first Huite Tribe was subordinated to Duerbote Tribe. Later Tuerhute Tribe moved into the territory of Russia. Then Huite Tribe became one of the four tribes of Elute. These four tribes roved around in different pasturelands in Qinghai.

The ancestor of the Dzungar Tribe was Bohan, the grand tutor of the Northern Yuan Dynasty (1368–1388). Heduoheqin, Bohan's descendent of the seventh generation, was the ruler of Dzungar. He had eleven sons. They were: Chechen, Zhuotebabatuer, Bandali, Zhuoliketuheshuoqi, Wenchun, Sengge, Galdan, Bumu, Duoerjizabu, Pengsukedashi, and Gaerma.

Galdan, the seventh son of Heduoheqin, was sent to Tibet to be a lama when he was young. He was a disciple of the 5th Dalai Lama. He became a good friend of Sangye Gyatso, Diba (the supreme chief executive) of Tibet.

In 1653 Heduoheqin, the ruler of Dzungar, died. Before he died, he appointed Sengge, his sixth son, as his successor. In 1671 Chechen, the eldest son of Heduoheqin, and Zhuotebabatuer, the second son of Heduoheqin, started a surprise attack on Sengge and killed him. When Galdan got this information, he came back from Tibet.

He commanded the troops formerly under Sengge to fight with the troops under Chenchen and Zhuotebabatuer. In a battle he defeated the troops under Chechen and Zhuotebabatuer and killed Chechen. Zhuotebabatuer ran away with the troops and people of his tribe. Very soon Galdan unified all the tribes of Dzungar. He claimed that the Dalai Lama had made him Boshuoketu Khan of Dzungar Khanate.

In the vast areas north to the Gobi Desert (in the south part of Mongolia) there lived the Khalkha Mongolians. In the area west of Hentiyn Mountains (in the mid-east part of Mongolia), east of Ongi River (in the mid-west part of Mongolia), north of the Gobi Desert, south of Chikoy River (flowing through the border between Russia and Mongolia), there lived the people of Tuxietu Khan Tribe of Khalkha Mongolians. In 1673 Chahunduoerji succeeded his father Gunbu as the head of Tuxietu Khan Tribe.

In the west part of what is now Mongolia there lived the people of Zasaketu Khan Tribe of Khalkha Mongolians. In 1670 Chenggun succeeded his brother Wangshuke as the head of Zasaketu Khan Tribe.

In 1684 Elinqin, a nobleman in Zasaketu Khan Tribe, held a rebellion. Chenggun defeated him. Elinqin and his subordinates ran away to Tuxietu Khan Tribe. Chenggun demanded Chahunduoerji, the head of Tuxietu Khan Tribe, to hand over Elinqin and the others to him. But Chahunduoerji refused to do so. From then on there were quarrels between Chenggun and Chahunduoerji. Kangxi sent Aqitugelong to mediate them. Kangxi also asked the Dalai Lama to sent envoys to carry out the mediation. At that time Chenggun died. Galdan planned to attack Khalkha. He induced Shala, Chenggun's son, to attack Chahunduoerji. Shala commanded his troops to Guerbanhegeer (a place in Altay Mountains, in the west part of Mongolia) to join forces with Galdan's army. Chahunduoerji was very angry. He commanded his army to fight with Shala's army and defeated them. He ran after Shala and killed him. In 1688 Galdan commanded an army of 30,000 men to attack Khalkha. Duoerjizabu, Galdan's younger brother, commanded some troops to loot the Khalkha Tribes headed by Putukeshen and Baerdan. He forced the people of these tribes to go with him taking the domestic animals of the people. Chahunduoerji led some troops to run after Duoerjizabu and killed him. He got back all the people and the domestic animals. Then Galdan divided his troops into three routes. He marched his troops from the area of Altay Mountains (in the west part of Mongolia) eastward into the territory of the Khalkha Mongolians claiming that he was determined to revenge his younger brother. Chahunduoerji and Luobuzanggunbu, the head of the Khalkha Tribe in Xihai (now Qinghai Lake, Qinghai Province), marched their troops to the place where Galdan's troops were stationed.

On their way they met with Xiletu, the envoy sent by the Dalai Lama. The envoy conveyed Kangxi's instruction that they should make peace with Galdan. During the peace talk, Zebutsundanba Khutukhtu was very disrespectful to Xiletu. Anyway the Khalkha Mongolians retreated to a place in the south of Hentiyn Mountains. Galdan's army marched to Hentiyn Moutains and attacked the Khalkha tribes. Gaerdan, the son of Chahunduoerji, fought with Galdan's troops, but was defeated. He had a very narrow escape. Danjinwenbu, Galdan's nephew, commanded a great army to take Kharkhorin (in Övökhangai Province, in the south part of Mongolia) where Erdene Zuu monastery was. Zebutsundanba Khutukhtu, the spiritual head of Tibetan Buddhism in Mongolia, sent an envoy to Kangxi asking him for help. In June 1688 Galdan attacked the people in Kharhkorin. Chahunduoerji commanded some troops to resist Galdan's army but was defeated. The people of Tuxietu Khan Tribe did not know whether Chahunduoerji still survived or not. Zebutsundanba Khutukhtu, taking Chahunduoerji's wife and children, and the other people ran away at night. All the people of Khalkha Khanate ran away southward, leaving all their yurts, their prosperities, horses, camels, cows and sheep behind. They rushed into the border area of Sonid (now Sonid Youqi and Sonid Zuoqi, Inner Mongolia Autonomous Region, China). Among them there were several heads of the subtribes of Khalkha Mongolians. The generals and officers of the Qing army defending the border area refused to let them come into the Chinese side. The heads of the Khalkha Mongolian Tribes said, "Our home places have been attacked by Galdan's army. We have no place to go but have to come to the border area. We are sure that when your emperor hears about this, he will have pity on us." The Qing troops tried to drive them away but they all refused to leave. Zebutsundanba Khutukhtu also led the people to the border area and stayed there. When this was reported to Kangxi, he said to Tong Guo Wei, the Commander-in-chief of the Imperial Bodyguards, and the other officials, "The officials of government affairs should discuss and make a decision whether we should drive away the people of Khalkha Mongolians who have been hunted down by the troops under Galdan and have come to our border areas or we should expend the area of the defense of the border area to include the places where the Khalkha Mongolians are staying. This is an important matter." Not long later the officials of government affairs reported the results of their discussion to Kangxi which read, "The Khalkha Mongolians have come in a very difficult situation. It would be unkind if we drive them away. But if they stay there for a long time, they would ruin the pasturelands. We suggest that we should let them stay there for a month. After that we shall make a decision as to how to settle the people of the Khalkha Mongolians." Emperor Kangxi agreed with their suggestion.

In July 1688 Haisandai, an official of the Hanlin Academy, went to the place where Zebutsundanba Khutukhtu was staying. On his way he met some officials of Elute Mongolians. They took a memorial written by Galdan to Kangxi. The memorial read, "Zebutsundanba Khutukhtu and Tuxietu Khan have gone against the teachings of the Dalai Lama. They were disrespectful to Xiletu, the envoy sent by the Dalai Lama. I told them that we should follow the rules of etiquette and make peace. But they disagreed with me. They led a great army to attack me. With the spiritual support by the Dalai Lama, I defeated them and ruined the places where they live. These two persons will not be accepted by anyone. They will have no place to go. And wherever they go, they will not be accepted."

Galdan asked Haisandai to tell Kangxi that if Zebutrundanba Khutukhtu went to the territory of the Qing Dynasty for protection, he should be refused to enter the border; or the officers of the Qing army defending the border area should arrest him and hand him over to Galdan. When Galdan's memorial was presented to Kangxi, he asked the kings and officials in charge of government affairs to discuss this matter. Very soon they reported the results of their discussion as follows, "Your Majesty regards all the states in the world as an integral whole. When the ruler of a state who has presented tributes to Your Majesty has come for protection in great difficult situation, he should be accepted and protected. Zebutrundanba Khutukhtu has come into our border area after he was defeated. We will certainly not arrest him and hand him over to Galdan. We should send an envoy to tell this to Galdan."

Kangxi sent Anada, a high ranking officer of the imperial bodyguard army, Shangnanduoerji, a lama, Xiola, Deputy Minister of Revenue, Langmuzhuhu, the Deputy Minister of Works, as his envoys to take Kangxi's imperial order to Galdan. Kangxi's imperial order read, "I rule over the whole world. I shall take good care of all the people in this world. I do my best to let them enjoy peace and tranquility and make sure that they will not suffer from war and the members of their families will not be separated from one another. The people of different countries should live in harmony. Each group of people has their proper place to live. I hear that recently the Elute Mongolians under you and the Khalkha Mongolians become enemies and are now at war. I considered that the Elute Mongolians and the Khalkha Mongolians were friendly with each other before. I am afraid that one of the two tribes will become extinct. Considering that the Dalai Lama takes care of all the people, I asked him to send envoys to mediate between the two sides. The Dalai Lama sent Qijiketalaikanbu. I sent Aqituzhuoerji and Baili to convey my order that the two sides should make peace. I have also sent envoys to take my order to Tuxietu Khan of the Khalkha Mongolians demanding him to make peace with you. Now Haisandai have come back to report to me and I know that you have reached the place where the Khalkha Mongolians live. Haisandai was not the envoy sent by me. He was sent by Alani, the minister in charge of the negotiations with the Russians. So he is not familiar with the conflicts between you and the Khalkha Mongolians. Both the people of the Elute Mongolians and the people of Khalkha Mongolians believe in Buddhism. The Dalai Lama has always cares about all the people. He does his best to let the people of different tribes to live in harmony so that no tribes would be perished. So he sent envoys to travel a long way to ask you to make peace. I still don't know the reason why the two sides are at war. Now I will send envoys to take my order to you. You should tell him why the two sides are fighting with each other. My envoys and the envoys sent by the Dalai Lama will follow the teachings of Buddhism to help the two sides of you to make peace."

In July 1688 Galdan attacked the subtribes of the Khalkha Mongolians and his army reached the area of Hulun Buir (in the northeast part of Inner Mongolian Autonomous Region, China). When this information was reported to Kangxi, he sent Jiertabu, a minister, Commander Bahai and Commander Tongbao to Horqin area (now Horqin Youyi Qianqi, Horqin Youyi Zhongqi, Inner Mongolian Autonomous Region) from Beijing to convey his order to Shalu, Tuxietu Prince of Horqin Mongolians, and Bandi, Daerhan Prince of Horqin Mongolians, that they should command 10,000 soldiers under them to prepare to resist Galdan's army. He ordered Mutai, the Deputy Commander-in-chief of the army stationed in Shengjing (now Shenyang, Liaoning Province), to command 1,000 troops to go the area of Horqin to prepare to resist the army under Galdan.

On 27 July 1688 Ananda, an officer of the Imperial Bodyguards, was sent with some officers to gather information about the movement of Galdan's army. They reached the northern bank of Herten River (a river which flowed from the east part of Mongolia to the northeast part of Inner Mongolian Autonomous Region, China). He found out that Galdan had commanded his army to retreat from Tuoerhui, a place on the north bank of Herten River, because the envoys sent by the Dalai Lama had come. He also got the information that Galdan had said to the envoys, "If I make peace with Tuxietu Khan, who would be responsible for the death of my brother Duoerjizabu? If I carry out the expedition for five more years, I will surely destroy Khalkha, and I will surely capture Zebutrundanba." He reported this information to the Ministry of Minority Affairs. The Minister of Minority Affairs suggested to Kangxi, "Now Galdan has retreated to Tula. His purpose is to look for Tuxietu Khan. We should send envoys to take an order of Your Majesty demanding them to stop fighting to Galdan before he fights with Tuxietu Khan." Kangxi granted an imperial order to Minister Alani to let the Horqin Mongolian troops withdraw.

On 3 August 1688 the army under Chahunduoerji, the head of Tuxietu Khan Tribe, and the army under Galdan met in Eluohuinuoer (a place in the middle part of Mongolia). A great battle broke out. The two armies fought with each other for three days. The troops under Galdan started a surprise attack on the camps of the army of the Khalkha troops at night. All the heads of the Khalkha tribes ran away in all directions. Chahunduoerji had no more power to fight any more. He went across the Gobi Desert and to the place where Zebutrundanba was staying. Ananda, the officer of the Imperial Bodyguards, reported all this to Kangxi. Kangxi said to Tong Guo Wei, the Commander-in-chief of the Imperial Bodyguards, Feiyanggu, Commander-in-chief of the Imperial Bodyguards, Mingzhu, Commander of the Imperial Bodyguards, and Minister Alani, "Now the Khalkha Mongolians and the Elute Mongolians are fighting with each other. We have to strengthen the defense of our border areas. The cavalrymen under the eight banners, the vanguard troops under the five banners will go to the strategic places outside Zhangjiakou and station there. They should get ready to be transferred to other places. The heads of the Mongolian tribes in Sonid Zuoqi and Sonid Youqi, Sizi Tribes in Tumd Youqi should send 2,000 troops. King Zamusa will be the commander of these troops; King Buomubuo will be the deputy commander. The heads of the Mongolians tribes in Darhan Qi, Muminggan Qi, Urad Qianqi, Urad Zhongqi and Urad Houqi should send 2,000 troops. These troops should be put under the command of Nuonei, the King of Darhan. The heads of the Mongolian tribes in Ordos Qi should send 2,000 troops. They will be put under the command of King Songalabu. These troops should be arranged in the strategic places along the border areas. The heads of the two Mongolian Tribes in Guihua should send 1,000 troops to station in the city of Guihua. They should be put under the command of Commander Alana."

In late August 1688 Galdan commanded his army in three routes to march to the border areas of the Qing Dynasty. These three routes of Galdan's army would meet in Aibihankalaebo (a place in Sonid Youqi, Inner Mongolian Autonomous Region, China). When this information was reported to Kangxi, he ordered to send 200 vanguard troops of the eight banners in Beijing, 1,000 soldiers who carried guns with 8 cannons to go to the border area within 5 days. He also ordered Bao Jing, the Commander-in-chief of the army stationed in Datong (in the north part of Shanxi Province), and Lan Li, the Commander-in-chief of the army stationed in Xuanfu (now Xuanhua, in the northwest part of Hebei Province), each to command 1,000 crack troops to Guihua (now Hohhot, Inner Mongolian Autonomous Region, China). Their troops should station in Guihua and get well preparation to resist Galdan's army. But on 3 September Kangxi ordered that the troops in Beijing and the troops in Datong and Xuanfu should stop going to the border areas and Guihua for the time being because Galdan had treated the envoys sent by Kangxi very politely and he had sent envoys to pay respects to Kangxi.

In September 1688 twenty-eight tribe heads of the Khalkha Mongolian Tribes led the people under them to enter the border areas and asked the officers of the Qing army to accept their surrender. When this was reported to Kangxi, he issued the order that the Khalkha Mongolians who had come to surrender should be allowed to rove around within the border areas for pasturelands. Then Chahunduoerji, the head of Tuxietu Khan Tribe, and his younger brother Xilibatuer led the Mongolian people under them to go into the border areas to beg the officers of the Qing army defending the border areas to accept their surrender. Zebutrundanba Khutukhtu, the spiritual leader of the Khalkha Mongolians, also led his followers to go into the border areas to beg the officers to accept their surrender. The Ministry of Minority Affairs reported all these to Kangxi. Kangxi ordered the kings and the officials of the government affairs to discuss this matter. They suggested, "The Elute Mongolians and the Khalkha Mongolians have always submitted to Your Majesty. They have paid tributes for many years. Now they have become enemies and fought against each other. The Khalkha Mongolians have been defeated by the Elute Mongolians. Chahunduoerji and Zebutrundanba Khutukhtu have sincerely asked Your Majesty to accept their surrender. We suggest that we should accept their surrender, let them stay within the border areas and provide for them. We suggest that Your Majesty should send Minister Alani to the border area to convey Your Majesty's intention to accept their surrender." Kangxi agreed with their suggestion and sent Minister Alani to the border area to accept their surrender.

Galdan sent envoys to pay tributes and pay respects to the Emperor. They begged Kangxi to allow them to carry out commercial activities in China as before. Kangxi ordered the kings and officials of the government affairs to discuss this matter. They suggested, "Galdan has expressed his sincere respect to Your Majesty and has paid tributes. He has asked Your Majesty to allow him to carry out commercial activities in China. Envoys should be sent to convey Your Majesty's permission to Galdan. But now the Khalkha Mongolians have rushed into our border areas. Your Majesty has sent Minister Alani to the border areas to arrange the settlement of the Khalkha Mongolians. We suggest that we may discuss later as to what to say to Galdan after Minister Alani has come back from the border areas." Kangxi agreed with their suggestions.

On 23 November 1688 Ananda, the officer of the Imperial Bodyguards, presented a memorial to Kangxi which read, "Galdan says, 'The people of the Khalkha Mongolians are not my enemies. But Chahunduoerji and Zebutrundanba Khutukhtu killed Shala, the head of Zasaketu Khan Tribe. They invaded my territory and looted my people. They killed my younger brother Duoerjizabu. They have started the war. I will not tolerate them anymore.' I asked Shangnanduoerji, the envoy sent by the Dalai Lama, to persuade him to give up the hatred. But Galdan said, 'I am very glad that you try to persuade me with the rules of etiquette. I don't mean to ignore the teachings of the Chinese Emperor and the Dalai Lama's rule of etiquette.' And Galdan sent an envoy to talk about the matter of paying tributes and commercial activities. Galdan says, 'We Elute Mongolians have always paid tributes and carried out commercial activities in China. But now we are not able to enter China. My people suffer a lot from this. I hope we will be allowed to do business in China as before.' He is now waiting for Your Majesty's decision." After Kangxi had read the memorial, he ordered the kings and officials of the government affairs to discuss this matter. Then they presented the results of their discussion to Kangxi which read, "Your Majesty cares about the two states and does not discriminate against anyone of them. Now Chahunduoerji and Zebutrundanba Khutukhtu went against the agreements of the peace talk, killed Shala, the head of Zasaketu Khan Tribe, invaded the territory of the Elute Mongolians, and killed Galdan's younger brother Duoerjizabu. They have really committed these offenses. We suggest that Your Majesty should send an envoy to ask the Dalai Lama to send a lama as his envoy to go with the officials sent by Your Majesty to hold a meeting with Galdan and Chahunduoerji and Zebutrundanba Khutukhtu. We should ask Chahunduoerji and Zebutrundanba Khutukhtu to admit all the offenses they have committed. Then we may make these two hostile states friendly forever. But before we send out the order, we should tell our plan to Chahunduoerji and Zebutrundanba Khutukhtu. If they agree with our plan and are willing to do what they should in the meeting of peace making, we may hold the meeting next year. If Chahunduoerji and Zebutrundanba Khutukhtu are not willing to do that, we may discuss this matter later. As for the matter that Galdan asked permission to carry out commercial activities in China, it will be discussed later." Kangxi agreed with their suggestion.

The Emperor sent an envoy to ask Chahunduoerji, the head of Khalkha Tuxietu Khan Tribe, whether he would take part in the peace talk with Galdan. Chahunduoerji presented a memorial to Kangxi to express that he found it difficult for him to take part in the peace talk with Galdan. After Kangxi read his memorial, he said to the kings and officials of the government affairs, "I am now ruling over the people of the world. I provide for the people in desperate conditions, let the people who are going to be extinct survive, let the people who are separated from one another come together, and make those people who are at war to live in harmony. I hope that all the people will live happily. Chahunduoerji and Zebutrundanba Khutukhtu went against the agreements of the peace talk, killed Shala, the head of Zasaketu Khan Tribe, invaded the territory of the Elute Mongolians, and killed Galdan's younger brother Duoerjizabu. Now they have been defeated by Galdan and rushed into our border areas and asked us to accept their surrender. I consider that they have paid tributes to us for many years and the State of Khalkha has been listed as a vassal state. So I have accepted their surrender and let them stay in our border areas. Now the people under them have run short of food and live in great difficulty, I have ordered to provide food for them. Now Chahunduoerji and Zebutrundanba Khutukhtu find it difficult for them to take part in the peace talk. I have accepted their surrender and have provided for them. I am not hardhearted enough to force them to take part in the peace talk. Now we should list all the offenses they have committed and send an envoy to take the list to Galdan. We should also send an envoy to ask the Dalai Lama to send an envoy to persuade Galdan to give up the hatred. Then this case can be closed."

On 9 December 1688 Shanbalingkanbu, the envoy sent by the Dalai Lama, went to the palace in Beijing to pay respects to the Emperor. He said to Kangxi secretly, "Before I set out for my journey, I went to the house where the Dalai Lama lives. But I did not see him. Sangya Gyatso went out and conveyed the Dalai Lama's words to me, 'You should ask the emperor of the Qing Dynasty to arrest Chahunduoerji and Zebutrundanba Khutukhtu and hand them over to Galdan. It will be beneficial to all the people. I will guarantee the safety of the lives of these two persons.'" (Actually by that time, the 5th Dalai Lama, had already died. Sangya Gyatso, Diba (the supreme chief executive) of Tibet, kept this secretly and did not declare the death of the Dalai Lama.) Then Emperor Kangxi sent envoys to the Dalai Lama with a letter which read, "I am ruling over all the people in the world. I will do my best to keep all the people living in harmony and to make sure that those people who are at war against each other will stop fighting and live peacefully. I will provide protection to anyone who has come to me when he is at the end of his resources. I will not discriminate against any group of people.

"You, Dalai Lama, believe in Buddhism and offer salvation to all the people. We cherish the same purpose. The State of Elute and the State of Khalkha both pay tribute to me. The people of both of the two states believe in Buddhism. When these two states were at war, both of us tried to persuade them to stop fighting and make peace. We sent envoys again and again. You and I knew that if the two states fought against each other, one of them would be defeated and lose its territory. You and I did our best to persuade them to stop fighting. But later they did not follow our advice and started war against each other. The State of Khalkha was defeated and the people were desperate. I accepted them and settled them in the border areas. I provided food. I think you would do the same if they had come to you for help. Now your envoy Shanbalingkanbu conveyed to me your intention that we should arrest Chahunduoerji and Zebutrundanba Khutukhtu and hand them over to Galdan, and you would guarantee their safety. That means you are partial to Galdan. Do you still hope that the State of Elute and the State of Khalkha will become friendly with each other again? The original intention of both you and me was not to be partial to any of the two sides. This is the reason why I have sent envoys again and again to persuade them to stop fighting with each other. Till today I still hope that they will make peace. Now I have sent Minister Alani to Galdan. He reports that Galdan was defeated by his nephew Tsewang Rabtan. His subbodinates have run away.

He is now in a very difficult situation. Since you often send envoys to Galdan, I suppose you already know this. If he comes to me for help, I will accept him and provide for him. I will certainly not arrest him and hand him over to his enemy. The Dalai Lama's purpose is to save all the people in the world; he will certainly not hand over anyone to his enemy. I suspect that the words conveyed by Shanbalingkanbu are not words said by the Dalai Lama. If these words were said by the Dalai Lama, he should have written them in a memorial. I have doubts about this. I will send envoys to take my letter to you. Please answer my questions in writing."

Tsewang Rabtan was the son of Sengge who had been the ruler of Dzungar from 1653 to 1671 and was murdered by his two brothers. He was Galdan's nephew. When his father was murdered, Tsewang Rabtan was still young. So he depended on his uncle Galdan. When he grew older, he found that Galdan had maltreated his nephews and had the intention to kill him. So in winter 1688 Tsewang Rabtan led all the people who had been under his father to leave Galdan and ran away to Boluotala (now Bole, in the northwest part of Xinjiang Uygur Autonomous Region). The heads of other subtribes of Dorbod Tribe followed Tsewang Rabtan to the area of what is now Xinjiang Uygur Autonomous Region. They roved in the area of Ertis River (in the northwest part of Xinjiang Uygur Autonomous Region). Galdan commanded troops and went after Tsewang Rabtan's forces, but he was defeated.

2. Emperor Kangxi's First Expedition against Galdan

News came that the army under Galdan started an offensive in the area where the Khalkha Mongolians lived. In December 1688 Emperor Kangxi ordered Wenda, the Deputy Minister of Minority Affairs, to go the place where the Khalkha people lived to collect information about Galdan. On 5 December 1688 they reached a river in the northeast part of Mongolia. They found that there were troops under Galdan. Wenda sent Shangnanduoerji to go back to report this information to Kangxi.

On 3 May 1690 Galdan commanded his army to cross Uldz River (a river in the northeast part of Mongolia). There were 30,000 men in Galdan's army. They were going to start an attack on the Khalkha Mongolians. Galdan sent an envoy to Nibuchu (now Nerchinsk, Russia) to ask the commander of the Russian army in Nibuchu to send Russian soldiers to join forces with him to attack the Khalkha Mongolians. When this information was reported to Kangxi, he ordered to send 2,000 soldiers from Horqin Youyi Qianqi and Horqin Youyi Zhongqi (in the east part of Inner Mongolian Autonomous Region, China) to Minister Alani who stationed his troops by Taolai River (now Tao'er River, in the east part of Inner Mongolian Autonomous Region, China). He ordered Shalu, Prince of Tuxietu, to command the Horqin troops to Taolai River as soon as possible. He also put 200 Manchu Vanguard troops under the Eight Banners under the command of Shalu; he ordered Zashi, the Prefecture King of Kalaqinduleng, to command 500 soldiers; he ordered Biligundalai, the Prefecture King of Duleng, to command 400 soldiers from Ongniud Qi (in the southeast of Inner Mongolian Autonomous Region, China), and Alabutan to command 400 soldiers from Bairin Qi (in the southeast part of Inner Mongolian Autonomous Region, China), all of them should go to the army under Minister Alani. He ordered Deputy Commander-in-chief Gaerma and Luo Man Se to command 200 soldiers with cannons to go there.

When Kangxi got the information that Galdan would ask the commander of the Russian army to send Russian soldiers to help him, he said to Jiliguli and Yifaniqi, the Russian Envoys who were in Beijing, "There was an internal disorder in the ruling classes of Dzungar Khanate. Galdan was defeat by his nephew Tsewang Rabudan. He could not go back to Dzungar Khanate and had to move to our territory. Now he said that he would join forces with your troops to attack Khalkha. The Khalkha Mongolians have come over to my dynasty. If you follow Galdan's words, you will go against your pledge and start war against us again. You should ride quickly to tell Yifan, the Commander-in-chief of the Russian army in Nibuchu, not to send Russian troops to help Galdan." Jiliguli and Yifaniqi rode very quickly to Nibuchu to convey Kangxi's words to Yifan.

In May 1690 Galdan's army pushed forward from Uldz River. Kangxi urged the Manchu troops under the Eight Banners to go to Taolai River where Minister Alani and his troops were taking cannons with them. He ordered Alanda to command the troops carrying cannons, and all the troops from Horqin Qi, Balin Qin and Ongniud Qi to hurry to Minister Alani's army.

In June 1690 Galdan commanded his army to cross Kerulen River (a river in the southeast part of Mongolia) and stationed his troops in a place to the south of the river. His army moved eastward along Kerulen River into the area of Hulun Buir (in the northeast part of Inner Mongolian Autonomous Region, China), then moved southward along Orchun River (a river in the area of Hulun Buir, Inner Mongolian Autonomous Region, China) to Khalkha River (a river in the border between Mongolia and China) into the border area of China. When this information was reported to the Emperor, he urged King Shajin to command all the Mongolian troops sent from Horqin Youyi Qianqi and Horqin Youyi Zhongqi to go forward to resist the troops under Galdan. He sent Tong Guo Gang and Commander Nuomai to command the troops of fireguns to go to the border area.

On 22 June 1690 Kangxi said to the officials of the Ministry of War, "Galdan has entered our border areas in pursuit of the Khalkha Mongolians. I will personally command the expedition against Galdan. The kings and princes who will go with me will march out of Xifengkou Pass. The troops under Gongsunu will go with me. Now I order that the kings should march their troops first. We must send an envoy to inform this to Minister Alani. The kings and officials of the government affairs should discuss and decide the dates of our departure." After discussion, the kings and officials of government affairs suggested to Kangxi that the troops under the kings and princes should set out on 4 July and Kangxi should set out on 6 July. When their suggestion was reported to Kangxi, Kangxi decided that the troops under the commanders should set out on 1 July; the troops under the kings should set out on 4 July; and Kangxi would set out on 6 July.

On 14 June the troops under Galdan reached a place called Wulanhada by the Ulgain River (situated to the west of Ulanhot, in the east part of Inner Mongolian Autonomous Region, China). They looted the Khalkha Mongolians there. Erdeni Bomubu, the spiritual leader of Buddhism in the area of Ujinqi (now Dong Ujinqi and Xi Ujinqi, in the east part of Inner Mongolian Autonomous Region, China), sent an envoy to see Galdan. Galdan said to the envoy, "I have come to attack my enemy Khalkha Mongolians. I dare not invade the territory of China. I hear that Minister Alani has commanded an army to march northward. Why? Where are Zebutsundanba Khutukhtu, Tuxietu Khan and Chechen Khan?" On 24 June Erdeni Bomubu reported this to Kangxi. Kangxi decided to increase the number of soldiers in the different routes of the troops and urged them to get ready to set out for the border areas.

Kangxi was about to set out for the expedition against Galdan. He sent an envoy to take an imperial order to Galdan which read, "I am ruling over all the people in the world and taking care of all the states in this world. All I hope is to let all the people live in their own places and they can live in harmony. Arms are a curse, and war is a dread thing. The hatred among peoples would last forever. This is not good. So I sent Minister Alani and others to persuade you to stop the war between the Elute Mongolians and the Khalkha Mongolians. You stopped the war. But now you have commanded a great army to attack the Khalkha Mongolians again. So I sent Minister Alani to lead some troops to prepare for any unexpected disturbance. Now you have entered my border area and looted the people in Ujinqi. You have gone against your own pledge to make peace. Now that you have entered my border areas, I will lead the kings, princes and heads of the tribes with great armies to fight against you."

At that time, Galdan's army marched along Khalkha River. They caught up with Kundulun Boshuoketu, the head of Saiyinnuoyan Tribe of the Khalkha Mongolians. Kundulun's troops could not resist the attack by Galdan's troops. After a battle, Kundulun's troops were defeated and he had a narrow escape. Minister Alani got the information that Galdan had stationed his troops by Suoyueerji Mountain (situated to the northeast of Dong Ujimqin Qi, Inner Mongolian Autonomous Region, China). He commanded his troops to go there intending to start a surprise attack on Galdan's troops at night. But when his troops reached there, he found that Galdan and his troops had left for Ulgain River. He sent an envoy to report this to Kangxi. Kangxi ordered him to follow Galdan's troops and report the information of the movement of Galdan's troops to him. And he ordered Alani not to fight with Galdan's troops before the troops commanded by Ehena arrived.

Galdan's troops moved 20,000 men slowly along the Ulgain River, forcing the men and women of the people of Ujinqi and their livestock to go with them. When Minister Alani got this information, he decided to start a surprise attack on Galdan's troops at night. In the early morning of 21 June his troops reached the camps of Galdan's troops by Ulgain River. He ordered 200 Zasake Mongolian soldiers to attack the enemy position and 500 Khalkha soldiers to go forward to get back the Khalkha women and children who had been forced to go with Galdan's troops. But after they had got back the Khalkha women and children, the Zasake Mongolian soldiers and the Khalkha soldiers began to fight with each other for the women and children. There was a great confusion in Alani's battle formation. Galdan's troops were divided into two wings. Alani ordered his troops to march forward. Galdan's soldiers fired fireguns. Alani's troops had to retreat. Then he ordered the Khalkha soldiers to attack the enemy positions. They were afraid of the fireguns of Galdan's troops and they refused to go forward and they retreated. Galdan's troops came in two wings to attack Alani's troops. There were no soldiers carrying fireguns in Alani's troops. They could not resist the attack by Galdan's troops. So Alani had to retreat to Eerzheyito, a place in Dong Ujimqin Qi, to wait for the main force to come. When Alani reported his defeat to Emperor Kangxi, he was very angry. He dismissed Alani from his post of Minister of Minority Affairs but still allowed him to command the troops.

In late June 1690 Galdan's army had reached the area of Xi Ujimqin Qi. On 2 July Kangxi appointed Fuquan, Prince Yu, (who was Kangxi's elder brother), as Grand General of Fuyuan (Fuyuan means "Pacification of the Faraway Places"); he appointed Yunzhi, his eldest son, as the Deputy Grand General. He ordered them to lead a great army to march out of the Great Wall from Gubeikou (situated in the north of Miyun, Beijing). He appointed Changning, Prince Gong, as Grand General of Anbei (Anbei means "Pacification of the North"); he appointed Yabu, Prince Jian, and Eza, Duoluoxin Prefecture King, as Deputy Grand Generals. He ordered them to command a great army to march out of the Great Wall from Xifengkou (situated in the north part of Qianxi, Hebei Province). Tong Guo Gang, Tong Guo Wei, Suoetu, Ming Zhu, Amida, Peng Chun and Tumai would go with the army as advisers.

On 14 July Kangxi set out for the border area. At night that day, he reached Niulanshan (in the north part of Shunyi District, Beijing). On 16 July he reached Gubeikou. On 17 July he reached Gulufuerjianjiahunga Mountain (a place outside the Great Wall). He ordered Jieshu, Prince of Kang, to command a great army to join forces with the army under Fuquan in Bairin (now Bairin Youqi, Inner Mongolian Autonomous Region, China). On 20 July Kangxi reached Boluohe Village (in Longhua, Hebei Province). On 22 July Kangxi fell ill. He had a fever and could not fall asleep. In the early morning of 23 July all the officials and bodyguards knelt down before Kangxi's bed asking him to go back to Beijing. Emperor Kamgxi agreed with them. On that day he started his journey back to Beijing. He issued an instruction to Fuquan which read, "You are getting closer and closer to the enemy. You should send out scouts to collect information of the movement of the enemy. You should do your best to delay the action taken by Galdan so as to wait for the troops sent from Shengjing and the Mongolian troops from Wula and Horqin."

On 29 July Fuquan got the information that Galdan's troops were stationed in Ulan Butung (situated in the southwest of Hexigten Qi, Inner Mongolian Autonomous Region, China) which was only 350 kilometers away from Beijing. He commanded his troops to march there in early morning of 1 August. At noon that day they could see Galdan's troops. Galdan's troops were in the bushes on the bank of a river. About 10,000 camels crouched on the ground forming a protection line for Galdan's troops. At three o'clock in the afternoon the battle began. The Qing troops under Fuquan fired cannons and fireguns. The cannon balls and bullets of the fireguns killed many camels and Galdan's soldiers. Galdan's troops fired back. Tong Guo Gang commanded his troops to attack the defense line of the enemy. But unfortunately he was killed in battle. The attack on the right wing was not successful. The troops could not get across the mud of the river bank. They had to turn back. In the evening the left wing of Fuquan's army broke into the enemy formation, defeated the enemy and killed many enemy soldiers. Fuquan wanted to carry on the momentum of the victory on the left wing and kill all the enemy troops. But it was already very late and dark. So he ordered the troops to withdraw.

Fuquan reported this great victory to Kangxi, the Emperor was very glad. He issued a commendation to him.

On 2 August Fuquan ordered his troops to march forward to attack the enemy. But Galdan's troops fought back resolutely. So Fuquan ordered the troops to halt temporarily. At that time Galdan sent Yilagukesan Khutukhtu, the senior lama of the Tibetan Buddhism in Mongolia, to see Fuquan. He conveyed Galdan's demand that the Qing government should hand over Zebutsundanba Khutukhtu and Tuxietu Khan to Galdan. He also told Fuquan that Jilong Khutukhtu, who had been sent by Sangye Gyatso, the supreme chief executive of Tibet, to Galdan, would come to make peace within one or two days. Fuquan listed all the crimes Galdan had committed and then sent him back. On 4 August Jilong really came with more than seventy followers to Fuquan's army. He said to Fuquan, "Galdan has come into the border area. His subordinates looted the people. This is certainly wrong. But His Majesty is the supreme ruler of the whole world. Galdan is just a small head of a tribe. He does not dare to act audaciously. He made the mistake of entering the border area only because he wants to catch Zebutsundanba Khutukhtu and Tuxietu Khan. Now he has given up the idea of catching Tuxietu Khan. He just hopes that His Majesty would arrest Zebutsundanba and send him back to the Dalai Lama. Then he will feel honored." Fuquan said, "Even if Tuxietu Khan and Zebutsundanba have committed crimes, they should be punished by His Majesty. It will be absurd to hand them over to the Dalai Lama in accordance with Galdan's words! Now you are coming back and forth. Can you guarantee that Galdan will not take the chance to escape and loot the people within our territory?" Jilong said, "If you follow His Majesty's instruction of benevolence and stop the military action, Galdan will not dare to take any action and will not run away." Fuquan said, "Although you have made the guarantee that Galdan will not dare to take any action, the different routes of our army are marching forward to attack Galdan. When they meet with the Elute troops, they will surely start their attack. Now I will follow His Majesty's instruction of benevolence and stop the battle. I will issue orders to stop their attack." Then Jilong sent some of his followers to tell Galdan the result of his talk with Fuquan. Fuquan reported all these to Kangxi and said in the memorial, "I think Galdan is a cunning man. What he said is not reliable. But after the battle on 1 August, he sent envoys to see me one batch after another. He must be in a very difficult situation. We wanted to start a fierce attack, but we were afraid that he will take advantage of the natural barrier and put up a strong defense. So we let his envoys come back and forth. We will start a fierce attack after the troops from Shengjing, Wula and Horqin have arrived. If chance permits, we shall destroy Galdan's army." When Kangxi got the report, he was very angry because Fuquan had missed the chance of winning the battle and destroying Galdan's army. He strictly ordered Fuquan to attack the enemy on 5 Augusty when the troops from Shengjing, Wula and Horqin arrived.

At night 4 August Galdan led his troops to escape. They crossed Xar Moron River (situated in the southwest of Hexigten Qi, Inner Mongolian Autonomous Region, China), went across a sandy area and reached Qagan Nur (a lake situated in the middle part of Inner Mongolian Autonomous Region, China). Fuquan wanted to command his troops to run after Galdan, but the horses in his troops were not strong enough to cross the sandy area. He was afraid that Galdan would escape faraway, so he and Jilong decided that Galdan should stay in a place not far away from the Qing army so that they can hold a peace talk. On 11 August Fuquan sent Wudan, an officer of the Imperial Guards, and Commander Saierji to go with Jilong to convey Fuquan's intention to Galdan. On 15 August Wudan, Saierge and Jilong came back with Daerhangelong and Xidaerkezaisang, the two envoys sent by Galdan with a memorial written by Galdan. They told Fuquan that Galdan had knelt down before an image of Buddha and swore that if he went against the words in the memorial, he would be punished by Buddha. The memorial read, "The Dalai Lama has sent Jilong to blame me for my going against the rules of etiquette. Now if Your Majesty grants me kindness, I will not attack the Khalkha Mongolians anymore." After Fuquan had read the memorial, he found that Galdan had not written down his words of swear in his memorial. He sent Jilong, Wudan and Saierji back to order Galdan to add the words of swear in the memorial. Then Galdan added his words of swear in the memorial.

After Emperor Kangxi had read the memorial, he ordered Fuquan to station his troops in Wulan Butung and to make sure that Galdan had really left the border area and gone far away.

Tsewang Rabtan, Galdan's nephew, took the chance that Galdan was fighting in Ulan Butung to occupy the whole area of Dzungar Khanate. He controlled a vast area west from Lake Balkhash (in southeastern Kazakhastan), east to Turpan (in the northeast part of Xinjiang Uygur Autonomous Region), north to Altay Mountains (which lie in the border areas of Xinjiang Uygur Autonomous Regen of China and the west part of Mongolia), and southwest to Chu River (a river in northern Kyrgyztan). From then on Galdan could not go back to Dzungar Khanate.

By the end of October Galdan had left the border and ran away to the area of Onon River (situated in the north part of Mongolia). Later in January 1691 Galdan and his troops moved to the southwest part of Mongolia.

On 22 November 1690 Fuquan and other generals who had carried out the expedition against Galdan in Wulan Butung came back to Beijing. Kangxi deprived Fuquan of the title of King of Government Affairs and forfeited his emoluments for three years as a punishment for his delay in attacking Galdan in Wulan Butung.

3. Emperor Kangxi's Second Expedition against Galdan

In February 1695 Galdan commanded his troops to Bayan Ulaan (situated by the upper reach of Kerulen River, to the southeast of Ulan Bator, Mongolia) from the southwest part of Mongolia. They looted the livestock of the local people along Kerulen River and prepared to spend the winter in the area of Bayan Ulaan.

On 4 November 1695 Emperor Kangxi decided to attack Galdan in three routes: General Sabusu would command the troops of the east route which was composed of 2,000 soldiers sent from Shengjing (now Shenyang, Liaoning Province) and 4,000 soldiers sent from Horqin (now Horqin Qi, Inner Mongolian Autonomous Region, China); they should march northward then along Kerulun River; General Feiyanggu would command the west route which would march from Guihua (now Hohhot, Inner Mongolian Autonomous Region, China); the middle route would march from Beijing, the capital. The officers and men of these three routes should carry food for 80 days.

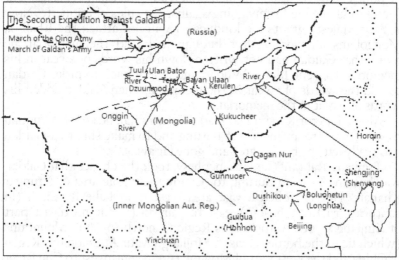

Kangxi decided to personally command the expedition. He ordered Yinreng, the Crown Prince, to stay in Beijing to take care of the state affairs. He ordered that the middle route should start from Beijing on 30 February 1696 and that Yinzhi (胤禔), his eldest son, Yinzhi (胤祉), his third son, Yinzhen, his fourth son, Yinqi, his fifth son, Yinyou, his seventh son, and Yinsi, his eighth son, should go with him. He ordered that the west route should start from Guihua on 18 February. He ordered General Sun Si Ke to command the troops in Shaanxi Province to Ningxia (now Ningxia Hui Autonomous Region) and then march out of Ningxia on 10 March to join forces with General Feiyanggu on his way to Onggin River (situated in the west part of South Hangay Province, Mongolia).

On 18 February the army under Feiyanggu marched northward from Guihua and the army under Sun Si Ke marched northward from Yinchuan (in the north part of Ningxia Hui Autonomous Region). On 11 April the army under Feiyanggu and the army under Sun Si Ke joined forces in the area by Onggin River. Then they marched towards Tuul River (a river which flows past Ulan Bator, Mongolia).

On 30 February 1696 Kangxi commanded the army of the middle route to march northward from Beijing. On 10 March the great army reached Dushikou (in the northwest part of Hebei Province) from which the great army marched out of the Great Wall. On 13 March Kangxi reached Boluohetun (in Longhua, Hebei province). On 15 March the great army reached Gunnuoer (situated to the southwest of Qagan Nur, Inner Mongolian Autonomous Region, China). On 14 April the great army marched out of the border area and towards Kerulen River. On 6 May Kangxi reached Kukucheer (a place to the south of Kerulen River, Mongolia). On 7 May scouts found that Galdan stationed his troops in a place on the north bank of Kerulen River. Then Kangxi commanded the vanguard troops to go forward first. The main force followed. On 8 May the great army reached Kerulen River. When Galdan got the information that Kangxi had come with a great army, he did not believe it. He went up Mengnaer Mountain and looked into the distance. He could see the wide spread camps of the great army under the command of Kangxi with many yellow banners for an emperor. He was greatly scared. He gave up the tents and military storages and ran away to the west. Emperor Kangxi ordered General Masika to command his troops to run after Galdan. He sent an envoy to Feiyanggu to order him to intercept the enemy. Then he commanded the main force to run after the enemy.

In May Feiyanggu's troops reached Tuul River. When he got the information that Galdan and his troops had reached Terelj (a mountain situated to the southeast of Ulan Bator, Mongolia), He sent Shuodai, the Commander-in-chief of the vanguards, and Deputy Commander-in-chief Alanda, to command their troops to go there to engage Galdan's troops. They fought with Galdan's army and they retreated while they fought. Galdan commanded his troops to pursue the Qing troops. In this way Shuodai and Alanda lured Galdan and his troops to Dzuunmod which was situated in the south of Hangayn Mountain and to the south of Tuul River. Feiyanggu had already arranged his troops in Dzuunmod. He divided his troops in three teams: the east team was arranged on a mountain, the west team was arranged along Tuul River, and the troops under Sun Si Ke were arranged in the middle. All the troops followed Kangxi's instruction that all the officers and men should get down from their horses and fight on foot and when they defeated the enemy, they should get on their horses to chase the enemy troops. There were still more than 10,000 men in Galdan's troops. When they reached Dzuunmod, they carried out a desperate fight. The battle began in 1 o'clock in the afternoon and lasted to 5 o'clock. The battle went on heatedly. Feiyanggu watched from afar and found that the back part of Galdan's battle formation was strongly defended and were unmoved. From this he knew that it was the place where the women and military supplies were. He ordered the picked troops on horseback to start a fierce attack on that part of the enemy battle formation. The enemy battle formation was in great confusion and collapsed. The enemy troops ran away to the northwest. Feiyanggu commanded his troops to give a hot pursuit. They chased the enemy for 15 kilometers to Terelji Mountain. They killed more than 3,000 enemy soldiers and captured more than 400 soldiers. Galdan's wife Anukatun was a very good fighter, but she was killed in the battle field. Galdan rode away with only several followers. Feiyanggu ordered Alanda to report the great victory to Kangxi. Then Kangxi ordered the troops to withdraw from the front.

4. Emperor Kangxi's Third Expedition against Galdan

After the defeat in Dzuunmod, Galdan escaped to the area of Tamir River (in Arkhangai Province, Mongolia). His subordinates also arrived there later. He held a meeting to discuss where they should go. He decided that they should loot the people around the Gobi Desert and rob all their food, then they should go to Hami (in the northeast part of Xinjiang Uyghur Autonomous Region). Danjinemubu, one of Galdan's general, said that there were villages in Hami and he was not used to live in villages. On 4 July 1696 he betrayed Galdan and ran away to the west. Galdan commanded some troops to run after him, but they could not catch him. Alabutan, another general under Galdan, also ran away. In September Galdan and his troops moved to a place near Altay (in Govi-Altay Province, in the west part of Mongolia).

When Emperor Kangxi got to know that Galdan was in Altay, on 21 October 1696 he sent Manji, one of Galdan's subordinates, who was captured in the battle of Dzuunmod, to take an imperial order to Galdan demanding him to surrender. On 25 September Galdan sent Geleiguying to see Kangxi to convey his intention to surrender. Kangxi said to Geleiguying, "Go back and tell Galdan to come to surrender personally. Otherwise I will personally command an expedition against him. He should come to surrender within 70 days. When the time limit of 70 days is over, my troops will march forward."

On 3 January 1697 Kangxi decided that his troops should start the expedition on 6 February. On 16 January Saibutengbalzhul, Galdan's son, was captured in Hami by the local people and was presented to the Qing army.

On 6 February Kangxi started his journey from Beijing towards Ningxia (now Ningxia Hui Autononmous Region) to carry out his expedition against Galdan. His eldest son Yinzhi went with him. In early March Kangxi reached the area of Yulin (in the north part of Shaanxi Province). On 3 March General Feiyanggu reported to Kangxi that Duoerji, an important general under Galdan, had surrendered with his wife and children. On 4 March Saibutengbalzhul, Galdan's son, was brought before Kangxi. He knelt on the ground and did not dare to look up. Kangxi asked, "Your father Galdan has come to the end of his resources. Will he come to surrender?" Saibutengbalzhul answered, "I am still young. I don't know clearly whether he will surrender. But I think he will surrender because Your Majesty is such a powerful emperor." Kangxi asked him about other things but he was so afraid that he could not answer any of them. Then Kangxi sent a party of soldiers to escort him to Beijing. On 19 March Kangxi reached Dingbian (in the northwest part of Shaanxi Province).

On 15 April Kangxi reached Bugutu (a place to the west of Yinchuan, Ningxia Hui Autonomous Region). There he got a memorial presented by General Feiyanggu which read, "On 9 April, I commanded my troops to Saqierbaerhasun. Danjila of the Elute sent nine envoys to me. They told me that on 13 the second March, Galdan reached Achaamutatai of Altay where he committed suicide by taking poison.

Danjila, Nuoyangelong and Lasilun, Danjila's son-in-law, are coming to surrender taking Galdan's dead body, bringing Galdan's daughter Zhongqihai and 300 households. Now Danjila and the others stay in Bayaenduer because they have run out of food and their horses are very tired." Kangxi ordered General Feiyanggu to command his troops to the place where Danjila and the others were. On 18 April Danjila sent Qiqierzaisang as his envoy to see Kangxi with a memorial which read, "Galdan died on 13 the second March. On that day we burned his dead body to ashes. We started from Achaamutatai to Bayaenduer. There are 400 able-body men, more than 1000 people, a horse for each man, and 150 camels in our group. Apart from these we have no other things." After reading the memorial presented by Danjila, Kangxi ordered General Feiyanggu to send Galdan's ashes to the place where the emperor was by post stations. Then Emperor Kangxi ordered his army to go back. On 16 May Emperor Kangxi arrived in Beijing.

SECTION SEVEN: EXPEDITIONS AGAINST TSEWANG RABTAN

1. Tsewang Rabtan Becomes the Khan of the Dzungar Khanate

After Galdan died, Tsewang Rabtan, who had actually controlled the vast areas of The Dzungar Khanate, became the actual ruler of The Dzungar Khanate.

To the northwest of the Dzungar Khanate there was the Kazakh Khanate (in what is now Kazakhstan). At that time, the ruler of the Kazakh Khanate was Tauke Khan. In the past Galdan had captured Tauke Khan's son and presented him to the Dalai Lama in Tibet (now Tibet Autonomous Region). After Galdan died, Tauke Khan sent an envoy to beg Tsewang Rabtan to help him to get back his son. Tsewang Rabtan sent envoys to the Dalai Lama and successfully got back Tauke Khan's son and he sent 500 officers and soldiers to escort him back to the Kazakh Khanate. When Tauke Khan got back his son, he killed all the 500 men in the escort. Then he sent troops to attack and kill Wulhedebaltu, the head of a subtribe of the Dzungar, and looted his people. He also sent troops to capture more than a hundred households in Uriankhai (a place in Altay Mountains, in the northwest part of Xinjiang Uygur Autonomous Region).

When Ayuqi sent his daughter to marry Tsewang Rabtan, he sent his son to escort her to Tsewang Rabtan. Tauke Khan sent troops to attack the team on their way. Tauke Khan also sent troops to attack Dzunger merchants who returned from Russia after business. So in 1698 Tsewang Rabtan sent General Tzeren Dondub to command a great army to attack the Kazakh Khanate. Tauke Khan was defeated and ran away. The Kazakh Khanate was split into three states: the Great Jüz, the Middle Jüz and the Little Jüz. These three states were submitted to Tsewang Rabtan.

2. Defeat of Tsewang Rabtan's Attack on Hami

Tsewang Rabtan thought that the Dzungar Khanate was powerful enough to contend with the Qing Dynasty. In March 1715 he sent troops to the northern part of Hami (in the Xinjiang Uygur Autonomous Region) and his troops attacked and looted five stockaded villages in that area.

On 25 March 1715 his troops reached the foot of Hami City. Emin, the king of Hami Hui Nationality Kingdom, reported this situation to Shiyide, the viceroy of Gansu. Shiyide sent Lu Zhen Sheng, the commander-in-chief of the Qing army stationed in Gansu, to command the troops to Hami. At the same time he sent a memorial to Emperor Kangxi to report this situation. Kangxi ordered General Xizhu to take 3,000 soldiers stationed in Xi'an (now in the south part of Shaanxi Province) to march quickly to reinforce Hami. He also sent orders to the generals of the Qing army stationed in the west part of Qinghai to prepare to resist an invasion by Tsewang Rabtan's army, because the west part of Qinghai was close to the Dzungar Khanate. He also sent envoys to notify the heads of the Khalkha Mongolian tribes in the west part of Mongolia to get ready to resist an attack by Tsewang Rabtan's army.

On 26 March 200 officers and men under Commander Pan Zhi Shan and Commander Bitiechangbaozhu, and the soldiers under Emin, King of Hami, fought against Tsewang Rabtan's troops outside Hami City. They defeated 2,000 enemy troops. About 90 Dzungar soldiers were killed. The enemy had to retreat 10 kilometers to the south. Lu Zhen Sheng sent his troops to go quickly from Gansu to reinforce Hami. On 12 April they reached a place which was 60 kilometers away from Hami City. When the people of Hami got this information, they were very happy. When Tsewang Rabtan's troops knew that the Qing reinforcement was coming, they all ran away.

In March 1717 Kangxi appointed Funingan, the Personnel Minister, as General of Pacifying the Rebels to command 8,500 officers and men to attack Urumqi (now the capital city of Xinjiang Uygur Autonomous Region) and Turpan (in Xinjiang Uygur Autonomous Region), the territory of the Dzungar Khanate. He ordered Kalunte, the commander-in-chief of the Qing army stationed in Xi'an (in Shaanxi Province) to go with Funingan. On 26 June Funingan commanded his troops to set out from Barkol (in the northeast part of Xinjiang Uygur Autonomous Region). The Qing army marched westward into the territory of the Dzungar Khanate. Very soon they took Urumqi. In 1720 Funingan sent troops to march southeast to attack Turpan. When the Qing troops reached Turpan, the chief of Turpan surrendered.

3. Defeat of the Invasion of Tibet by Tsewang Rabtan's Army and the Pacification of Tibet

Tibet (now Tibet Autonomous Region) was situated in the southwest part of China. It was adjacent to Qinghai (now Qinghai Province) in the north and Western Region (now Xinjiang Uygur Autonomous Region) in the northwest. The capital city was Lhasa. The Tibetan people believed in Tibetan Buddhism. The Dalai Lama was the religious leader and the actual ruler of Tibet. During the reign of Emperor Kangxi, Lobsang Gyaco was the 5th Dalai Lama. In his later years he devoted most of his time writing books. So he entrusted all the power to Sangye Gyatso, Diba (the supreme chief executive) of Tibet. Galdan, Khan of the Dzungar Khanate, was once a disciple of the 5th Dalai Lama when he was young. During the war between Galdan's Dzungar Khanate and the Khalka Mongolian Tribes and the war between Galdan's Dzungar Khanate and the Qing Dynasty, Sanye Gyatso always supported Galdan and falsely conveyed the 5th Dalai Lama's words that he supported Galdan (actually the 5th Dalai Lama had already died by that time). So when Galdan was defeated by the Qing army in 1696 in the area by Kerulen River (in the east part of Mongolia) and ran away, he tried to inspire his disheartened subordinates by saying, "This action was not my own intention. I took this action because the Dalai Lama sent an envoy to tell me that the southern expedition was highly auspicious. This is the reason why I have carried out the southern expedition."

Kangxi suspected that the Dalai Lama had already died. He sent an envoy to take a letter to Sanye Gyatso which read, "I learned from the captured Mongolians that the Dalai Lama died long ago. But you never reported this to me. When the Dalai Lama was alive, there was peace in the areas outside the Great Wall for more than 60 years. It is you who have instigated Galdan to start wars with the Khalkha Mongolians." In the letter Kangxi sternly demanded Sangye Gyatso to tell the truth. In 1697 Sangye Gyatso had to send a memorial to Kangxi which read, "Unfortunately the 5th Dalai Lama died in 1682, fifteen years ago. I was afraid that there would be disturbances among the local people, so I did not announce his death. I will announce it in October this year." He begged Kangxi not to reveal this to the public. Kangxi promised to keep this secret till October. In 1697 Sangye Gyatso made Cangyang Gyaco the 6th Dalai Lama.

Lha-bzang Khan was the ruler of the Khoshut Khanate which covered the most part of Tibet and the south part of Qinghai. He held the military power of Tibet. Sangye Gyatso thought that Lha-bzang Khan would be a threat to him. So in 1705 he tried to murder him by poison. But his plan was not successful. Then he sent troops to drive Lha-bzang Khan out. Lha-bzang Khan gathered a great army to carry out an expedition against Sangye Gyatso and killed him. Lha-bzang Khan sent a memorial to Kangxi to ask permission to depose the 6th

Dalai Lama made by Sangye Gyatso. Kangxi ordered to escort the 6th Dalai Lama to Beijing, the capital of the Qing Dynasty. But in 1707 when the 6th Dalai Lama reached Qinghai (now Qinghai Province) on his way to Beijing, he died. He died at the age of twenty-five.

By that time Lha-bzang Khan was nearly 60 years old. His second son commanded some troops to station in Qinghai. His eldest son Galdanzhong had gone to the Dzungar Khanate to marry Tsewang Rabtan's daughter. Kangxi worried that Tsewang Rabtan would detain Lha-bzang Khan's eldest son in the Dzungar Khanate in the pretext that he loved his son-in-law. Then Lha-bzang Khan would be alone and be in a dangerous situation. If there was any contingency, the Qing army could not save him because he was more than 5,000 kilometers away. So he sent an envoy to ask Lha-bzang Khan to make good preparation for any contingence.

In 1717 Tsewang Rabtan sent Tzeren Dondub to command 6,000 men to invade Tibet in the pretext that they would escort Lha-bzang Khan's eldest son Galdanzhong and his wife back to Tibet. They started from Ili (now Yining, the capital city of Ili Kazakh Autonomous Prefecture, in the west part of Xinjiang Uygur Autonomous Region), went past the desert (Taklimakan Desert) in the south part of Xinjiang, and then they went over the snowy mountains in the south of Hotan (in the southwest part of Xijiang Uygur Autonomous Region). They concealed themselves by daytime and marched by night time. After a long march they reached the area of Shigatse (in the south part of Tibet Autonomous Region) which was situated to the west of Lhasa (the capital city of Tibet Autonomous Region) where Lha-bzang Khan was. Lha-bzang Khan did not make any preparation to fight because he believed that Tsewang Rabtan's troops were escorting his son and his daughter-in-law back to Tibet. When the Dzungar troops reach Damu (in Damxung, Tibet Autonomous Region) situated to the north of Lhasa. It was at this point that Lha-bzang Khan realized the true intention of the Dzungar troops under the command of Tzeren Dondub. He and his younger son Soerza commanded their troops to resist the enemy troops. They fought with enemy troops for two months. They were defeated. They had to go to Potala which was situated in the northwest of Lhasa and defended this city. Lha-bzang Khan immediately sent an envoy to take a memorial to Kangxi asking him for help. Tseren Dondub induced Lha-bzang Khan's subordinates to surrender. At night of 28 January 1718 several of the high ranking officials under Lha-bzang Khan opened the northern gate of Potala. The Dzungar troops entered Potala City and killed Lha-bzang Khan. Lha-bzang Khan's son Soerza tried to run away with 30 men, but he was caught by the Dzungar soldiers. The Dzungar soldiers searched the treasuries from the temples and sent them back to Ili.

Elunte, General of Xi'an, commanded the troops in Xining (now Xining, in the east part of Qinghai Province) and the troops in Songpan (in the north part of Sichuan Province) to rescue the army of Tibet. In September 1718 they reached Kala River (in the area of Nakchu, in the north part of Tibet Autonomous Region). They fell into an ambush of the Dzungar army. General Elunte fought bravely, but he was killed in battle. The troops under him were destroyed.

Emperor Kangxi pondered the fact that Tibet was adjacent to Qinghai in the north, Sichuan and Yunnan in the east. If the Dzungar army occupied Tibet, these border provinces would be threatened. If the Dzungar soldiers could cross the snowy mountains and crossed the perilous places, so could the Qing army and when the Dzungar troops got the information that the Qing army had come, they would surely run away. So he decided to send a great army to march into Tibet. After they had entered Tibet, they should put the Dalai Lama on the throne, and the Qing army should be stationed in Tibet for a long time. The Tibetan troops would be put under the command of the Qing generals. If the Dzungar army came again, the Qing army could wait at ease for the exhausted enemy.

So he issued an imperial edict to make Gäsang Gyaco, who was at that time in Qinghai, the 6th Dalai Lama.

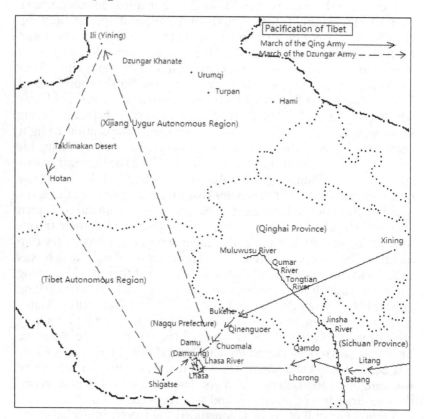

In January 1720 Emperor Kangxi appointed his 14th son Yinti (胤禵) as the Grand General of Pacifying the Far Away Places (撫遠大將軍). He ordered Yinti to stay in the area of Muluwusu River (which was the ancient name for the upper reach of Qumar River, in the southwest part of Qinghai Province) to attend to the commanding of the army and to arrange the soldiers' pay and provisions. He ordered Yan Xin, the General of Pacifying the Rebels (平逆將軍), to command a great army to march into Tibet from Qinghai. In February 1720 he ordered Galbi, the General of Tranquilizing the West (定西將軍), to command a great army in Sichuan (now Sichuan Province) and Yunna (now Yunnan Province) to march into Tibet from Sichuan (now Sichuan Province). The Tibetan people in Qinghai knew that the Dalai Lama in Qinghai was the true Dalai Lama and the Dalai Lama in Tibet was a false one. They asked Kangxi's permission to let them carry the true Dalai Lama into Tibet in a meditation bed. Kangxi gave his permission and issued a gold seal to the true Dalai Lama. Many Mongolian Khans, kings and tribe heads commanded their troops to go into Tibet with the Qing army.

Tzeren Dondub, the commanding general of the Dzungar army, personally commanded some troops to resist the Qing army coming from Qinghai. He sent his adviser Sang to command 3,600 men to resist the Qing army coming from Sichuan. General Galbi offered amnesty to the Tibetan people in Litang County and Batang County (these counties are now in Ganzi Tibetan Autonomous Prefecture, in the west part of Sichuan Province) and enlisted their services. Then the Qing army marched to Qamdo (in the northeast part of Tibet Autonomous Region). Then they marched to Lhorong (to the southwest of Qamdo). They marched to the southwest quickly. On 22 August they crossed Lhasa River and took Lhasa. General Galbi gathered all the local officials and chiefs and lamas of the temples in Lhasa together to hold a meeting. In the meeting he declared openly Kangxi's intention to save the people of Tibet. Then he ordered to seal all the government warehouses. He sent troops to station in the critical points near Lhasa. He arrested 101 Dzungar lamas. Among them five had been appointed by Tzeren Dondub as leaders of these lamas, so these five lamas were executed. The rest were kept in jail. He adopted many measures to stabilize the situation in Lhasa.

The Qing army under General Yan Xin marched from Qinghai. On 15 August 1720 they reached a place by Bukehe (in Nagqu Prefecture, in the north part of Tibet Autonomous Region). That night Tzeren Dondub commanded his troops to start a surprise attack on the Qing army. The Qing troops fought bravely and defeated the Dzungar troops. On 19 August the Qing army started from Bukehe. On 20 August they stationed in Qinenguoer (a place in Nagqu Prefecture). At midnight, about 2,000 Dzungar soldiers came to attack the Qing troops. The Qing Troops resisted the attack bravely. The Dzungar troops were defeated and ran away. On 21August they marched from

Qinenguoer. On 22 August they stationed in Chuomala (in Nagqu Prefecture). Early next morning about 1,000 Dzungar troops started a surprise attack on the camps of the Qing army. They were found out by the guards. The Qing soldiers fired guns and cannons. Many enemy soldiers were killed or wounded. The remaining enemy soldiers ran away. Since Lhasa was already taken by the Qing army under General Galbi, the Dzungar troops under Tzeren Dondub were attacked from the front and from the back. They were utterly defeated and ran away to the northwest. On their way, many of them died of hunger and cold. Only less than half of the Dzungar troops could get back to Ili. On 8 September General Yan Xin started from Damu (now in Damxung, Tibet Autonomous Region) to escort the newly made Dalai Lama to Lhasa.

On 15 September 1720 the 6th Dalai Lama was escorted to Potala Palace and put on the throne. Awangyishi Gyaco, the Dalai Lama set up by Lha-bzang Khan, was deposed and was escorted to Beijing, the capital of the Qing Dynasty. Kangxi ordered to leave 4,000 Mongolian, Sichuan and Yunnan soldiers to station in Tibet. He appointed Gongcewang Nuoerbu to command all the Qing troops stationed in Tibet. Abao, Kangxi's son-in-law, and Commander Wuge were appointed as military advisers for Gongcewang Nuoerbu. Albuba, a Tibetan official, who had submitted to the Qing Dynasty and had accompanied the Qing army to take Tibet, and Kangjinai, a Tibetan official, who had commanded his troops to intercept the Dzungar troops, were made kings. Longbunai, who had submitted to the Qing Dynasty, was appointed as Regent to manage the government affairs of Front Tibet (the area of Lhasa). Poluonai was made First Class Taiji (the highest title for nobilities) to manage the government affairs of Back Tibet (the area of Shigatse).

SECTION EIGHT: KANGXI'S SONS COMPETE FOR THE THRONE

1. Emperor Kangxi's Sons

Emperor Kangxi had 35 sons, but some of them died young. The important surviving sons are listed here:

- Concubine Hui gave birth to Yinzhi (胤禔), the First Son;
- Empress Xiaochengren gave birth to Yinreng (胤礽), the Second Son;
- Concubine Rong gave birth to Yinzhi (胤祉), the Third Son;
- Empress Xiaogongren gave birth to Yinzhen (胤禛), the Fourth Son, Yinzuo (胤祚), the Sixth Son, Yinti (胤禵), the Fourteenth Son;
- Concubine Cheng gave birth to Yinsi (胤禩), the Eighth Son;
- Concubine Yi gave birth to Yintang (胤禟), the Ninth Son;
- Concubine Wenxi gave birth to Yin'e (胤䄉), the Tenth Son;

- Concubine Jingmin gave birth to Yinxiang (胤祥), the Thirteenth Son;
- Concubine Shunyimi gave birth to Yinxie (胤祄), the Eighteenth Son.

2. Emperor Kangxi Makes Yinreng the Crown Prince

Although Yinzhi (胤禔) was Emperor Kangxi's eldest son, he was not made crown prince because his mother was only a concubine.

Yinreng, Kangxi's second son, was born to Empress Xiaochengren, who tragically died after giving birth. In December 1675 Kangxi decided to make Yinreng Crown Prince when he was two years old. On 13 December 1675 a ceremony was held. Kangxi sat on his throne and all the Kings, Beiles, Beizis and Dukes (the high ranking nobility of the royal clan), and all the civil and military officials, attended the ceremony and presented their congratulations. On that day Kangxi issued an imperial edict which read, "Since ancient times emperors have ruled over the whole country. An emperor must designate his successor to the throne so that the country can be stable and prosperous and the royal clan can last forever. I have to attend to a lot of state affairs. I have to work assiduously day and night. With the blessing of my ancestors, I am able to undertake this important task. My son Yinreng is a good looking and clever boy. Now I am following the orders of the Grand Empress Dowager and the Empress Dowager to make Yinreng Crown Prince. A grand ceremony has been held. And I now solemnly inform Heaven, the Earth, and the Ancestral Temple, that on 13 December 1675 I granted Yinreng the seal and made him Crown Prince. He will be placed in the Eastern Palace so as to show his importance as the successor to the throne."

When the Crown Prince was young, Kangxi instructed him personally. When he was six years old, Kangxi appointed Zhang Ying and Li Guang Di, both of whom were Grand Secretaries, as his teachers. He ordered Xiong Ci Lü, a Grand Secretary, to give the Crown Prince lessons on Neo-Confucianism (a philosophy school founded by Cheng Hao, Cheng Yi and Zhu Xi of the Song Dynasty). In 1686 Tang Bin, the Minister of Rites and Supervisor of the Household of Crown Prince, recommended Dao Geng Jie to be the Vice Supervisor of the Household of the Crown Prince as the tutor of the Crown Prince. But very soon Dao Geng Jie resigned because he fell ill. The next year Tang Bin died. The Crown Prince could understand Chinese characters and Manchu characters. He was good at riding horses and shooting arrows. He often accompanied Kangxi on inspection tours. When Kangxi made poems on the way, Yinreng could compose poems in reply using the same theme and rhyme used by Kangxi.

In July 1690 Kangxi personally commanded the expedition against Galdan, the Khan of the Dzungar Khanate. When he reached Boluohe Village (in Longhua, Hebei Province) which was situated outside the

Great Wall, he fell ill. He summoned the Crown Prince and Yinzhi, his third son, to the place where he stayed. When the Crown Prince saw his ill father, he did not show any anxiety and concern. This made Kangxi very unhappy, and he sent the Crown Prince back to Beijing.

In 1694 the officials of the Ministry of Rites was preparing the rites for offering sacrifices for the ancestors. They suggested that the mattress for the Crown Prince to kneel down on when doing his devotions should be kept inside the doorsill. But Kangxi told Shamuha, the Minister of Rites, that the mattress should be moved outside. Shamuha said, "Shall I write down Your Majesty's words in the records?" Kangxi was very angry and ordered Shamuha to be dismissed from his post. In 1695 the Crown Prince married a girl by the name of Shi. Kangxi made her Crown Princess.

In February 1696 Kangxi carried out the second expedition against Galdan. He ordered the Crown Prince to carry out a ceremony of offering sacrifices to gods in the city outskirts for Kangxi. Then he issued an imperial order that all the memorials by the ministries should be presented to the Crown Prince and handled by him. As for important matters, the officials should discuss these matters and make decisions on these matters, and then they should report their decisions to the Crown Prince.

In June Kangxi defeated Galdan and returned to Beijing triumphantly. The Crown Prince led all the officials to meet him outside Beijing. In 1697 Kangxi commanded a great army to march to Ningxia (now Ningxia Hui Autonomous Region), and again he ordered the Crown Prince to handle state affairs in Beijing. While Kangxi was out in Ningxia, the Crown Prince ganged up with some officials to form a clique to plan some schemes. This was reported to Kangxi, and when he came back to Beijing, he ordered to those high ranking officials arrested and punished them according to the law. From then on the Crown Prince was out of favor with Emperor Kangxi.

3. Emperor Kangxi Deposes Yinreng

In August 1708 Emperor Kangxi had a hunting trip in the north part of Hebei Province. Yinxie, his eighteenth son, who was eight years old, fell ill on the way and had to stop in Yong'anbai'ang'a (a place near Weichang Manchu and Mongol Autonomous County, in the north part of Hebei Province). Kangxi was very anxious and stayed by his bedside day and night. He ordered the doctors to do their best to cure him. But later Yinxie's illness turned worse. On 2 September Kangxi summoned all the officials who had followed him on the hunting trip and said to them, "Since the Eighteenth Prince fell ill, I have hoped that he would recover. But today his illness has become more serious. I think there is no hope to save him. I, as the emperor, have great responsibilities. I have worries about the old Grand

Empress Dowager. And I have to take care of all the ordinary people. I am the only person who should be responsible for them. Compared with these responsibilities, my young son is not so important. I have to bear the pain of giving up my son. We shall go on our way now." On that day they marched for ten kilometers and reached Bulinhasutai (in Weichang Manchu and Mongol Autonomous County, in the north part of Hebei Province).

On 4 September Kangxi summoned the kings, ministers, imperial guards and the military and civil officials to his temporary residence in Bulinhasutai. He ordered Yinreng, the Crown Prince, to kneel down before him. Kangxi said with tears in his eyes, "Forty-eight years have passed since I inherited the great cause passed down from Taizu, Taizong and Shizu. I have worked cautiously and conscientiously. I have treated my officials kindly and have enabled my people to lead a good life. What I have done is for the tranquility of the whole country. Now Yinreng does not act according to the morality passed down from the ancestors and does not follow my teachings. He willfully maltreated his subordinates. He is brutal and licentious. I am too embarrassed to list all his evil conduct. I have tolerated him for twenty years. He has become even more brutal. He has insulted the kings, nobles, ministers and officials in court. He tried to arrogate all powers to himself. He ganged up with his followers. He has pried into my personal affairs and tried to get information about my daily life.

There is only one emperor in the country. How can Yinreng insult and maltreat the kings, nobles, ministers and officials at his own will? Nalsu, Ping Prefecture King, Haishan, a Beile, and Duke Puqi were beaten by him. He has maltreated many ministers, officials and soldiers. I have learned many of his ill doings. He hated those officials who reported his ill doings to me and he would give them a good beating. So I did not ask the officials about his ill doings. During the period of my inspection tours to Shaanxi Province, the areas to the south of the Yangtze River and Zhejiang Province, when I lived in houses or travelled on boats, I seldom stepped outside so as not to give trouble to the ordinary people. But Yinreng and his subordinates did all kinds of bad things to the people. I feel shame for him. He also sent his subordinates to intercept the envoys of foreign states who escorted tributes to me. They stole the horses the Mongolians paid me as tributes. This made the Mongolians very unhappy. His evil conduct are too varied to mention one by one. Still I cherished hope that he would reform. This is the reason why I have tolerated his bad conducts till today. I know that Yingreng is a luxurious person. I appointed Lingpu, his nanny's father, as the manager of the Imperial Household Department so that Yinreng could easily get what he wanted. But unexpectedly Lingpu was even greedier. All the bondservants working in the Imperial Household Department hated him. I personally taught Yinreng since he was a child that all the things we use are the hard-won possessions of the ordinary people.

We should be frugal. But he has not followed my teachings. He leads a life of extravagance and depravity.

He never cares about his brothers. When Yinxie fell seriously ill, all the people around me were all worried for me because I am old. Yinreng is Yinxie's blood brother. But he did not show any fraternal love to Yinxie. When I criticized him about this, he suddenly flared up. What is even stranger is that every night he got close to my tent and spied on me through the seam of the tent. In the past Suo'etu secretly helped Yinreng to carry out a scheme to take the throne from me. I got word of this and put Suo'etu to death. Now Yinreng has ganged up with the members of his clique to avenge Suo'etu's death. Now I am uncertain whether I will be poisoned to death today or murdered tomorrow. I feel ill at ease day and night. How can I entrust the great cause passed down from the ancestors to such a person?

When Yinreng was born, his mother died. His birth caused his mother's death. He is an unfilial person. Since I ascended the throne, I have led a life of frugality. When I sleep, I cover myself with old quilts. I wear socks made of cloth. All the things used by Yinreng are much better than mine. But still he was not satisfied. He spent the money in the treasury at his own will. He interfered in state affairs. He will ruin our country and do great harm to the people in the end. If such an unfilial and heartless person is made emperor, the great cause passed down from the ancestors will surely be ruined."

After saying all this, Kangxi cried so bitterly that he fell on the ground. The officials went forward and helped him up. Then Kangxi said, "The great country created by Taizu, Taizong and Shizu and made prosperous by me will certainly not be entrusted to such a person. When I go back to the capital, I will hold a ceremony to tell Heaven, the Earth and the ancestors that Yinreng has been deposed from the position of the crown Prince.

"I ordered Yinzhi, Zhi Prefecture King, to protect me. But I did not have the intention to make Yinzhi crown prince. Yinzhi is an impetuous, ignorant and stubborn person. How can such a person be made crown prince? No action will be taken against those who joined Yinreng's clique because they were forced to. Suo'etu's sons Ge'erfen and A'erjishan, and Yinreng's guards Su'erte, Hashitai and Sa'erbang'a will be executed. Du Mo Chen, Ajintai and Suhechenniyahan will be sent in exile to Shengjing. Deposing the crown prince is an important matter which will affect the life of the ordinary people. I must make a decision on this matter when I am still in good health. Now I order you to arrest Yinreng immediately. All the kings, ministers and officials may present your memorials about this matter impartially."

The kings, ministers and officials touched their heads to the ground with tears in their eyes. They said, "Your Majesty's decision is insightful and wise. All the ill doings of the Crown Prince cited by Your Majesty are all actual facts. We do not have any objection."

The next day Yinxie died of his illness.

Since Kangxi had deposed Yinreng as crown prince, he felt depressed. He could not sleep for six nights. He summoned the officials to his tent and said to them, "As I observe, Yinreng has been acting quite strangely, like a lunatic. It seems that demons have seized him."

Yinreng, the deposed crown prince, was arrested. The Emperor ordered Yinzhi, his eldest son, to guard Yinreng. When Yinreng was escorted back to Beijing, he was kept in a tent set up by the side of Shangsiyuan, that is, the office in charge of the management of horses used by the royal house. Kangxi ordered Yinzhen, his fourth son, together with Yinzhi, to guard Yinreng.

On 16 September 1708 Emperor Kangxi summoned all the kings, ministers and officials to Meridian Gate (the front gate of the Forbidden City, Beijing). The Emperor's imperial edict was read to them, "The position of the crown prince is very important. I have studied all the history books and I know this very well. I will not take any actions lightly. When Yinreng was young, I personally taught him the Book of Songs and the Book of History. Then I ordered Zhang Ying, the Grand Secretary, to teach him. I also ordered Xiong Ci Lü to teach him books about Neo-Confucianism. I ordered an old scholar of the Hanlin Academy to accompany him day and night. He gave Yinreng many good advices. Yinreng should have learned the principles of righteousness. He is good at riding horses and shooting arrows. He is also a learned man. But now he is seized by demons. He has lost his sense. He suddenly gets up and suddenly sits down. His speeches and behaviors are abnormal. He sometimes saw demons and felt uneasy to stay in his bedroom. He moved his dwelling place several times. He eats eight bowls of rice, but he did not feel full. He could drink thirty cups of wine but he was not drunk. Weird things also happened to his personal attendants. From these things we can see that he has become a lunatic.

"At first I intended to depose Yinreng after I had come back to the capital and held a ceremony in Fengxian Hall. But I could not wait any longer. So I ordered to arrest him when we were on our way back to the capital. You kings, Beiles, ministers and officials may express your ideas about this freely." All the kings, Beiles, ministers and officials knelt down and said, "Your Majesty has done your best to teach the crown prince about benevolence and righteousness. But in the recent years Yinreng caught an illness and became a lunatic. He has been seized by demons and acted abnormally. Your Majesty puts the interests of the nation and the life of the people in the first place and takes the action of deposing the crown prince. We shall assist Your Majesty to carry out your decision." Then Emperor Kangxi said, "I have made up my mind. A ceremony will be held to tell Heaven, the Earth and the ancestors that the Crown Prince has been deposed and has been put under house arrest."

On 18 September Kangxi sent officials to hold a ceremony in the Temple of Heaven (situated in the southeastern part of the Forbidden City, Beijing) to offer sacrifices to Heaven. In the ceremony Kangxi's sacrificial address was read out, "I have been on the throne for 47 years. I have worked conscientiously day and night for the national well-being and the people's livelihood. I always refer to the history books before I take any action. I know very well that the one who won over the hearts of the people would rule over the nation; and the one who lost the hearts of the people would lose the nation. I always take this as a warning. I am afraid that the great cause passed down from the ancestors may be ruined by me. Although I am not a highly virtuous man, I hold great power in my hands. I personally attend to the state affairs. I am impartial in dealing with matters. I alone make all the decisions about important state affairs. I work very hard. I will do my best for the nation till my heart stops beating. With the blessings of Heaven, my country has become much more prosperous under my reign. I will work for the benefit of the people all my life.

"But I don't know what crime I have committed that I have a son such as Yinreng. He is neither filial nor righteous. He did all kinds of strange things that no other people would do. He is extremely brutal. He is seized by demons and has become a lunatic. I think Heaven knows this very well. Now Yingreng does not say anything about devotion and loyalty. He does not do any acts of virtue and righteousness. He has committed many crimes. It is impossible to let him succeed to the throne. So I have made this sacrificial address to tell Heaven that Yinreng has been deposed from the position of the crown prince so as to avoid any harm to the nation and people. Although I have many sons, none of them is as good as me. If the Qing Dynasty can last a long period of time and my life can be prolonged, I will work even harder and carry out the cause to the end. I have written this sacrificial address to inform Heaven that I have deposed Yinreng from the position of crown prince."

At the same time sacrificial ceremonies were also held in the Temple of Earth (in the Forbidden City, Beijing) and Imperial Ancestral Temple (just outside the Forbidden City), and the same sacrificial address was read out, but the word "Heaven" in the address was changed into "Earth" and "Ancestors" respectively.

4. Emperor Kangxi's Sons Compete to Be Named Crown Prince

After Yinreng had been deposed, Yinzhi, Kangxi's eldest son, said to his father, "Yinreng behaved despicably. He is discreditable. Sorcerer Zhang De Ming once read Yinsi's face and predicted that Yinsi (Kangxi's eighth son) would become an extremely noble man. If Yinreng should be put to death, it is not necessary for Your Majesty to do anything." When Kangxi heard these words, he was very surprised and angry. On 25 September Kangxi summoned all his sons before him and told them what Yinzhi had said. Then he went on saying, "I think Yinzhi is a ferocious and ignorant person. He does not know any principles of righteousness. If he forms a clique with Yinsi and his party and kills Yinreng, he will be acting violently and he will not be thinking of my feelings. He does not know the principles of relations between the emperor and his subjects. He does not consider the feelings between father and sons. Such a person will surely become a traitor and an unfilial son. Heaven will not tolerate such acts. He will be punished by laws."

After Yinreng was deposed, Kangxi gave a warning to his sons. "Any of you who schemes to be the crown prince will be regarded as a rebel and will be punished." Yinsi, Kangxi's eighth son, was made Beile (the third rank of the nobility of the royal house) in March 1698, and he was appointed as General Manager of the Imperial Household Department. After Yinreng was deposed from the position of the crown prince, Yinsi did his best to take the position as the crown prince. Yintang, Kangxi's ninth son, Yin'e, Kangxi's tenth son, Yinti, Kangxi's fourteenth son, and high ranking officials Aling'a, Elundai, Kuixü and Wang Hong Xü were on the side of Yinsi. Yinzhi, Kangxi's eldest son, told Kangxi that Sorcerer Zhang De Ming had said that Yinsi would be extremely noble. This made Kangxi very angry. It happened that Lingpu, a manager of the Imperial Household Department, was arrested because he was a member of the party of Yinreng, the former crown prince. Lingpu's home was searched and his properties were confiscated.

But Yinsi did his best to protect Lingpu. Kangxi reproached him by saying, "Lingpu is a greedy man. He has become very rich by corrupt practices. His properties have not yet been totally confiscated. Yinsi often does his best to win fame for himself. He takes all the credits to himself for all the kindness I show to the people. He has become another crown prince! Anyone who praises Yinsi will be put to death." The next day, Kangxi summoned all his sons before him and said, "When Yinreng was deposed as crown prince, I told you all that any of you who tried to gain the position of the crown prince would be regarded as a rebel and be punished by law. Yinsi is sly. He cherishes the purpose of becoming the crown prince. He ganged up with the members of his party and tried to murder Yinreng. Now his plot has been revealed. Arrest Yinsi and hand him over to the Department of Governmental Affairs to be tried." Yintang secretly urged Yinti to go forward to save Yinsi. Kangxi was very angry. He drew out his sword, intending to kill him. Yinqi, Kangxi's fifth son, knelt before him and begged him not to. Kangxi said that Yinsi could not be pardoned for his crimes; and Yinsi was deprived the title of Beile.

On 2 October Emperor Kangxi said to the ministers and the officials, "Before Yinreng was deposed from the position of the crown prince, Zhang Ming De had planned a scheme to assassinate Yinreng. If he carried out the action, I would surely be threatened. It is said that there are 16 persons in his assassination group. Two of them were already in the palace. They tried to recruit more members from my guards. But all my guards are devoted to me. None of them joined his group. When Zhang Ming De did the fortune telling for Yinsi, he must have said something to Yinsi. Yinsi must have passed what Zhang Ming De's words to Yintang and Yinti. Otherwise they would not have told me what Zhang Ming De had said. Zhang Ming De has committed a serious crime and should be executed."

In October 1708 Yinzhi (胤祉), Kangxi's third son, reported to Kangxi that Yinzhi (胤禔), Kangxi's eldest son, had instigated Bahange, a lama, to practice witchcraft to bewitch Yinreng. Kangxi ordered to have Yinreng's living place searched. More than ten small wooden human figures with needles on their heads and backs were found. Kangxi ordered to detain Yinzhi (胤禔), Kangxi's eldest son. He deprived Yinzhi the rank as a king. Yinreng was kept in house arrest. Kangxi summoned Yinreng to the palace and let him live in Xian'an Hall in the palace. Kangxi said to the ministers and officials, "Recently I summoned Yinreng before me and asked him about the things happened in the past. He practically does not know anything happening in the past. He has really been bewitched by the witchcraft. Now with the blessings from Heaven he has recovered from lunatic disease. He has returned to normal. I will make a decision about him later." Some officials suggested that Kangxi should put Yinreng back to the position of the crown prince. But he turned down their suggestion.

On 16 November 1708 Kangxi summoned Yinreng, the deposed crown prince, and all his sons, kings and the officers of the Imperial Guards before him. Kangxi said, "When I commanded the middle route of the expedition army against Galdan, I left the Crown Prince to attend to the state affairs. All the officials in the court said that the Crown Prince was good at handling the state affairs. But when I commanded the army to march to Ningxia, the Crown Prince listened to the words of some wicket persons and behaved badly. He did many evil things. From then on I lost heart on him. I punished several of his subordinates in accordance with the laws. So some people said that the Crown Prince was not filial. The Crown Prince was unrepentant. He seemed to have become a lunatic. This was the reason why I ordered to take him into custody. Although Yinreng has beaten people when he was in violent rages, he has never beaten anyone to death. He has never interfered in the state affairs. All his abnormal behaviors were caused by the witchcraft practiced by Bahange instigated by Yinzhi. When the Crown Prince was arrested and was escorted back to Beijing, I ordered the guards to protect the deposed Crown

Prince carefully. Otherwise the deposed Crown Prince would have been killed by Yinzhi on the way. When the deposed Crown Prince was escorted back to Beijing, I ordered to let him live in Xian'an Hall because I worried that the deposed Crown Prince would be murdered by Yinzhi. I have been so worried about the deposed Crown Prince that I fell ill. I feel a pity that the Crown Prince has been deposed. I reported my feelings to the Empress Dowager. She said that she also feels a pity. Now I declare to release you in front of all the people. You may express your feelings to all of them." Yinreng said, "Your Majesty is most sagacious and intelligent. I have done many evil things. I will reform. Otherwise the providence would not forgive me. I don't cherish any hope that I would be put back to the position of the crown prince. And I think you all should not have any hope that I would be put back to the position of the crown prince." Then Kangxi said to the kings, ministers and officials, "I have read many history books. I know, since ancient times no deposed crown princes could survive. After the deposed crown princes had died, the emperors all regretted having deposed the crown princes. Since Yinreng was put in custody, I have felt uneasy all the time. Since I fell ill, I felt better each time I summoned the deposed crown prince before me. Many of my sons were brought up by others. My eldest son brought up by Galu, the General Manager of the Imperial Household Department. My third son was brought up by Zhuo'erji, Official of the Imperial Household Department. Only my fourth son was brought up by myself. When he was young, he was a bit moody. He understands my intentions best. He loves me very much. He is devoted and filial. My fifth son was brought up in the palace of the Empress Dowager. He is a good hearted man. He is pure and simple. My seventh son is keen in learning. He is genial and affable. All the officials say that my eighth son is a virtuous man. Prince Yu told me that he was a man of good character. With the help of all of you he will make great progress." Then Kangxi said to Yinreng, the deposed crown prince, "Now I release you from custody. You should remember my kindness shown on you. You should not hate those who have revealed your bad behaviors. I hope you will reform yourself thoroughly. You should read more books on rational knowledge. From now on I will not mention any of your past evil behaviors." On the same day, Yinzhen, Kangxi's fourth son, presented a memorial to Kangxi which read, "I have the chance to attend upon Your Majesty and have received many instructions from Your Majesty. Today Your Majesty commented on me with words of praise. I feel greatly honored. Your Majesty pointed out that I was a bit moody when I was young. Now more than ten years has past. During this period Your Majesty has never pointed out that I have any moody acts. I have corrected this weak point. Now I am over thirty years old. I think I have become a steady man. The word 'moody' has a lot to do with my future. I earnestly request that the words about 'moody' be deleted from the record of the talk of Your Majesty." Then Kangxi gave words to this effect which read, "During the period of these more than ten years, my fourth son has not acted moodily. I incidentally mentioned the word 'moody' today just for the sake of encouraging him. No reference to his being 'moody' should be put in the transcript of my talk."

Then Kangxi announced, "When Yinreng was kept in custody, no one said anything in favor of him. Only my fourth son was especially courageous and righteous. He spoke several times in favor of Yinreng in front of me. He is really a great man."

In December Kangxi fell ill. He ordered the officers of the Imperial Guards, Grand Secretaries of the Manchu Nationality and Han Nationality and ministers to recommend one of his sons to be the crown prince. They all recommended Yinsi, Kangxi's eighth son. On 21 January 1709 Kangxi summoned all the important people to come before him. Kangxi asked them, "Last winter I fell ill. I ordered you to recommend one of my sons to be the crown prince. Why did you only recommend Yinsi? He has offended me. His mother was from a humble family. How can he be the crown prince? Yinsi ganged up with Yinzhi, who once suggested to me to make Yinsi the crown prince. He also said that you would assist Yinsi. From this I can see that you are planning a conspiracy. You must tell me who first nominated Yinsi for crown prince." After investigation Kangxi found out that it was Maqi, a Grand Secretary. Kangxi was very angry and ordered to discharge Maqi from the position of Grand Secretary and put him in jail.

5. Yinreng Is Re-Instated as Crown Prince

In January 1709 some kings and officials of the Manchu Nationality and Han Nationality presented a memorial to Kangxi to suggest that Yinreng should be put back as crown prince. Kangxi gave them an imperial edict which read, "Yinreng should be put back to the position of the crown prince right away. It has been delayed because the officials of the Manchu Nationality and the Han Nationality suggested that Yinsi should be put in the position of the crown prince. I was very angry. I wanted to wait till I recovered from my illness and found out who was the first to nominate Yinsi for crown prince. Now with the blessings of Heaven, the Earth and the ancestors, I have recovered from my illness and I have found out who was the first to nominate Yinsi for crown prince. During the several months when I was ill, Yinreng attended to me day and night and served medicine and food to me. He has totally recovered from the state in which he was possessed by witchcraft. This is because Heaven, the Earth and the ancestors have seen that I have worked very hard to attend to the state affairs all these years. I will order to hold ceremonies to tell

Heaven, the Earth and the ancestors that Yinreng has been re-instated as crown prince."

On 9 March 1709 Kangxi sent officials to hold sacrificial ceremonies in the Temple of Heaven, the Temple of Earth and the Imperial Ancestral Temple to tell Heaven, the Earth and the ancestors that Yinreng had been put back to the position of the crown prince. Kangxi's sacrificial address was read out in the Temple of Heave, "With the help of Heaven I have successfully ruled over this vast country. I know very clearly that my successor is very important to the country. More than thirty years has passed since I promoted my son Yinreng to the position of the crown prince. But unexpectedly Yinreng suddenly became brutal and lunatic. The great cause passed down from my ancestors and the people's livelihood must come first. I could not tolerate his evil acts. I deposed him from the position of the crown prince. I told you about this in the former sacrificial address. Later I looked into this matter. I found out that some wicket people ganged up together to set Yinreng up. They stirred up troubles. I thought that the situation would develop into a mess. I made a thorough investigation. At last I found out the source of Yinreng's disease. I did my best to cure him. With the blessing of Heaven Yinreng completely recovered from his illness.

"During this period I was so worried that I fell ill. I considered that it would be very difficult to recover from my illness. I worried that the great cause passed down from my ancestors would be affected. I must appoint the successor to the throne. Among my sons Yinreng enjoys the highest status. Although he was once possessed by witchcraft, he has completely recovered from it. So I summoned the officials before me to tell them about my decision. From then on he has worked hard. He is very worried about my health. He personally attends to me and does his duty as a filial son. He insists in doing so for a long time. I believe that he will cultivate his moral character and will have the ability to succeed to the throne. Now a ceremony is held on 9 March 1709 to respectfully tell Heaven that Yinreng has been restored to the position of the crown prince. I hope Heaven will bless him." Ceremonies were also held in the Temple of the Earth and in the Imperial Ancestral Temple. The sacrificial addresses were similar to that which read out in the Temple of Heaven, but the word of Heaven was changed into Earth or Ancestors.

On the same day Kangxi made his third son Yinzhi (胤祉), his fourth son Yinzhen, his fifth son Yinqi Princes (the highest rank of nobility of the imperial house). He made his seventh son Yinyou and his tenth son Yin'e Prefecture Kings (the second rank of nobility of the imperial house). He made his ninth son Yintang, his twelfth son Yintao and his fourteenth son Yinti Beizi (the third rank of nobility of the imperial house).

In order to prevent Yinzhi (胤禔), Kangxi's eldest son, to do more harm to the crown prince, Kangxi ordered to continue to keep him in house custody.

Kangxi ordered that Bahangelong, the lama who had practiced witchcraft on Yinreng, the crown prince, should be put to death by a thousand cuts.

6. Yinreng Is Deposed Again

In 1711 Emperor Kangxi was already on the throne for 50 years. In October this year, Emperor Kangxi found out that many ministers and high ranking officials formed a clique to conspire to put Yinreng on the throne. After investigation, he found out that the main members of this clique were: Tuoheqi, the Infantry Commander, Geng'e, Personnel Minister, Qishiwu, Minister of Justice, Eshan, a commander, and Yatu, a commander. Kangxi ordered to arrest all of them. Tuoheqi, Qishiwu and Geng'e were executed by hanging. Eshan was removed from office and put in jail. Yatu was sent to attend to the grave of Prince An. Kangxi said, "All these wicked persons worked for Yinreng. Yinreng is neither benevolent nor filial. He promised to give them handsome rewards. So they passed secrets to him. He is extremely audacious."

On 30 September 1712 Kangxi said to his sons, "Since Yinreng was restored as crown prince, he has not recovered from his lunatic disease. He has let me down. I will not entrust to him the great cause passed down from the ancestors. I have reported this to the Empress Dowager. Now I order that Yinreng be arrested and taken into custody."

Kangxi issued an imperial edict on 1 October 1712 to inform all the kings, Beiles, Beizis and all the officials that he had already deposed Yinreng as crown prince. The imperial edict read, "In the past Yinreng behaved abnormally. So he was put in custody. But later I fell ill. Considering the sentiment between father and son, I set him free. I told you all that he would reform. He also swore before the Empress Dowager, and all the kings and officials that he would reform. I expected that he would repent thoroughly of his misdeeds. But on the day when he was set free, he showed signs that he still behaved abnormally. During these several years his lunatic disease still existed. He cannot distinguish right from wrong. He has let me down. I did my best to tolerate him because I still hoped that he would correct his errors. But now I can see that it is impossible for him to correct his errors even if I teach him every day. Now I am already 60 years old. I don't know how many more years I can live. The great cause created by my ancestors was passed down to me. I have been on the throne for more than 50 years. I work hard day and night and exhaust all my energies attending to state affairs. Still I cannot say that I have done a satisfactory job.

"Yinreng is a lunatic and cannot win the support of the people. How can I entrust the great cause on him? So I have deposed Yinreng from the office of the crown prince and have kept him in custody. I have issued this imperial edict to let everyone know my decision."

On 19 October 1712 Kangxi ordered that Yinreng, the deposed crown prince, should be taken into custody in Xian'an Hall of the palace.

On 16 September Kangxi sent officials to the Temple of Heave, the Temple of Earth and the Imperial Ancestral Temple to hold ceremonies to tell Heaven, the Earth and the ancestors that he had deposed Yinreng from the position of the crown prince and had kept him in custody.

SECTION NINE: EMPEROR KANGXI PASSES AWAY

On 9 November 1722 Emperor Kangxi ordered Yinzhen (胤禛), his fourth son, to hold a sacrificial ceremony in the Temple of Heaven on 15 November for him because he was ill at that time and could not hold the ceremony personally. Considering that Kangxi was ill, Yinzhen sincerely asked his father's permission to let him attend to him. Kangxi said to Yinzhen, "I cannot go to hold the ceremony to offer sacrifices to Heaven personally. So I have ordered you to hold the ceremony in my place. Before the ceremony you must strictly fast so as to show your sincerity. Then you may hold the sacrificial ceremony for me." Yinzhen accepted his father's order and went to the fasting room in the east part of Beijing to fast. He had to stay there till 15 November.

On 10, 11, 12, November, three days in a row, Yinzhen sent his guards and eunuchs to Changchun Yuan (an imperial garden in the northwestern part of Beijing) where Kangxi was staying, to convey his best regards to his father. Kangxi sent word that he was getting better.

At 3 o'clock in the morning of 13 November, Kangxi became seriously ill. He sent a man to the fasting room to urge Yinzhen to hurry back. He sent other officials to hold the sacrificial ceremony in the Temple of Heaven. At 5 o'clock Kangxi summoned Yinzhi (胤祉), his third son, Yinyou (胤祐), his seventh son, Yinsi (胤禩), his eighth son, Yintang (胤禟), his ninth son, Yin'e (胤䄉), his tenth son, Yintao (胤祹), his twelfth son, Yinxiang (胤祥), his thirteenth son, and Longkeduo, the Minister of Minority Affairs, before his bed. Kangxi said to them, "My fourth son Yinzhen is a man of excellent character. He is very similar to me. He will surely be able to inherit the great cause. Now I order that he is to to succeed me to the throne as emperor of the Qing Dynasty."

Yinzhen rode very quickly from the fasting room to Changchun Yuan. At nine o'clock in the morning he hurried into the bedroom. Kangxi told him that he had become seriously ill. Yinzhen went into the bedroom three times to express his best regards to his father. At nine o'clock that evening, Kangxi passed away.

Kangxi left a posthumous edict which read, "All the emperors in history ruled over the realm with the principals of respecting Heaven and following the examples of the ancestors. In order to respect Heaven and follow the examples of the ancestors, an emperor should be friendly with the people in the faraway places, provide for the people, work for the interests of all the people, unify all the people, protect the country when it faces danger, practice good governance and make the country prosperous and in tranquility. I have worked hard day and night for the interest of the country. I am already 70 years old. I have been on the throne for 61 years. I can be on the throne for such a long time because Heaven, the Earth and my ancestors have granted me blessings. I learn from the history books that there have been 301 emperors since the Yellow Emperor during the period of more than 4,350 years. Very few of them could be on the throne as long as I. When I was on the throne for 20 years, I did not dare to think that I could be on the throne for 30 years. When I was on the throne for 30 years, I did not dare to think that I could be on the throne for 40 years. Now I have been on the throne for 61 years.

The Book of History mentions five blessings: the first is longevity; the second is wealth; the third is health and peacefulness; the fourth is morality; the fifth is natural death at old age. Natural death at old age ranks the fifth in the five blessings because it is very difficult to obtain. I am 70 years old this year. I own the whole nation. I have more than 150 children and grandchildren. Now the whole country is in peace and prosperity. I have enjoyed great blessings. I am at ease, even if I should die now. Since I sat on the throne, the life of the people has become much better than before. In order to realize my ancestors' aim of making the nation prosperous and letting the people enjoy life, I have been working hard day and night. All these years I have done all I can. I have spared no efforts. Zhuge Liang once said, 'I will bend to the task and spare no effort unto my dying day.' Only Zhuge Liang could do so as an official. An emperor takes up the heavy responsibility. He can not share his responsibility with anybody else. An official may work as an official and he may resign from office. He may retire when he is old and stay at home and enjoy his old age with his sons and grandsons. He can spend his life leisurely and carefree.

An emperor is busy all his life and does not have a day's rest. Emperor Yao made many inspection tours to all the corners of the country. He died in Cangwu, a faraway place. Emperor Yu spent all his life controlling the floods and he at last died in Kuaiji. They attended to the state affairs industriously. They could not lead a peaceful and quiet life. The divinatory symbols of retreat in the Book of Changes give advice to officials on how to avoid danger, but it does not give any advice to emperors on avoiding danger. From this we can see that an emperor has no way to rest or to avoid danger. An emperor has to bend to his task and spare no effort unto his dying day. Our Qing Dynasty took over the whole realm in the most proper way. At first Emperor Taizu and Emperor Taizong did not have the intention to take the whole realm. Taizong once led the army to the foot of the city of Beijing. All the officials said that the Qing army should take Beijing. But Emperor Taizong said, 'The Ming Dynasty and our state have not been friendly. It is easy to take it. But considering that the emperor of the Ming Dynasty is the ruler of China, I am not hard hearted enough to take it.' Later Li Zi Cheng took Beijing and Emperor Chongzhen of the Ming Dynasty committed suicide by hanging himself to death. His officials came to ask our army to enter Shanhaiguan Pass. Then our army defeated Li Zi Cheng and took over the whole realm. Emperor Chongzhen was buried with a proper funeral ceremony for an emperor. In the past Emperor Gaozu of the Han Dynasty was only a lowest ranking official in charge of a small area of five square kilometers in Sishui County. Emperor Taizu of the Ming Dynasty was only a monk in Huangjue Temple. Xiang Yu rose in arms to attack the Qin Dynasty. But in the end the whole realm belonged to Liu Bang who established the Han Dynasty. By the end of the Yuan Dynasty Chen You Liang rose up and took vast areas of the realm. But in the end the whole realm belonged to Zhu Yuan Zhang who established the Ming Dynasty. The ancestors of our dynasty acted in accordance with the will of Heaven and the desire of the people and owned the whole realm. From this we can see that all the treacherous local strongmen were doomed to be destroyed by the true masters.

The life of an emperor is granted by Heaven. If he should enjoy longevity, nobody can prevent him from enjoying longevity. If he should enjoy peace and tranquility, nobody can prevent him from enjoying peace and tranquility. I have read books since I was a child. I know the principles of the ancient times and those of the present days. In the prime of my life I could draw strong bows and shoot many arrows. I am good at fighting wars. But I have never killed anyone without reason. I made strategic plans to pacify the revolt of the three feudatories and defeat Galdan in the north of the great desert. All the money has been spent for the army in wars or for disaster relief. I have never wasted the money because the money has been collected from the ordinary people. I just spent no more than 20,000 taels of gold a year in making inspection tours and hunting. Every year more than 3,000,000 taels of gold have been spent in water control works. So the money spent for my inspection tours is less than one percent of the money spent in water control works. Emperor Xiao Yan was the founder of the Liang Dynasty. When he was old he was persecuted by Jing Hou, the premier. He at last died in Taicheng. Yang Jian, Emperor Wen of the Sui Dynasty was the founder of the Sui Dynasty. But he could not predict the evil doings of his son Yang Guang, Emperor Yang of the Sui Dynasty. At last Yang Guang died a violent death. I am already 70 years old. I have more than a hundred children and grandchildren. After I die, you should live in harmony and take care of yourselves. Then I may die in peace. My fourth son Yinzhen is a person of excellent character. He is quite similar to me. He will surely be able to succeed the great cause. Now I order that he should ascend the throne and be the emperor. He should wear the mourning apparel for 27 days according the rules. This should be publicized to all the people so that they all know my intention."

Emperor Kangxi was given the posthumous title of Emperor Ren (Chinese characters: 仁皇帝, meaning "Emperor of Benevolence"). His temple title was Shengzu (Chinese characters: 聖祖, meaning "Sacred Ancestor"). On 1 September 1723 Kangxi was buried in Jingling Mausoleum (located in Zunhua, Hebei Province).

Historians highly praised Kangxi. They said, "Shengzu was benevolent and filial in nature. He was intelligent and valiant. He succeeded to the throne when he was young. He was diligent in administration and for the benefit of the people. He was an emperor with civil and military abilities. He unified the whole realm. Kangxi was an emperor who maintained the achievements of his predecessors. But his contributions were so great that he could be regarded as the founder of a dynasty. He had profound learning. He respected Confucianism and Taoism. He was open minded. He persistently implemented his policies. He did his best to reform the society. Under his reign the people enjoyed their life and the whole realm was in great peace and tranquility. The prosperous period under the reign of Kangxi has great influence in history. People today still long for that prosperous period. The Book of Great Learning states, 'As a monarch, he devoted himself in practicing benevolence.' It also states, 'The people will never forget the monarch who was virtuous.'"

CHAPTER THREE: AISIN GIORO YINZHEN, EMPEROR YONGZHENG OF THE QING DYNASTY

SECTION ONE: THE REIGN OF AISIN GIORO YINZHEN

1. Aisin Gioro Yinzhen Ascends the Throne

On 20 September 1722 Yinzhen ascended the throne of the Qing Dynasty at the age of forty-five. He decided that the title of his reign was Yongzheng (雍正), and the year of 1723 would be the first year of Yongzheng. Historians use his reign title and refer to him as Emperor Yongzheng, or the Yongzheng Emperor.

According to the rule that no one could have any word in his name the same with that of the name of the emperor, all his brothers had to change their names. Yinzhi (胤禔) was changed into Yunzhi (允禔); Yinreng (胤礽) was changed into Yunreng (允礽); Yinzhi (胤祉) was changed into Yunzhi (允祉); Yinqi (胤祺) was changed into Yunqi (允祺); Yinzuo (胤祚) was changed into Yunzuo (允祚); Yinyou (胤祐) was changed into Yunyou (允祐); Yinsi (胤禩) was changed into Yunsi (允禩); Yintang (胤禟) was changed into (允禟); Yin'e (胤䄉) was changed into Yun'e (允䄉); Yinzi (胤禌) was changed into Yunzi (允禌); Yintao (胤祹) was changed into Yuntao (允祹); Yinxiang (胤祥) was changed into (允祥); Yinti (胤禵) was changed into Yunti (允禵).

Emperor Yonzheng appointed his younger brothers Yunsi and Yunxiang, Maqi, a scholar, and Minister Longkeduo to manage the government affairs. In December he made Yunsi as Prince Lian, Yunxiang as Prince Yi, Yuntao as Prefecture King Lü, Hongxi, Yunreng's son, as Prefecture King Li. He appointed Longkeduo as the Personnel Minister, Yunsi as the Minister of Minority Affairs and Zhang Ting Yu as the Minister of Rites.

6. Aisin Gioro Yinzhen, Emperor Yongzheng of the Qing Dynasty

2. Measures Taken by Emperor Yongzheng to Consolidate His Rule

During the reign of Kangxi, when Yingreng was deposed from the position of the crown prince, Yunsi planned a scheme to take the position of the crown prince. Emperor Yongzheng disliked what Yunsi had done in that time. Yunsi knew clearly that Yongzheng disliked what he had done. So he was often discontented and unhappy. When Yongzheng issued the order to make him Prince Lian, his wife said to those who came to express their congratulations, "What's the use of expressing congratulations? I am afraid that sooner or later he will be put to death." When Yongzheng heard about this, he disliked Yunsi all the more.

In January 1724 Emperor Yongzheng said, "Yunsi has always been insidious and crafty. Father Emperor knew this very well. He issued many imperial edicts to condemn Yunsi. Since I ascended the throne, I have treated Yunsi very well. I made him a prince. Later I appointed him to manage the government affairs. But he did not do his best to serve me. He still cherished the hope of taking the throne. He tried in every way to provoke me to anger so that I would punish him. He did this in order to charge me with the crime of doing harm to my brothers. Among my brothers, Yunsi is quite capable of managing government affairs. I valued his ability. He was much better than Yuntang and Yun'e. So I often advised him to reform. I have to do this because I am responsible for the ancestors and the whole realm."

In February 1724 Yunsi was not given any awards because he just worked for his own interests. Later Emperor Yongzheng issued several imperial edicts to blame Yunsi because the ancestor plates for the Ancestral Temple and the weapons for the army stationed in Altay (in the north part of Xinjiang Uygur Autonomous Region) made by the Ministry of Works were of very low quality. Yunsi proposed to Yongzheng that the number of armors for the Imperial Household Department should be reduced. But very soon he suggested to Yongzheng that the amount of armor for each basic unit should be increased from 50 suits to 90 suits.

His two suggestions conflicted with each other. Yongzheng said, "Yunsi is the most treacherous person."

One day a group of soldiers in the Imperial House Department gathered before the residence of Yunsi and made a lot of noise. The next day the same group of soldiers gathered before the house of Li Yan Xi, the Deputy Commander of the troops of the Imperial Household Department, and looted his house. Yongzheng ordered to arrest these soldiers. They were interrogated. One of them confessed that Yunsi had instigated them to make trouble in the house of Deputy Commander Li Yan Xi. Yongzheng ordered Yunsi to execute the leaders of this group. Yunsi presented to Yongzheng a list of five persons. Yongzheng found that one of them was the one who had made the confession. One of them insisted that he had not taken part in the looting of the house because he had been ill and had stayed at home. Yongzheng blamed Yunsi for presenting a false list. The Imperial Clan Court suggested that Yunsi should be stripped of the title of a prince. Yongzheng ordered to spare him. Yunsi had beaten 96 guards to death. The Imperial Clan Court again suggested that Yunsi should be stripped of his title of a prince. But Yongzheng again spared him.

In January 1726 Emperor Yongzheng summoned all the kings and the ministers to the palace to expose Yunsi's crimes to them. He said, "During the reign of Shengzu, Yunsi did a lot of things that made

Shengzu unhappy. When Yunreng was deposed from the position of the crown prince, Shengzu ordered Yunsi and me to manage the government affairs. We presented many memorials to Shengzu. Shengzu wrote his comments on each of the memorials and returned them to us. Yunsi kept all these memorials. Later when I asked Yunsi where those memorials were, he said, 'When father emperor was angry, I was afraid that the memorials might cause trouble. So I burned all the memorials with all the comments written by father emperor.' After Shengzu passed away, I considered that Yunsi was a capable man. I hoped that he would repent thoroughly of his misdeeds and work for the state. I let him manage the government affairs and made him a prince. I treated him with sincerity. During these three years, the Imperial Clan Court and the ministers suggested to me many times that I should punish him. But I did my best to tolerate him. Yunsi is treacherous and insidious. He entertains rebellious schemes in his mind. I ordered the officials in the Imperial Household Court to interrogate him why he had burned all the memorials with the comments written by father emperor. He said, 'At that time I was seriously ill. I burned all the memorials when my mind was in great confusion.' When I interrogated him personally, he swore that what he had said was true. He has alienated himself from Heaven and from the Ancestors. He has also alienated himself from me. It is impossible for him to be a member of the Imperial Clan. According to the instruction of father emperor and following the rule of stripping the membership of the Imperial Clan, now I declare that Yunsi has been stripped of the membership of the Imperial Clan."

In February 1726 the kings and the ministers suggested to Emperor Yongzheng that Yunsi should be executed. Yongzheng did not agree. He just ordered to strip Yunsi's title as a king and keep him in the jail of the Imperial Household Court. In June 1726 the kings and the ministers listed Yunsi's 40 crimes and suggested to execute Yunsi. Yongzheng just allowed the officials to announce Yunsi's crimes to the public. In September Yunsi fell ill. He kept vomiting. Yongzheng ordered the doctors to treat him. But not long later he died in jail.

Yuntang, Kangxi's ninth son, and Yun'e, Kangxi's tenth son, were diehard followers of Yunsi. In January 1726 Yuntang was stripped of the membership of the Imperial Clan. In June the kings and the ministers accused Yuntang of having committed 28 crimes and they suggested to Emperor Yongzheng that Yubtang should be executed. Yongzheng did not agree. He just ordered to put Yuntang in jail in Baoding (now Baoding, Hebei Province). In August he fell ill and died of stomachache. Yun'e was stripped of membership in the Imperial Clan and put in jail in April 1724. He was lucky enough to live until the reign of Emperor Qianlong and he was released in 1737.

SECTION TWO: THE DEFEAT OF LOBSANG TENDZIN AND THE
PACIFICATION OF QINGHAI

1. The Rise of Lobsang Tendzin in Qinghai

Lobsang Tendzin's father Dashbaatar was the head of the Mongolian Khoshut Tribe in the east part of Qinghai (now Qinghai Province, in the northwest part of China). In November 1697 Dashbaatar led all the heads of subtribes to Beijing to have an audience with Emperor Kangxi. He granted Dashbaatar royal costumes and court beads. In January 1698 Kangxi issued an imperial edict to make Dashbaatar a prince.

In 1714 Dashbaatar died. Lobsang Tendzin inherited his father's title of a prince and became the head of the Mongolian Khoshut Tribe. In 1720 he commanded his troops to join in the Qing army's action of escorting the 7th Dalai Lama into Tibet. When he came back to Qinghai from Tibet, he attempted to be the head of the whole Qinghai and Tibet area. He secretly asked Tsewang Rabtan, Khan of the Dzungar Khanate, to help him. He seduced the heads of the subtribes to support him. He abandoned the title of prince granted by the emperor of the Qing Dynasty and named himself Khong Taiji (the Mongolian title for crown prince, the highest rank for the Mongolian nobles). Erdeni Erketoketonai, a prefecture king, would not submit to him and he led his people to move to the area controlled by the Qing army for protection.

2. The Defeat of Lobsang Tendzin and the Pacification of Qinghai

In 1723 Lobsang Tendzin led the heads of the subtribes of Khoshut Tribe to rebel against the Qing Dynasty. He led his troops to attack his close relative Chahan Tendzin. Chahan Tendzin had to lead his people to go the area controlled by the Qing army for protection. Yongzheng issued an imperial edict to Nian Geng Yao, the Governor of Sichuan and Shaanxi, which read, "Lobsang Tendzin's grandfather Güshi Khan had been respectful and submissive. His father Dashbaatar came over and submitted to our Dynasty and was made a prince. Later Lobsang Tendzin inherited his father's title of a prince. He should have been thankful to the kindness granted to him and complied with the law. But now he is so brutal as to suppress his close relatives Prince Chahan Tendzin and Prefecture King Erdeni Erketoketonai. He has held a rebellion. When I got the information that he had attacked his close relatives, I sent an envoy to persuade him to stop the action and make peace. But he led his army to attack Chahan Tendzin and Erdeni Erketoketonai. They had to come to our territory for protection. He has betrayed me. He has gone against the law of Heaven. He must be seriously punished. Now I appoint you as Grand General of Pacifying the Far Away Places. You should command the army to carry out a punitive expedition against Lobsang Tendzin. If he dares to resist, you may just exterminate him. You may spare those who were forced to join in the rebellion if they come to surrender. Those who can kill Lobsang Tendzin will be awarded handsomely."

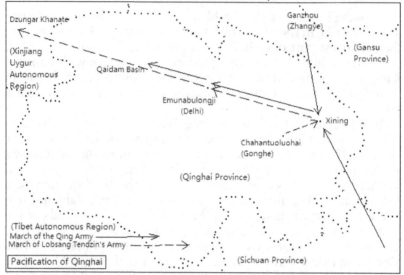

Lobsang Tendzin pretended to have stopped the rebellion. He lured Changshou, Emperor Yongzheng's envoy, to Chahantuoluohai (a place in Gonghe, in the east part of Qinghai Province) and detained him. In October 1723 Nian Geng Yao commanded his army to march from Ganzhou (now Zhangye, Gansu Province) to Xining (now Xining, in the east part of Qinghai Province). He asked Emperor Yongzheng to put Commander Sudan and Yue Zhong Qi, Sichuan provincial Governor, under his command.

When Nian Geng Yao reached Xining, his main force was still on the way. Lobsang Tendzin got this information and sent his troops to attack the strongholds around Xining and took them all. Then he commanded his troops to attack the city of Xining. Nian Geng Yao and the generals under him sat on the tower on the top of the city wall calmly and commanded his troops to resist the attack. Then Lobsang Tendzin had to give up the attack of the City of Xining and turned to surround the stronghold to the south of the City of Xining. Lobsang Tendzin forced his troops to go forward. The troops under Nian Geng Yao fired cannons and killed many enemy soldiers.

In November 1723 Yue Zhong Qi commanded his troops to reach the City of Xining. He ordered his troops to attack the camps of Lobsang Tendzin's army. Lobsang Tendzin was defeated and ran away. Yue Zhong Qi commanded his troops to pursue the enemy. Lobsang Tendzin had a narrow escape with only 100 soldiers.

In March 1724 Yue Zhong Qi marched the army under him to Emunabulongji (in the north of Delhi, in the mid-north part of Qinghai Province) where Lobsang Tendzin and his army stayed. He sent a detachment to prevent Lobsang Tendzin from escaping into Qaidam Basin (in the west part of Qinghai Province). Lobsang Tendzin escaped into Qaidam Basin. Yue Zhong Qi commanded his army to pursue him. In Qaidam Basin the Qing troops captured Lobsang Tendzin's mother Altaihatun and his relatives. They also captured many people and numerous cows, sheep, horses and camels. The heads of the subtribes of the Khoshut Tribe who had joined in the rebellion were killed or surrendered. Lobsang Tendzin escaped with 200 men to the Dzungar Khanate (in Xingjiang Uyghur Autonomous Region). Then the whole area of Qinghai was pacified. From then on Qinghai was put under the direct control of the government of the Qing Dynasty.

SECTION THREE: THE REFORMS CARRIED OUT BY EMPEROR YONGZHENG

1. The Replacement of the Native Chieftains by Officials Appointed by the Government

In places where the people of minority nationalities lived, the people were ruled by their native chieftains. In May 1724 Emperor Yongzheng issued an imperial edict to the governors of Sichuan, Shaanxi, Hunan, Guangdong, Guanxi, Yunnan and Guizhou which read, "I know that the native chieftains in different places ignore the laws. They levy a heavy tax on the native people. The tax they levied is more than twice of the tax levied by the government. They rob the people of their horses and cows. They take away the children of the people. They killed people at their own will. The native people suffer a lot from the suppression by the native chieftains. The people feel indignant but not dare to say anything against them. I am doing my best to let all the people enjoy their life. But the native people are still living in suffering. I feel sad for them. From now on the governors should be strict with the native chieftains under them and should not allow them to treat the people brutally."

Xiang Guo Dong, the native chieftain of Sangzhi (now in the northwest part of Hunan Province), and Peng Yu Bin, the native chieftain of Baojing (now in the northwest part of Hunan Province) treated the native people cruelly. They killed the native people at their own will. In August 1728 Emperor Yongzheng issued an imperial edict to the governor of Hunan to give his consent to replace the native chieftains of Sangzhi, Baojing and Yongshun (in the northwest part of Hunan Province with officials appointed by the government who had a term of office. In May 1729 Yongshun became Yongshun

County; Baojing became Baojing County; and Sangzhi became Sangzhi County. An official was appointed to each of these counties to be the magistrate of the county. The Qing government sent 800 officers and men to station in Yongshun County, 400 officers and men in Baojing County, and 300 officers and men in Sangzhi County.

2. Reform of the Tax System

In the past governments of different dynasties practiced the "head tax" system. Tax was levied on grown-up males. Many grown-up males did not have any farmland. They could not get money to pay tax. They lived in suffering. In July 1723 Li Wei Jun, Governor of Hebei Province, presented a memorial to Emperor Yongzheng to ask his permission to substitute head tax by levying tax according to farmland in the area of Hebei Province. Emperor Yongzheng let the Ministry of Revenue to discuss this matter.

In September 1723 the Ministry of Revenue reported the result of their discussion to Emperor Yongzheng which read, "Li Wei Jun, Governor of Hebei Province, asked permission to substitute head tax by levying tax according to farmland. We suggest that Your Majesty should grant him the permission. And this policy should be carried out at the beginning of next year. By that time head tax will be replaced by levying tax according to farmland. The amount of farmland owned by each person should be registered in books and tax will be levied according to the amount of farmland registered in these books." Emperor Yongzheng let the Nine Ministers to discuss this matter.

On 22 September 1723 the Nine Ministers reported to Yongzheng that they supported Li Wei Jun's suggestion to substitute head tax by levying tax according farmland. Then Yongzheng ordered Li Wei Jun to carry out this tax reform in Hebei Province from the beginning of 1724. Gradually this policy was carried in the whole realm.

3. Melting Silver Pieces to Make Silver Bars; New Tax and New Benefits to Officials to Encourage Honesty

In the past the people paid tax with small pieces of silver. The local officials of the county level had to melt these small pieces to make silver bars so as to present them to the provincial government. During this procedure about 10% of the silver would be lost. If the tax was paid with grains, birds and rats would take the grains during transportation of these grains. So there would be 10% loss during the transportation of the tax grains. In order to make up the loss, the local officials would levy 30% to 40% more of the tax from the people. The local officials took the extra tax silver for themselves or used it to bribe their upper level officials. During the Qing Dynasty, the officials got low pay. So they accepted bribes from the officials under them and became corrupted.

In June 1724 Nuomin, the Governor of Shanxi Province, and Gao Cheng Ling, the Administrative Commissioner of Shanxi Province, presented memorials to Emperor Yongzheng in which they suggested that the additional tax should be levied by the officials of counties and should be transferred to the treasury of the provincial government. The additional tax could be used to increase the income of officials so as to nourish honesty. And it could be used for special expenditures so that it was not necessary for the counties and prefectures to levy extra tax for the special expenditures. In this way the additional tax would not be taken as their private property.

In July 1724 Emperor Yongzheng issued an imperial edict to ratify the suggestion by Nuomin and Gao Cheng Long. He allowed the officials of other provinces to carry out this policy. Several years later, the national treasury was full. The people's burden was lightened.

SECTION FOUR: THE DEMISE OF EMPEROR YONGZHENG

On 21 August 1735 Yongzheng fell ill. But he still attended to the state affairs. On 22 August he became seriously ill. His fourth son Hongli, Prince Bao, and his fifth son Hongzhou, Prince He, attended to him day and night. At 8 o'clock that night, Yongzheng summoned Yunlu, Prince Zhuang, Yunli, Prince Guo, Grand Scholars Eltai and Zhang Ting Yu, Ministers Fengsheng'e, Naqin and Langhaiwang to his bedroom. Eltai and Zhang Ting Yu took out the imperial edict written by Yongzheng personally which read, "I now appoint my fourth son Hongli as the crown prince. He may ascend the throne now." Not long later the crown prince came out to convey Yongzheng's order to appoint Yunlu, Prince of Zhuang, Yunli, Prince of Guo, Grand Scholars Eltai and Zhang Ting Yu as regents.

On 23 August Yongzheng passed away at the age of fifty-eight. He had been on the throne for 13 years. In November that year he was given the posthumous title of Emperor Xian (in Chinese character: 憲). His temple title was Shizong (in Chinese characters: 世宗). He was buried in Tai Mosolium in the Western Qing Tombs (in Yixian, Hebei Province).

Historians highly praised Emperor Yongzheng. Emperor Yongzheng practiced strict rule. He was a hard working emperor. He attended to the state affairs till late at night. He carried out several reforms that made China strong and stable. The people lived in peace and prosperity. Some historians said that he was an emperor as great as Emperor Wen (Liu Heng, 202 BC–157 BC) and Emperor Jing (Liu Qi, 188 BC–141 BC) of the Western Han Dynasty (202 BC-8 AD) who created the prosperity period of Wen and Jing.

CHAPTER FOUR: AISIN GIORO HONGLI, EMPEROR QIANLONG OF THE QING DYNASTY

SECTION ONE: AISIN GIORO HONGLI ASCENDS THE THRONE

In the early morning of 3 September 1735 all the officials gathered in the court. Aisin Gioro Hongli in white clothes went to the place where the coffin of the late emperor was. He knelt before the coffin and touched his head to the ground nine times. He told his late father that he was going to ascend the throne in accordance with his order. After that he changed clothes and donned the robes of an emperor. Then he accompanied his mother to Yongshou Palace (the Palace of Eternal Longevity). He helped his mother into her chair. He knelt before his mother and touched his head to the ground nine times. After that he went to Taihe Hall (the Hall of Supreme Harmony) in the palace where he ascended the throne of the Qing Dynasty. All the kings, ministers and officials came up to express their congratulations. He declared that the title of his reign was "Qianlong" (Chinese characters: 乾隆). The word "Qian" (乾) means "Heaven"; the word "Long" (隆) means "prosperous" or "prosperity". The two words put together may mean "As prosperous as Heaven" or "May Heaven grant prosperity to our country". Then 1736 became the first year of Qianlong. Historians use this reign title, Qianlong, to refer to this emperor.

7. Aisin Gioro Hongli, Emperor Qianlong of the Qing Dynasty

SECTION TWO: PACIFICATION OF TIBET

1. The Situation in Tibet

Polhanas was one of the four Kalöns (administrative officials) of Tibet. He worked very hard and made great contribution in administrating Tibet. In 1740 Emperor Qianlong made him a Prefecture King. Polhanas had two sons. The elder one was Gyurme Cebudeng. The younger one was Gyurme Namgyal. Emperor Qianlong would appoint one of them to inherit Polhanas' title of prefecture king. The elder son Gyurme Cebudeng offered the chance to his younger brother. Polhanas liked his second son better than the first son and he asked Emperor Qianlong to let his second son inherit the title. Qianlong gave his consent. He also issued an imperial edict to make Polhanas' first son a duke and ordered him to guard Ngary Prefecture (in the west part of Tibet Autonomous Region). In 1748 Polhanas died of illness. Gyurme Namyal succeeded his father as Prefecture King. And he also took the position of a Kalön (administrative official in Tibet).

2. Pacification of the Rebellions in Tibet

In 1751 Gyurme Namyal commanded his troops to Ngary Prefecture and killed his elder brother Gyurme Cebudeng. He reported to the court of the Qing Dynasty that Gyurme Cebudeng had died of serious disease. Then he took his army to Back Tibet (in the area of Shigatse, in the south part of Tibet Autonomous Region) where Gyurme Cebudeng's two sons were. He killed Gyurme Cebudeng's first son Pengsukewangbu. Gyurme Cebudeng's second son ran away to be a lama under Panchen Lama and he escaped death.

In November 1751 Fu Qing, the Commander-in-chief of the Qing army stationed in Tibet, and Labudun, Supervisor of the Qing army stationed in Tibet, knew that Gyurme Namgyal would take the whole area of Tibet and rebel against the Qing Dynasty. They reported this to Emperor Qianlong. They made a plan to kill Gyurme Namgyal. On 14 November they summoned him to the office of the Official of the Qing Government in Tibet. They waited for him on the second floor of the office. When Gyurme Namgyal arrived, he was asked to go up to the second floor. Then Fu Qing went forward and held Gyurme Namgyal's arms. Labudun drew out his sword and killed Gyurme Namgyal. Robsang Zashi, Gyurme Namgyal's subordinate, commanded 1,000 soldiers to surround and attack the office. They gathered firewood on the first floor and set fire on the office. Fu Qing and Labudun fought very bravely. But they were killed. On 15 November Emperor Qianlong ordered Celeng, the Governor of Sichuan Province, and Yue Zhong Qi, the Commander-in-chief of the army stationed in Sichuan to command the army in Sichuan to march into Tibet. Before the Qing army under Celeng and Yue Zhong Qi reached Tibet, Bandida, the Duke of Tibet, put down the rebellion and captured Zuoni and Robsang Zashi, the two heads of the rebellion. Bandida and his troops waited for the Qing army to come. When Celeng got the information, he ordered the main force to stay in Dajianlu (now Kangding, in the west part of Sichuan Province). He commanded only 800 men to march quickly to Tibet. When Celeng reached Tibet, he discussed with Zhaohui, a minister of the Qing government, Namuza'er, the Qing imperial resident in Tibet, and Bandida to make rules and regulations to cope with the aftermath of the rebellions in Tibet. According to the rules and regulations there should be four Kalöns to attend to the administration affairs in

Tibet. The four Kalöns should be put under the leadership of the Qing imperial resident in Tibet and the Dalai Lama. The Qing government should send 1,500 officers and men to station in Tibet. From then on the rule of the Qing government in Tibet was strengthened and Tibet became stable.

SECTION THREE: THE CONQUEST OF THE DZUNGAR KHANATE

1. The Situation in the Dzungar Khanate

In 1727, Tsewang Rabtan, Khan of the Dzungar Khanate, died. His son Galdan Tseren succeeded his father and became Khan. In September 1745 Galdan Tseren died. His two sons Lama Dorji and Tsewang Dorji Namjal fought against each other to be the khan. In 1750 Tsewang Dorji Namjal was murdered by his subordinates. So Lama Dorji succeeded to be khan. In 1752 Dawachi, the grandson of Teren Dondub (who was Tsewang Rabtan's younger brother), supported by Amursana, the head of the Khoid Tribe, got the power and became Khan. In March 1754 Dawachi and Amursana became enemies and began to attack each other. In June 1754 Amursana was defeated by Dawachi and escaped to the area of Irtysh River (in the north part of Xinjiang Uyghur Autonomous Region). He intended to surrender to the Qing government. Qianlong ordered General Celeng to help him. In July 1754 Amursana with his troops came to surrender. Qianlong ordered Amursana to come to have an interview with him. On 12 November Qianlong reached Chengde Mountain Summer Resort (now in Chengde, in the northeast part of Hebei Province). On 19 November Amursana and his subordinates arrived at the Summer Resort. Qianlong received them in a hall in the Summer Resort. He made Amursana as a prince. He made Amursana's subordinates as prefecture kings, Beiles and dukes.

2. Pacification of Ili and the Capture of Dawachi, Khan of the Dzungar Khanate

In January 1756 Emperor Qianlong appointed Bandi as General of Dingbian (Dingbian means Pacification of the Border Area), and Amursana as the Left Deputy General of Dingbian. He ordered them to command the troops under them to attack the Dzungar Khanate from the north route. They should start their march from Ullaangom (in the west part of Mongolia). He appointed Yongchang as General of Dingxi (Dingxi means Pacification of the West) and Sala'er as his deputy. He ordered Yongchang and Sala'er to command the troops under them to attack the Dzungar Khanate from the west route. They should start their march from Barkol (in the northeast part of Xinjiang Uygur Autonomous Region). The two routes of army should join forces in Bortala (now the capital city of Bortala Mongol Autonomous Prefecture, in the western Xinjiang Uygur Autonomous Region), then they should start an attack on Ili, the Dzungar capital.

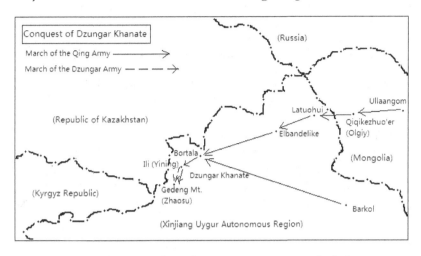

In February 1756 Bandi and Amursana commanded their troops to march to the Dzungar Khanate from Ullaangom. Amursana commanded 6,000 men to go first. Bandi commanded 2,000 men started later. When Bandi reached Qiqikezhuo'er (a place near Ölgiy, in the west part of Mongolia), he found that there were not enough horses for his troops. So he left 500 men behind to wait for the horses. He commanded 1,500 men to go first. He caught up with Amursana in Latuohui (a place in the north part of Xinjiang Uygur Autonomous Region). Emperor Qianlong had told Bandi that he should let Amursana to go first because the Dzungar people knew Amursana and Amursana could persuade the Dzungar officers and men to submit and that it was not necessary for Bandi to go together with Amursana. So when they reached Elbandelike, Bandi ordered Amursana to go first. In April the troops under Bandi reached Bortala. They caught the officials sent by Dawachi to recruit soldiers. From these officials Bandi found out that Dawachi did not know that the Qing troops were coming and had not prepared to defend Ili. Bandi sent an envoy to urge the troops of the west route to march quickly to Bortala. In May, the two routes of the troops joined forces and started a fierce attack on the city of Ili and took it. Dawachi commanded 10,000 men to retreat to Gedeng Mountain (in Zhaosu County, in the west part of Xinjiang Uygur Autonomous Region). Commander Ayuxi commanded 25 cavalrymen to start a surprised attack on the enemy troops at night. The Dzungar soldiers were scared and ran away. When the victory was reported to Emperor Qianlong, he made Bandi Duke of Chengyong (Chengyong means Honest and Brave). Bandi knew that the provision in Ili was poor. It could not provide enough food for the great army. So he suggested to Emperor Qianlong that 500 soldiers could stay in Ili area and the main force may withdraw back to Barkol. Qianlong accepted his suggestion and ordered Bandi and Erong'an, the adviser of the army, to stay in Ili with 500 soldiers. The main force began to withdraw. In June the Qing troops captured Dawachi. On 17 October Dawachi was escorted to Beijing. On 28 October a ceremony of presenting captives was held. Qianlong sat on a chair on the tower of the city wall of Beijing to receive the captives. After the ceremony Qianlong spared Dawachi and made him a prince. From then on the Dzungar Khanate was pacified.

3. Putting Down Amursana's Rebellion

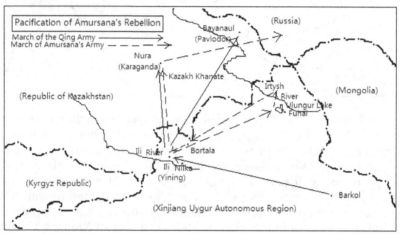

When the Qing army started to march to the Dzungar Khanate, Emperor Qianlong had sensed that Amursana had his own secret purpose. He ordered Bandi to keep Amursana under strict control. When the Qing army took Ili, Emperor Qianlong intended to make the heads of the four subtribes of the Khoshut Tribe khans of the four subtribes. He planned to make Amursana Khan of the Khoid Tribe. But Amursana wanted to be the general head of all the four subtribes. So he was quite unhappy with Emperor Qianlong's decision. He did not use the seal of the Deputy General of Dingbian. He used the seal of Galdan Tseren, the former Khan of the Dzungar Khanate, to show to the local people of the subtribes of the Khoshut Tribe. He concealed the fact that he had surrendered to the Qing Dynasty. He told the local people that he had brought the Chinese soldiers to pacify the Dzungar area. So it became clear that he was going to rebel. After Ili had been taken, Emperor Qianlong summoned Amursana to go back. He planned to have an interview with Amursana and other heads of the subtribes of the Khoshut Tribe in Chengde Mountain Summer Resort in September 1756. By that time he would hold a grand ceremony to make them khans. Sebuteng Ba'erzhu'er, an official in the army, was going back first. Amursana asked him to beg Emperor Qianlong to make him Khan of the Khoshut Tribe so that he could be the general head of all the four subtribes. When Sebuteng Ba'erzhu'er reached Beijing, he did not dare to convey Amursana's desire to Emperor Qianlong. Emperor Qianlong sent an envoy to ask Bandi to urge Amursana to go to Chengde Mountain Summer Resort. And he ordered Elinqin Duo'erji, an adviser of the army, to accompany him. Amursana had to start his journey back unhappily. Qianlong expected that Amursana would rebel in the end. So he ordered Bandi to act before Amursana rebelled. When Qianlong's order reached Bandi, Amursana had already started his journey back.

In August 1756, when Amursana reached Ulungur (now Ulungur Lake, in Fuhai, in the northwest part of Xinjiang Uygur Autonomous Region), he took out the seal of the Left General of Dingbian and gave it to Elinqin Duo'erji who was accompanying Amursana back to Chengde Mountain Summer Resort. Amursana asked him to give the seal back to Emperor Qianlong. Then Amursana rebelled. He commanded his troops to the area of Irtysh River (in the northwest part of Xinjiang Uygur Autonomous Region). Keshimu, Balang, Dunkeduomanji and Wuketu were Amursana's followers. On 24 August they held a rebellion in Ili. Bandi and Erong'an commanded the 500 soldiers to resist them. The enemy force was too strong. So they retreated eastward to the area of the upper reach of Ili River, then to Nilka (a place to the east of Yining, in the west part of Xinjiang Uygur Autonomous Region). The enemy troops came and surrounded them. Bandi and Erong'an would rather die than be captured. They drew out their own swords and killed themselves.

In late August Amursana and his troops came to Bortala (in the west part of Xinjiang Uygur Autonomous Region). In January 1757 Amursana and his troops came back to Ili. In March Emperor Qianlong ordered Celeng, General of Dingxi (Dingxi means Pacification of the West), to march from Barcol to take back Ili and capture Amursana. In the same month Celeng commanded his troops to Ili and defeated Amursana and recovered Ili. Amursana ran away to the Kazakh Khanate (now Republic of Kazakhstan). Ablai, Khan of the Kazakh Khanate, united with Amursana to resist the Qing army. He married his daughter to Amursana. Celeng commanded his troops to march to the border between China and the Kazakh Khanate. Qianlong ordered him get ready to march into the territory of the Kazakh Khanate to capture Amursana and escort him to Beijing. In April 1757 Qianlong sent an envoy to take a letter to Ablai, Khan of the Kazakh Khanate, urging him to capture Amursana and escort him to Beijing, otherwise he would order 10,000 Qing soldiers to enter the territory of the Kazakh Khanate to capture Amursana. In August Hadaha, the Left Deputy General of Dingbian, defeated Ablai's troops in Bayanaul (in the south part of Pavlodar, in the northeast part of the Republic of Kazakhstan). In the same month Daledang'a, General of Dingxi, defeated the troops commanded by Amursana in Nura (a place in Karaganda in central Kazakhstan). In July 1758 Ablai sent seven envoys to see Qianlong to express his intention of surrendering to the Qing Dynasty with all the territory of the Kazakh Khanate. Qianlong accepted his surrender and ordered him to capture Amursana. Amursana found that he could not stay in the Kazakh Khanate any more. In September 1758 he escaped to Russia. In January 1759 the Russian official in charge of the border area informed the Chinese that Amursana had died from smallpox. The Russians transported Amursana's body to Kyakhta (a Russian place by the northern border of Mongolia). They asked the Qing government to send officials to examine the corpse and verify its identity. Emperor Qianlong sent officials who knew Amursana well; they examined the remains and confirmed that Amursana had really died.

SECTION FOUR: THE COMPILATION OF SIKU QUANSHU (四庫全書)
(COMPLETE LIBRARY IN FOUR SECTIONS)

In China, there were many books on Confucian classics, history, philosophy, literature, various schools of thought, astronomy, geography, medical science and doctrines both Buddhist and Taoist. In 1403 Emperor Zhu Di (1360–1424), the third emperor of the Ming Dynasty (1368–1644), ordered the scholars to put all the books together and compile one complete set. The scholars worked very hard for several years. In winter 1408, they finally completed compiling the great set of books. Emperor Zhu Di named it Yongle Dadian (the Yongle Great Encyclopedia, 永樂大典). This massive work contained 22,933 sections bound into 11,095 books with 370 million characters.

In November 1773, Zhu Jun, the director of education and imperial examination in Anhui Province, presented a memorial to Emperor Qianlong stating that the collection lacked some important books. He suggested that a search for such books should be carried out in all the provinces; there were very few books of the Han Dynasty (202 BC–220) and Tang Dynasty (618–907) left; there had been no officially published books of commentary on classics and history written in the periods of Liao Dynasty (916–1125), Song Dynasty (960–1279), Jin Dynasty (1115–1234) and Yuan Dynasty (1271–1368). He suggested that the government should seek out and buy such books from the people and make officially published copies. He also stated that it was problematic that books in Yongle Dadian were classified by the four tones of the sound of the first character in the titles of the books, so the books in the same classification were not the same kind of books; he suggested that the new set of books should be divided into four parts: Jing (經) (Confucian Classics), Shi (史) (History), Zi (子) (Masters, Schools of Thought), and Ji (集) (Literary Collections).

In March 1774, Emperor Qianlong ordered the court officials and scholars to check and proofread Yongle Dadian and to select the books in it to make copies. He ordered them to put all the copies selected in Yongle Dadian, together with the books collected from different provinces and all the books stored in the Imperial Library to compile a whole set of books. All the books were classified into four categories as described. He named this great set of books Siku Quanshu (四庫全書), meaning "the Complete Library in Four Sections."

Emperor Qianlong appointed Grand Scholars Liu Tong Xun, Liu Lun and Lu Min Zhong as the General Managers in charge of compiling the great books. He appointed Ji Yun and Lu Xi Xiong as Chief Editors, with forty more officials and scholars under them; 3,800 officials were in charge of copying the books. More than 300 scholars proofread the output. All the people worked very hard for nine years. In January 1783 the compilation of Siku Quanshu was completed. This great work included 3,500 volumes, 78,000 chapters, and 36,000 titles with 800 million Chinese characters. It was the greatest written work in the world at that time.

In order to store the copies of Siku Quanshu, Emperor Qianlong had ordered four libraries built. They were: Wenyuan Ge (文淵閣) in the Forbidden City; Wensu Ge (文溯閣) in Shengjing (now Shenyang, Liaoning Province); Wenyuan Ge (文源閣) in Yuanming Yuan (圓明園) (now the Old Summer Palace in Beijing); and Wenjin Ge (文津閣) in Chengde, Hebei Province. In July Qianlong ordered that those copies of Siku Quanshu that were already finished should be stored in these four libraries. At the same time he ordered that three more copies be made to store in Wenhui Ge (文匯閣) in Yangzhou, Jiangsu Province, Wenzong Ge (文宗閣) in Zhenjian, Jiangsu Province, and Wenlan Ge (文瀾閣) in Hangzhou, Zhejiang Province.

SECTION FIVE: EMPEROR QIANLONG LEAVES THE THRONE TO HIS 15TH SON AISIN GIORO YONGYAN

By 1796 Emperor Qianlong had been in power for 60 years, and he was already 86 years old. On 3 September 1796 Qianlong sat on the throne in Qinzheng Hall by Zhongnanhai, Beijing. He summoned all his sons, grandsons, kings, dukes and the court officials to have an audience with him. He declared that he had decided to name his 15th son Aisin Gioro Yongyan as the Crown Prince. He would pass the throne to him the next year, and the new emperor's reign title would be Jiaqing.

He said to all the people present, "When I ascended the throne, I prayed to Heaven to grant me blessings so that I could stay on the throne for 60 years, when I would pass the throne to my son. My grandfather stayed on the throne for 61 years. I do not dare to stay on the throne as long as my grandfather did. And now I am already 86 years old. It is time for me to pass the throne to my successor."

On 1 December 1796 Qianlong issued an imperial edict saying that once he had passed the throne to his successor, all memorials and reports presented to him should be addressed to Taishang Huangdi (上皇帝) (Emperor's Father).

On 1 January 1797 a grand ceremony was held in the palace. Emperor Qianlong granted the imperial seal to the Crown Prince. The Crown Prince accepted the seal and ascended the throne and became the emperor. He respected his father and said that all memorials about important military and state affairs should be presented to Taishang Huangdi, who would make the decisions on these matters.

8. The Throne of the Emperors of the Qing Dynasty

After Taishang Huangdi relinquished the throne, he still worked very hard to attend to state affairs. In the winter of 1799 he felt unwell, but he was still holding interviews with court officials. On 2 January 1800 he became seriously ill. On 3 January he passed away at the age of eighty-nine. He was given the posthumous title of Emperor Chun (純, meaning "Pure"). His temple title Gaozong (高宗) means "Ancestor with Great Success").

Historians highly praised Emperor Qianlong. They said, "Gaozong was an immensely successful emperor. He did all he could to make the country prosperous. He extended the territory of China. He made great political and military achievements and led great cultural developments. He had reigned for 60 years and his longevity benefited our nation."

Printed in the United States
By Bookmasters